IN THEIR OWN WORDS

Annexed to a letter addressed to the Rt Honble the Secretary of State Home Dept

List of various Street Nuisances

1 Organs. Hurdy-gurdys. Fiddlers. Harps &c &c — [These are innumerable]

2 Brass bands of various kinds with from 3 to 12 performers [These are numerous and frequent]

3 Fantocini. Various exhibitions usually accompanied by shrill fifes and noisy drums. [These are frequent]

4 Monkey and fiddle dancing. or with gun or sword performing exercise.

5 Scotch Bagpipes disturbing at a great distance

6 Impostors with Bagpipes more disagreeable even than the genuine performers.

7 The same accompanied by dancers who are either part of the troop or are collected from the children and idlers of the neighbourhood.

8 Black or colored men beating a monotonous drum called a Tom-Tom to no time, but audible at a great distance.

10 Tumblers of various kinds generally with music or the audience collected by music.

11 Tall men on stilts looking inquisitively into drawing rooms windows.

12 Young girls on shorter Stilts

13 Children playing in the Streets at all sorts of games — always making a great noise, occasionally breaking a window and sometimes putting out the eye of a passenger.

14 Amateurs performers parading the streets with Accordions, flutes whistles and other instruments for their own instruction or pleasure.

IN THEIR OWN WORDS

Letters from history

The National Archives

BLOOMSBURY
LONDON • OXFORD • NEW YORK • NEW DELHI • SYDNEY

The National Archives

Conway
An imprint of Bloomsbury Publishing Plc

50 Bedford Square
London
WC1B 3DP
UK

1385 Broadway
New York
NY 10018
USA

www.bloomsbury.com

First published 2016

British Library Cataloguing-in-Publication Data
A catalogue record for this book is available from the British Library.

Library of Congress Cataloguing-in-Publication data has been applied for.

ISBN: HB: 978-1-8448-6285-6
ePDF: 978-1-8448-6287-0
ePub: 978-1-8448-6286-3

2 4 6 8 10 9 7 5 3 1

Page design by Nicola Liddard, Nimbus Design

Printed and bound in China by C&C Offset Printing Co.

Contents

Allies, diplomacy and foreign relations

Protest, revolution and rebellion

Scandals, loopholes and murder

Cultural, technological change

Introduction

In times past, letters were the medium that brought news which could make or break an individual or a family's fortunes. When wives on the home front during the First World War hovered by their front gates to wait for the postman, they hoped his arrival would bring the happy news that their husbands were still alive and well, and dreaded the knock at the door bringing them the earth-shattering news of a fatality. In today's world, there are multiple ways to contact people immediately across the globe, but for hundreds of years, letters were the main way to bridge distances.

In his novel *The Go-Between* (1953), LP Hartley famously stated that 'the past is a foreign country. They do things differently there'. Recapturing that 'foreign country' is of enduring interest, as it deepens our understanding of where we have come from, and where we might be going to. When seeking to build a picture of the past, few historical sources are as immediate and compelling as letters. They contain the full array of human emotions, from love to hate, from fear to excitement. All aspects of humanity are featured, and the highs and lows of life are described by its protagonists – all through the medium of pen and paper. Similar to eavesdropping or to reading a private diary, leafing through past correspondence indulges our 'natural inquisitiveness' or, put less charitably, our nosiness.

Reading the letters of others can feel like stepping into a time machine, taking us back to the moment when the author set down his thoughts and feelings on paper. As fellow humans, we can often relate to the emotions described in such letters, despite a gulf of sometimes hundreds of years. At the same time, letters from the past are so fascinating because they give fresh and intimate insights into very different worlds from our own. Letters by the well-known heroes and villains of history add colour and detail to our existing perceptions, and may reveal overlooked personality traits or foibles. Correspondence written by more ordinary folk, by contrast, reveals invaluable evidence of how life was once lived: of how our ancestors dressed, what they ate and what they believed.

While the words on the page offer precious glimpses into the thoughts of people long gone, letters tell us much more than what is written down. Merely by seeing the handwriting of a famous figure in history, and by examining their signature, we feel closer to who that person was – a unique part of the historical puzzle not captured by a portrait, a photograph or an eye-witness account. In this way, once-seemingly abstract historical figures come to life.

Letters leave further clues, aside from the words and the handwriting. They have a sort of body language all of their own: we cannot help but draw conclusions based on the colour or quality of the paper. And the conventions used at the beginnings and ends of letters can also reveal a great deal about the author, and his or her feelings towards the recipient. For all of these reasons, there is much to learn and enjoy from reading historical letters.

The delights and rewards of accessing the past through letters are counterbalanced with some interesting challenges. For as vivid and intriguing as they are, letters are far from transparent windows on to the past. Personal letters, and perhaps especially love letters, draw the reader in because they offer a glimpse into an intimate, private world and seem to tell us a lot about the author at their most heartfelt and open. Certainly, such letters can reveal the spontaneous expression of an individual's feelings, but it is worth bearing in mind that their expressions might not be as unique as they initially appear. Any individual letter from a given era will most likely share commonalities with other correspondence from the time, relating to what was considered appropriate or relevant to discuss. Therefore letters can tell us as much, if not more, about the prevailing cultural attitudes of the time, as a specific individual's outlook.

When determining what we can learn from historical letters, it is important to consider the author's intended audience. Depending on who they were writing to, in a private letter to a close family member or an open letter to be published in a newspaper, authors may have had a specific agenda in mind – be it to present themselves in a certain light, or to influence the behaviour of the recipient. What authors chose to leave out in their letters can often be just as revealing as what they included, and, in circumstances of war for example, official censorship combined with self-censorship could certainly distort a true depiction of day-today experiences. Frequently too, only one side of the correspondence survives, since, in most cases, people are more likely to keep letters which they have received than to make copies of letters which they have written themselves. And even one-sided correspondence may be incomplete, if family members have deliberately removed or destroyed letters that paint their ancestors in a bad light. There have always been gaps in the historical record, but the paper trail left by letters for most of history has predominantly been the preserve of the white, educated elite. Looking at letters in isolation can therefore inadvertently render voiceless whole sections of a population who lacked the education or means to correspond with others. For the historian on a quest to recapture the sense of a bygone era, correspondence is most valuable when considered alongside other types of source.

Irrespective of the relative strengths and weaknesses of using correspondence to enhance our understanding of the past, there is no doubting that letter-writing has a long and illustrious history. It was in the 10th century that cotton paper first arrived in Europe from the Far East. For the next few hundred years, this remained the main writing material, before the introduction of paper made from linen rags in the 14th century. By the time Gutenberg produced his first Bible in around 1456, most letters were written on vellum – a fine parchment made from the skins of calves, lambs and kids. As an expensive material, vellum was the preserve of the elite. Cheaper, paper alternatives became more readily available over the course of the 15th century however, and this changed the nature of correspondence from matters confined purely to governance and business to more personal letters.

Dipping a feather quill into ink was the most common way of penning a missive until the late 19th century, when New Yorker Lewis Edson Waterman invented the modern fountain pen. By creating a special device to slow the feed of ink to the nib, Waterman hugely reduced the chances of unwanted ink leaking on to the page. Half a century later, the Hungarian inventor Laszlo Biro created the fast-drying ballpoint pen, which was an overnight success. 'Biros' were widely used by British and American soldiers during the Second World War, and have been popular with letter-writers ever since.

The way letters have made their way from writer to recipient has also significantly evolved over time. Under the Roman Emperor Trajan, letter-carriers with chariots, known as 'positus', were stationed at regular intervals to transport important messages, and indeed this is where the word 'post' originally came from. Chariots were replaced with coaches and horse-riders over the centuries, and it was common practice for the recipient to pay for the letter upon arrival, with fees varying according to the number of pages and the distance the letter had come. In many cases, letters were kept private by the writer using a coloured wax seal on the outside of their correspondence. In the Middle Ages, this practice was often set aside, and messengers entertained people they met en route by reading out the content of letters. The author's decision about whether or not to seal a letter no doubt shaped what and how they wrote. It was not until May 1840, in Queen Victoria's reign, that a nationwide postal delivery service using prepaid stamps was introduced. The so-called 'Penny Black' stamp, bearing a portrait of the young Queen Victoria, was brought in for letters under half an ounce, and the 'Twopenny Blue' stamp was used where correspondence weighed more. All of this meant that people could buy stamps in advance, send cards at Christmas, and put letters into pillar boxes on the street. And countries around the world soon began to operate similar systems. Interestingly though, it was not until 1966 that households across the UK were assigned postcodes to help with the delivery of mail, and it was only in 1968 that the option of sending post either first or second class was introduced. Sending and receiving mail had become a lot more sophisticated than it was in Emperor Trajan's day.

This anthology of letters, which spans nearly 1,000 years of history, has been selected from the 126 shelf-miles of documents held within The National Archives' extensive collection. We learn about the foibles of great leaders, who were human too, in spite of their illustrious positions; we learn about the heroism and bravery of those tested by extreme circumstances; we learn about crime and injustice from both victims and perpetrators; and we learn about the prevailing attitudes and values of societies very different from our own. Brought together, these letters show just how much can be gleaned about the past from delving into the surviving pen-and-paper exchanges sent between men and women who are no longer with us.

Companions,

comrades,

lovers

Medieval family politics

Letter from Isabelle of Angoulême to Henry III

1220

In this tiny letter, Isabelle of Angoulême writes to her son Henry III, the young King of England, to explain why she had remarried without his knowledge or permission. Even to modern eyes, it may seem odd that a widowed mother might remarry without talking to her son about it (even if today she would not be expected to ask permission) – and this marriage was not just a family affair, but a matter of international politics.

When King John died in October 1216, his kingdom was in a state of civil war, with many barons in rebellion due to John's tyrannical methods of rule. His heir, Henry, was just nine years old. John's death did much to take the impetus out of the baronial rebellion, and through a combination of military victory and diplomacy, the royal councillors who had taken charge of the child King's government gradually made peace with the barons and brought the rebellion to an end.

However, they managed no such feat with the young King's widowed mother. Isabelle of Angoulême was a French heiress. As a child she was betrothed to the influential Poitevin baron, Hugh de Lusignan. However, John thought that this union of Hugh's lands with Isabelle's would make Hugh too powerful. To counter the threat, John simply married Isabelle himself.

Isabelle was much younger than her new husband, and seems to have had little involvement in government. But she was close to Henry, and may have expected a role in his government after her husband's death. However the royal councillors, led by the formidable William Marshall, had other ideas. They snubbed Isabelle, and in 1217 she returned to France, turning her attention to the administration of her family lands in Angoulême.

Three years later, she married Hugh de Lusignan – the son of the man to whom she was betrothed many years before – thereby creating the combined territories that John had sought to prevent. Worse, Hugh now demanded the lands in England and France that Isabelle had been given by John as part of her dower settlement.

Hugh and Isabelle detained Henry's younger sister, Joan, as a hostage until the dower lands were released. This complicated matters for Henry even further: a few years before, Joan was promised in marriage to Hugh himself, but Hugh abandoned this plan when her mother (who after all was an anointed Queen) became available. Henry III and his council then negotiated a marriage between Joan and Alexander II of Scotland, a match vital to establishing good relations between England and its northern neighbour. The marriage of Isabelle and Hugh at once made Hugh threateningly powerful, gave him grounds to demand further lands in England and France, and jeopardised Henry's plans to create a marital union with the Scottish King.

It is hardly surprising, then, that in this letter Isabelle tries to justify her actions to her son and explain how she had done it all for him. She tells Henry that Hugh needed a wife to give him heirs, that Joan was too young a wife to realise his hope of having a child soon, and that Hugh's friends had suggested that he should take a French wife. Isabelle, she claims, knew that this could be bad for Henry – and so stepped in, and married Hugh herself. She then explains that Hugh wants to serve Henry faithfully, and that he will do so once he receives the money and possessions owed to him by right of his marriage to Isabelle. Once this is done, Isabelle and Hugh will also return Joan to Henry.

There was little that Henry III could do. Following intervention from the Pope, and assurances about the dower lands, Hugh and Isabelle allowed Joan to return to England, and she married Alexander II in 1221. As to Isabelle, she continued to be an unreliable ally, and her and Hugh's political manoeuvring caused many problems for Henry III over the years.

It is easy to be cynical about the motives that Isabelle cites to justify her actions. It is reasonable to assume that her decision to return to France in 1217 was distressing for her young son. And it is certain that her second marriage and actions thereafter caused him and his allies a huge amount of trouble. But as a woman, Isabelle had far fewer weapons in her armoury than her male counterparts. By taking control of her own second marriage and the marriage of her daughter, Isabelle gained influence that she had never been allowed by John. Isabelle's power may have been based within the family – but it was power nonetheless.

To her dearest son, Henry, by the grace of God, king of England, lord of Ireland, duke of Normandy and Aquitaine, count of Anjou, Isabella, by the same grace queen of England, lady of Ireland, duchess of Normandy and Aquitaine, countess of Anjou and Angoulême, sends health and her maternal benediction. We hereby signify to you that when the Counts of March and Eu departed this life, the lord Hugh de Lusignan remained alone and without heirs in Poitou, and his friends would not permit that our daughter should be united to him in marriage, because her age is so tender, but counselled him to take a wife from whom he might speedily hope for an heir; and it was proposed that he should take a wife in France, which if he had done, all your land in Poutou and Gascony would be lost. We, therefore, seeing the great peril that might accrue if that marriage should take place, when our counselors could give us no advice, ourselves married the said Hugh, count of March; and God knows that we did this rather for your benefit than our own. Wherefore we entreat you, as our dear son, that this thing may be pleasing to you, seeing it conduces greatly to the profit of you and yours; and we earnestly pray you that you will restore to him his lawful right, that is, Niort, the castles of Exeter and Rockingham, and 3500 marks, which your father, our former husband, bequeathed to us; and so, if it please you, deal with him, who is so powerful, that he may not remain against you, since he can serve you well – for he is well-disposed to serve you faithfully with all his power; and we are certain and undertake that he shall serve you well if you restore to him his rights, and, therefore, we advise that you take opportune counsel on these matters; and when it shall please you, you may send for our daughter, your sister, by a trusty messenger and your letters patent, and we will send her to you.

A doomed queen
Catherine Howard's letter to her lover Culpepper

1541

On 28 July 1540, an ageing King Henry VIII married his fifth bride, the 19-year-old Catherine Howard. He declared her his 'rose without thorn' and was apparently infatuated with her. Yet less than two years later, the marriage was over and the young Queen had met her fate on the scaffold.

Catherine was the daughter of Lord Edmund Howard, the second Duke of Norfolk's youngest son. Although members of a noble family, Catherine's parents were far from wealthy, and Catherine was sent to live in the household of her grandmother, the dowager Duchess of Norfolk. Her father could not afford her upbringing, but in her grandmother's household Catherine lived comfortably (although by all accounts not under close supervision).

As Catherine grew into a young woman, there were tales of numerous indiscretions with admirers. Certainly there had been some sort of flirtation with her music teacher Henry Mannox, followed by a more serious relationship with Frances Dereham. But by 1539 Catherine's affection for Dereham had waned, and she had met and fallen in love with Thomas Culpepper, a gentleman of the King's Privy Chamber.

Catherine arrived at court as a lady-in-waiting to Anne of Cleves in early 1540, and quickly caught the eye and heart of the King. By July of the same year, Henry's marriage to Anne of Cleves had been annulled and he had wed Catherine, making her his fifth wife. Henry was thrilled with his new bride, and although Catherine too seemed content, all was not quite as it appeared. Just months after her wedding, Catherine penned her infamous letter to Culpepper. In it, she writes of her great concern for Thomas following a bout of illness, and of her desire to see him and to speak with him. She laments that it 'makes my heart die to think what fortune I have that I cannot be always in your company', and signs the letter 'Yours as long as life endures, Kathryn'.

This letter is all the more poignant as it was subsequently used as evidence of Catherine's treason against the King. Rumours about Catherine's behaviour as a young woman in her grandmother's household had led to investigations about her life before marriage, and eventually turned to her life as the wife of the King. Catherine's supposed 'relationship' with Culpepper was subsequently revealed, and her affectionate letter full of her love for Thomas helped to seal both of their fates.

Henry was the most powerful man in England. He had previously executed his second wife, Anne Boleyn, for adultery, and divorced two further wives. Catherine's letter to Culpepper had put her in a precarious position and led to not only the end of her marriage to the King of England, but also the end of her short life: Culpepper was executed in December 1541 and Catherine in February 1542.

Master Coulpeper, I hertely recomend me unto youe praying you to sende me worde how that you doo. Yt was showed me that you was sike, the wyche thynge trobled me very muche tell suche tyme that I here from you praying you to send me worde how that you do. For I never longed so muche for [a] thynge as I do to se you and to speke wyth you, the wyche I trust shal be shortely now, the wyche dothe comforthe me verie much whan I thynk of ett and wan I thynke agan that you shall departe from me agayne ytt makes my harte to dye to thynke what fortune I have that I cannot be always yn your company. Y[e]t my trust ys allway in you that you wolbe as you have promysed me and in that hope I truste upon styll, prayng you than that you wyll com whan my lade Rochforthe ys here, for then I shalbe beste at leaysoure to be at your commarendmant. Thaynkyng you for that you have promysed me to be so good unto that pore felowe my man, whyche is on of the grefes that I do felle to departe from hym for than I do know noone that I dare truste to sende to you and therfor I pray you take hym to be wyth you that I may sumtym here from you one thynge. I pray you to gyve me a horse for my man for I hyd muche a do to gat one and thefer I pray sende me one by hym and yn so doying I am as I sade afor, and thus I take my leve of you trusting to se you s[h]orttele agane and I wode you was wythe me now that yoo maitte se what pane I take yn wryte[n]g to you.

Yours as long as
lyffe endures
Katheryn

One thyng I had forgotten and
that hys to
instruct my man to tare here wyt[h] me still, for he
sas wat so mever you bed hym he wel do et and [...]

XVI. 1134

13

Master Culpeper I hartely recomend me vnto you prayng you to sende me worde how that you doo yt was showed me that you was seke the wyche thynge trobled me very myche tell suche tyme that I here from you praying you to send me worde how that you do for I never longed so myche for thynge as I do to se you and to speke wyth you the wyche I trust shal be shortely now the wyche dothe comforthe me vere myche when I thynke of ytt and wan I thynke a gen that you shall departe from me a gayne ytt makes my harte to dye to thynke what fortune I have that I cannot be always yn your company yt my trust ys allway in you that you wolbe as you have promysed me and in that hope I truste vpon styll prayng you than that you wyll com when my lade Rochforthe ys here for then I shallbe beste at leysoure to be at your commandment thankyng you for that you have promysed me to be so good vnto that pore felowe my man whyche ys on of the greffes that I do felle to departe from hym for than I do knoe noone that I dare truste to sende to you and therfor I pray you take hym to be wyth you that I may sumtyme here from you one thynge I pray you to gyve me a horse for my man for I hade myche a do to gat one and therfor I pray sende me one by hym and yn so doyng I am as I sayde afor and thus I take my leve of you trustyng to se you shortely a gayne and I wode you was wyth me now that you myghte se what payne I take yn wryteng to you

yours as long as lyffe endures Katheryn

one thyng I had forgotten and that hys to [redacted] tret my man to tare here wyth me stell for he ses whatsoever you byd hym he wel do yt a

14

Lean meals for the Earl of Leicester

Elizabeth I drafts a playful thank-you letter

1577

Here at The National Archives we hold a rare draft letter written by Queen Elizabeth I to the Earl and Countess of Shrewsbury that can be deliciously contrasted to the final, sent version (now held at Lambeth Palace Library).

The letter was intended to thank the Earl and Countess for the hospitality they had given to Elizabeth's favourite, Robert Dudley, Earl of Leicester, during his stay at Buxton, one of their Derbyshire residences. The Earl and Countess owned many properties in Derbyshire, and the Countess may be more familiar to you as Bess of Hardwick, the indomitable matriarch and builder of both Chatsworth House and Hardwick Hall.

The draft is dated 4 June 1577 and we think it is written in Elizabeth's own hand. It begins by thanking the Earl and Countess for how 'honorably' Leicester was 'received and used by you our cousin the Countess at Chatsworth and how his diet is by you both discharged at Buxtons'. As Elizabeth holds Leicester in such high favour, she is particularly pleased with their kindnesses towards him and writes what begins as a straightforward letter of thanks. However, Elizabeth quickly begins to play around with the convention of thanks and obligation, writing that as she considers herself in debt to them for their hospitality, there is a danger that '*unless you cut off some part of the large allowance of diet you give him ... the debt thereby may grow to be so great as we shall not be able to discharge the same, and so become bankrupt*'.

To prevent this fiscal disaster Elizabeth has a practical suggestion. Instead of providing him with a luxurious menu they should instead restrict his diet, allowing him two ounces of meat a day – and not the good stuff. For drink he can have '*the twentieth part of a part of a pint of wine to comfort his stomach*'. On festival days they can be more generous, and he is allowed for his dinner '*the shoulder of a wren, and for his supper a leg of the same*'.

Elizabeth is poking fun at Leicester's reputation as a healthy eater as he was known for his preference for light suppers over feasts, and he may even have been responsible for setting an early fashion for salad. While jokes about Leicester's eating habits may have amused the Earl and Countess, her references to the debt she owes them would have been no laughing matter. As the guardians of Mary Queen of Scots the couple had been forced to foot the bill for the Queen's imprisonment, with Elizabeth providing little in the way of financial aid.

So jokes about limiting the diets of their guests probably cut rather too close to the bone. In the sent version of the letter, dated 25 June 1577, we can see that Elizabeth (or perhaps her close advisor, William Cecil) decided it was a safer bet to stick with a more conservative letter. She begins the letter in a similar style by aligning any service done to Leicester with a service done to herself, describing him rather wonderfully as 'another ourself'. But instead of teasing the Earl and Countess she reiterates her debt to them for their care of Mary Queen of Scots and states how this has enabled the country to 'enjoy a peacable government, the best good hap that to any prince on earth can befall', and promises to repay them 'when time shall serve'. Despite this promise they never did fully recover their costs and eventually the financial and political pressures of their role as guardians, and the constant need to defuse her various plots and intrigues, took its toll on their relationship, and ultimately led to their separation.

In the draft we see Elizabeth's mischievous and whimsical side, and a rare instance when Elizabeth relates to her subjects on a more equal level. It stands in stark contrast to the final version of the letter, suggesting that the draft process could serve as a creative outlet for its own sake, and would never have been intended to be sent. Elizabeth's affection for Leicester is evident, and although he is the subject of the letter the tone so captures the flirtatious and affectionate dynamic of their relationship that it is almost as though she is writing with him in mind as her audience.

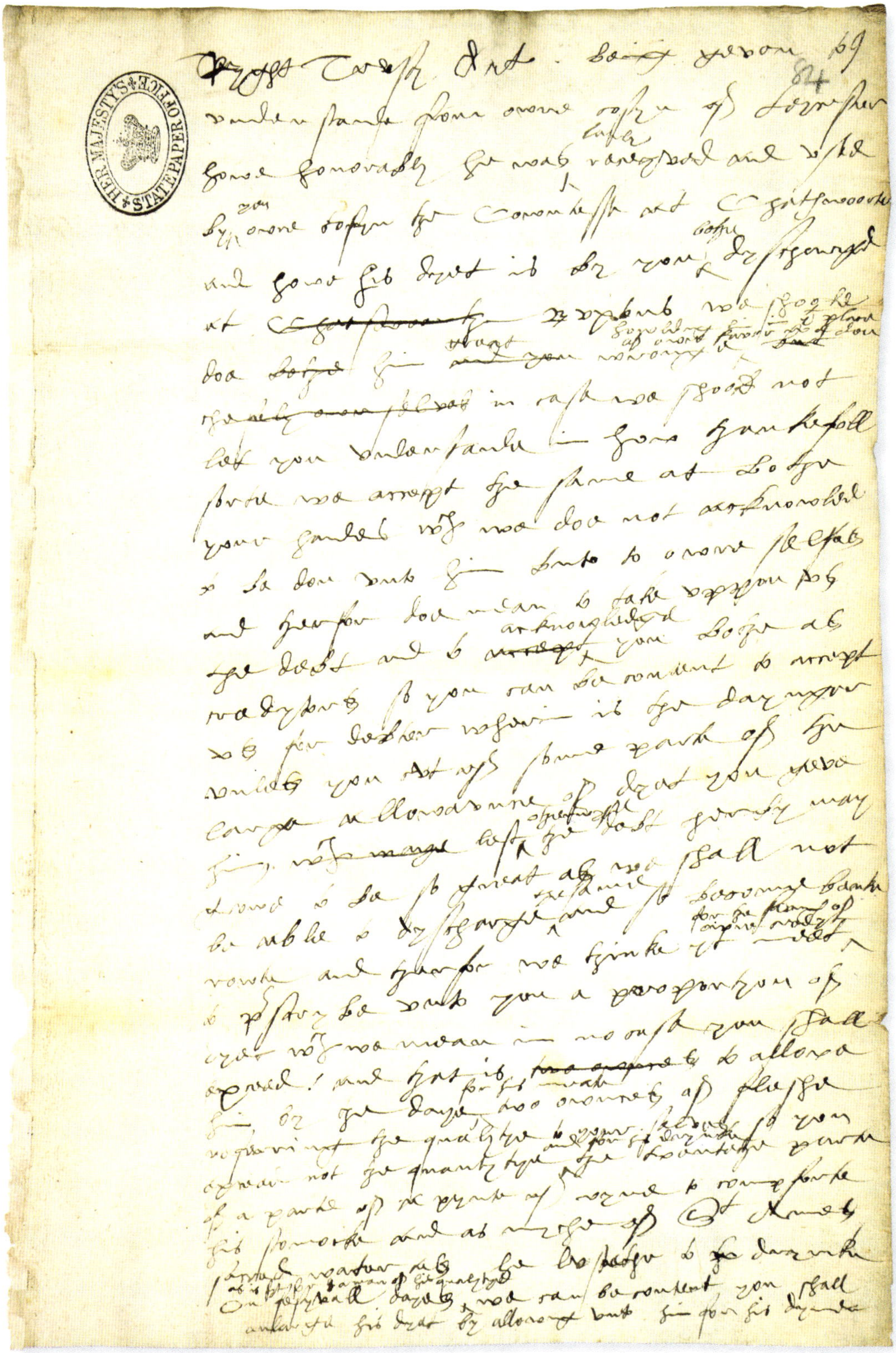
HER MAJESTY'S STATE PAPER OFFICE

10

~~of his his ordenarie allowance~~
the shoulder of a mutton and for his supper
a legg of the same besides his ordinary
allowance. the like proportion we would you
shall allowe unto our brother of warwicke
seing that we thinke it meat in respect
that his bodie is more replete then
~~others~~ his brothers that the mutton lefte
allowed at supper on fysshe dayes be
abated for that eight suppers a weeke
be to muche of flesshe. This order
more necessary yf is you shall inviolably
observe and so may you right well
assure your selfe of a most thankfull
detter & I will deservinge rewardes.

Right trusty etc. Being given to understand from our cousin of Leicester how honourably he was lately received and used by you our cousin the Countess at Chatsworth and how his diet is by you both discharged at Buxtons, we should do him great wrong (holding him in that place of our favour as we do) in case we should not let you understand in how thankful sort we accept the same at both your hands. Which we do not acknowledge to be done unto him but to ourselves, and therefore do mean to take upon us the debt and to acknowledge you both as creditors so you can be content to accept us for debtor, wherein is the danger unless you cut off some part of the large allowance of diet you give him lest otherwise the debt thereby may grow to be so great as we shall not be able to discharge the same, and so become bankrupt. And therefore we think it meet for the saving of our credit to proscribe unto you a proportion of diet which we mean in no case you shall exceed: and that is to allow him by the day for his meat two ounces of flesh reserving the quality to your selves so you exceed not the quantity. And for his drink the twentieth part of a part of a pint of wine to comfort his stomach, and as much of St Anne's sacred water as he lusteth to drink. On festival days, as is fit for a man of his quality, we can be content you shall enlarge his diet by allowing unto him for his dinner the shoulder of a wren, and for his supper a leg of the same besides his ordinary ounces. The like proportion we mean you shall allow unto our brother of Warwick, saving that we think it meet, in respect that his body is more replete then his brother's, that the wren's leg allowed at supper on festival days be abated, for that light suppers agreeth best with rules of physic. This order our meaning is you shall inviolably observe and so may you right well assure yourselves of a most thankful debtor to so well deserving creditors.

'Slaving during master's pleasure'
Bonded labour in eighteenth century Maryland

1756

The iniquities of slavery are universally acknowledged. But how many people realise that alongside the hundreds of thousands of Africans enslaved in the British colonies of North America and the Caribbean in the 18th century, many thousands of white English, Welsh, Scottish and Irish men, women and children worked in cotton fields and tobacco plantations, on comparable terms of bondage?

'Indentured servants' sold themselves into what was effectively slavery for a fixed period (typically seven years) in exchange for their passage to America and the promise (frequently unfulfilled) that when they had served their time they would be given a plot of land, seed and tools, with which to build a new life in the New World. Other bonded labourers were convicts, guilty of sometimes quite petty crimes, transported to the colonies and sold to landowners to work their land. Still others were waifs and strays, London's street-children and vagabonds, or simply unfortunates who fell victim to unscrupulous ships' captains and crimps who kidnapped them and carried them off in chains across the Atlantic, to be knocked down to the highest bidder in Maryland, Virginia or Barbados.

Her being '*forever banished*' for her '*former bad Conduct*' might suggest Elizabeth Sprigs, writer of this letter, had been sentenced to transportation for some crime, but no record of a conviction has come to light and there is not actually enough evidence in the letter to say whether she was a convict or an indentured labourer.

Elizabeth, who is clearly in a desperate state, describes the conditions in which she lives and works, and the treatment she receives at the hands of her master and mistress, and begs her father for help. Tied up, whipped, abused, over-worked, under-fed, ill-housed and inadequately clothed – her characterisation of her treatment lends credence to her assertion (supported by other contemporary accounts) that '*many neagroes [sic] are better used*'.

This is the only known surviving trace of poor Elizabeth's wretched existence. We can deduce from it nothing of her origins beyond her being the daughter of a London metal-worker. The letter does, however, contain the information that her master was Richard Cross, about whom something *is* known. Cross was one of four sons of a Maryland planter family, and Elizabeth would have lived and worked at one of the

Cross's plantations near Baltimore — probably either Cross's Park or Cross's Lot. 'Mr Lux', the Baltimore merchant (probably William Lux) is also a name to conjure with. The Lux family had long-established connections with the convict trade: from 1720 to 1737, first Darby Lux then Francis Lux had commanded a succession of ships bringing convicts from England, most notably the *Patapsco Merchant*, and in 1752, the *Lux* was plying the same trade out of Annapolis.

Like so much about her, we can only guess at Elizabeth's level of literacy, but despite some vivid invective breaking through in places, surely straight from her own tongue, this letter has the hallmarks of one written for her by a third party – and there is some evidence of whom that might have been. The handwriting, layout, paper and several distinctive turns of phrase match two other letters from the mailbag of the same ship that carried Elizabeth's letter. One is from a William Hodgeon, in which he asks his wife to send him a copy of *The Whole Duty of Man*. Anyone who could contemplate reading a stodgy High Church treatise like that would not have needed assistance with letter-writing, so it seems reasonable to guess that he may have been the one who penned all three letters.

Whoever actually put pen to paper, we do know that once written, along with 300 other items of mail for England, the letter was entrusted to the *Enterprize*, a British ship which had brought to Annapolis, among other passengers, one indentured servant and four convicts, and was returning to England (with this letter) when captured on 8 December 1756 by the French privateer *L'Aurore*, and then retaken on 17 December by the British privateer *Blakeney*. Kept by the High Court of Admiralty until eventually transferred to The National Archives, the *Enterprize*'s mail was never delivered.

The saddest thing about this affair is that Elizabeth would not have been aware that her appeal never reached her father. We cannot know whether there would have been a family reconciliation had it not been for the intercession of chance, in the form of *L'Aurore*. Neither has it been possible to discover her ultimate fate, or how long she went on toiling in those atrocious conditions, every day hoping for the news from her family that she was, if not forgiven her trespasses (whatever they may have been), at least not entirely abandoned.

News that never came.

Black and white slave labourers on a plantation.

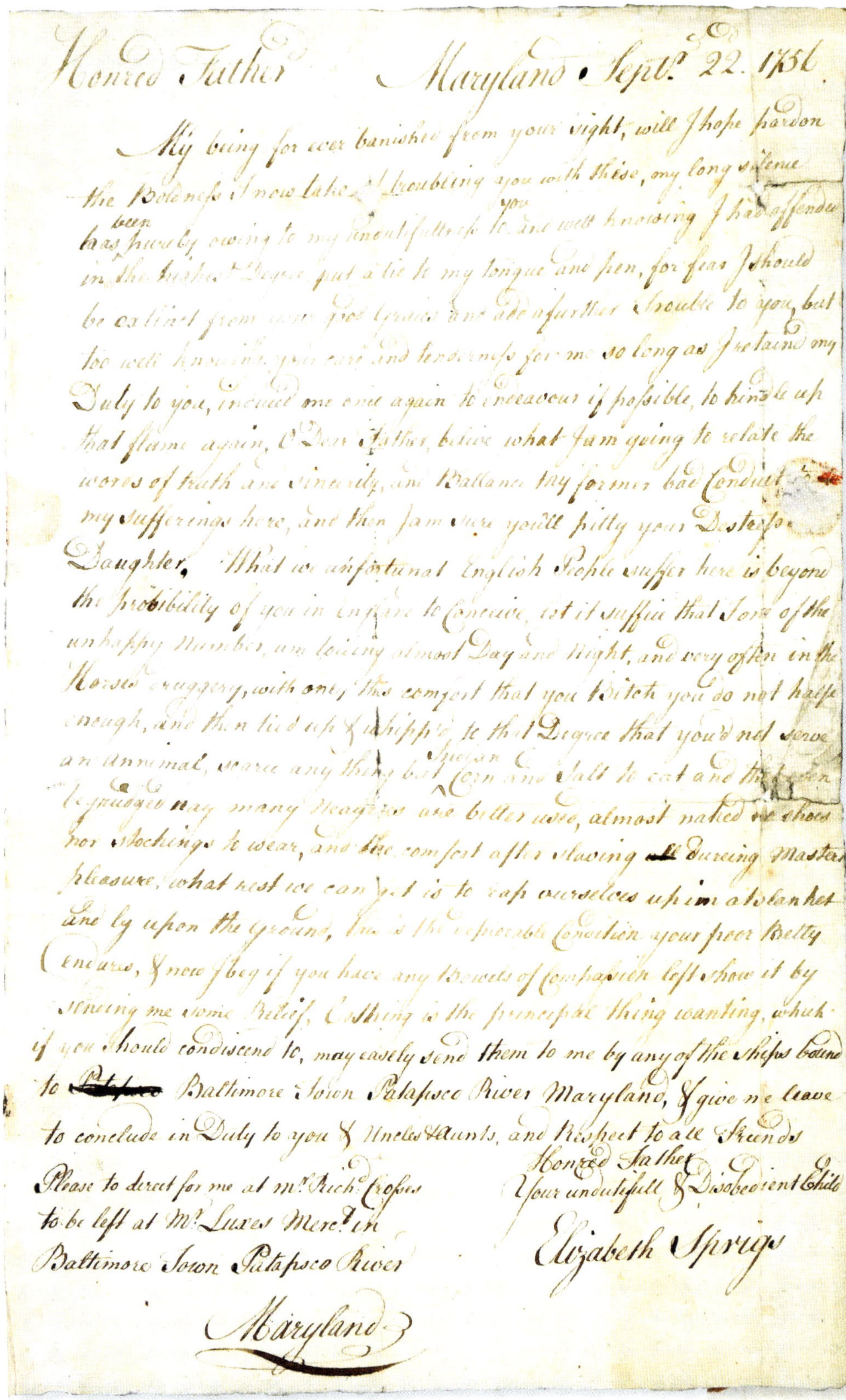

Honred Father Maryland Septr. 22. 1756

My being for ever banished from your sight, will I hope pardon the Boldness I now take of troubling you with these, my long silence has been purely owing to my undutifullness to you, and well knowing I had offended in the highest Degree, put a tie to my tongue and pen, for fear I should be extinct from your good Graces and add a further Trouble to you, but too well knowing your care and tenderness for me so long as I retaind my Duty to you, induced me once again to endeavour if possible, to kindle up that flame again, O Dear Father, belive what I am going to relate the words of truth and sincerity, and Ballance my former bad Conduct my sufferings here, and then I am sure you'll pitty your Destress Daughter, What we unfortunat English People suffer here is beyond the probibility of you in England to Conceive, let it suffice that I one of the unhappy Number, am toiling almost Day and Night, and very often in the Horses druggery, with only this comfort that you Bitch you do not halfe enough, and then tied up & whipp'd to that Degree that you'd not serve an Annimal, scarce any thing but Indian Corn and Salt to eat and that even begrudged nay many Neagroes are better used, almost naked no shoes nor stockings to wear, and the comfort after slaving ~~all~~ dureing Masters pleasure, what rest we can get is to rap ourselves up in a blanket and ly upon the ground, this is the deplorable Condition your poor Betty endures, & now I beg if you have any Bowels of Compassion left show it by sending me some Relief, Clothing is the principal thing wanting, which if you should condiscend to, may easely send them to me by any of the ships bound to ~~Patapsco~~ Baltimore Town Patapsco River Maryland, & give me leave to conclude in Duty to you & Uncles & Aunts, and Respect to all Friends

Honred Father
Your undutifull & Disobedient Child
Elizabeth Sprigs

Please to direct for me at Mr. Richd. Crosses
to be left at Mr. Luxes Mercht. in
Baltimore Town Patapsco River
Maryland

To
Mr John Sprigs
White Smith in White Cross Street
near Cripple Gate
London

To
Mr. John Sprigs
White Smith in White Cross Street
near Cripple Gate
London

Honred Father Maryland Septr 22d 1756

My being for ever banished from your sight, will I hope pardon the Boldness I now take at troubling you with these, my long silence has been purely owing to my undutifullness to you and well knowing I had offended in the highest Degree, put a tie to my tongue and pen, for fear I should be extinct from your good Graces and add a further Trouble to you, but too well knowing your care and tenderness for me so long as I retaind my Duty to you, induced me once again to endeavour if possible, to kindle up that flame again. O Dear Father, belive what I am going to relate the words of truth and sincerity, and Ballance my former bad Conduct to my sufferings here, and then I am sure you'll pitty your Destressed Daughter. What we unfortunat English People suffer here is beyond the probibility of you in England to Conceive, let it suffice that I one of the unhappy number, am toiling almost Day and Night, and very often in the Horses druggery, with only this comfort that you Bitch you do not halfe enough, and then tied up & whipp'd to that Degree that you'd not serve an annimal, scarce any thing but Indian Corn and Salt to eat and that even begrudged nay many neagroes are better used, almost naked no shoes nor stockings to wear, and the comfort after slaving dureing masters pleasure, what rest we can get is to rap ourselves up in a blanket and ly upon the Ground, this is the deplorable Condition your poor Betty endures, & now I beg if you have any Bowels of Compassion left show it by sending me some Relief, Cothing is the principal thing wanting, which if you should condiscend to, may easely send them to me by any of the ships bound to Baltimore Town Patapsco River Maryland, & give me leave to conclude in Duty to you & Uncles & Aunts, and Respect to all Friends

Honred Father
Your undutifull & Disobedient Child
Elizabeth Sprigs

Please to direct for me at
Mr Richd Crosses to be left
at Mr Luxes Merct in Baltimore
Town Patapsco River
Maryland

Britain versus the South Pole

Telegram sent to Captain Oates' mother announcing his death

1913

This momentous telegram was sent on behalf of the War Office and is date-stamped 11 February 1913. It was addressed to a Mrs Oates at Gestingthopre Hall, Castle Hedingham, Essex. The content of the telegram is brief, but to the recipient, it would have been heartbreaking.

It reads: *'Deeply regret to inform you telegram received from Commander Terra Nova reports that your son Captain L.E.G. Oates 6 Inniskilling Dragoons died 17 March 1912'.*

The telegram is as significant a piece of correspondence as it is brief. Captain Lawrence Edward Grace Oates was a serving cavalry officer in the 6th Inniskilling Dragoons and a member of the famous Terra Nova Expedition led by the celebrated 'Scott of the Antarctic'.

The expedition, formally named the British Antarctic Expedition, was a trip with various objectives, both scientific and geographical. One of these was to become the first group to reach the geographical South Pole.

Following their departure from base camp on 1 November 1911 as a larger group of intrepid explorers, a streamlined five-man polar party remained on course for the South Pole on 4 January 1912. The polar party included the leader, Captain Robert Falcon Scott, Lt Henry Bowers, PO Edgar Evans, Dr Edward Wilson and Captain Lawrence 'Titus' Oates.

The group was successful in reaching the South Pole on 17 January 1912, but were in fact the second team to achieve this goal (Roald Amundsen's Norwegian contingent completed the feat a mere 34 days earlier). However, it was the death of all the members of the polar party on the return journey that ensured this story was viewed as a great heroic tragedy in the eyes of the British public at the time.

Indeed, members of the search party, set up to retrieve the bodies of the lost explorers, are recorded as noting that 'the Empire – almost the civilised world – [was] in mourning'.

What makes Captain Oates's story extraordinary is the fact that he sacrificed himself on the return journey when he knew his frostbite and general condition were holding

Captain Oates pictured in Antarctica in 1911.

back the party, who he calculated may have lived without him slowing them down. Edgar Evans had already died, and the memory of his dying teammate slowing the group's progress would have weighed heavily on him.

Legend has it, having woken up on 17 March 1912 during a blizzard, Captain Oates announced, 'I am just going outside and I may be some time.' He left the tent and walked alone to his certain death, in the hope that he would find peace and his comrades a smoother journey to their safety. Unfortunately, despite bravely facing death head-on, his sacrifice could not save Scott and the others. They too perished by the end of March 1912.

Captain Scott wrote that Oates's last thoughts were of his mother, and he states that Titus Oates 'took pride in thinking that his regiment would be pleased at the bold way in which he met his death'. Perhaps then, this short telegram to his mother has a bold simplicity to it. It informed his mother that her son, a Captain in the 6th Inniskilling Dragoons, had met his death. It was with deep regret that this was the case, but his bravery and self-sacrifice were a testament to his character, and is the reason he has a special place in the pantheon of 'stiff upper lip' British heroes today.

Captain Oates with some of the expedition ponies and dogs in Terra Nova.

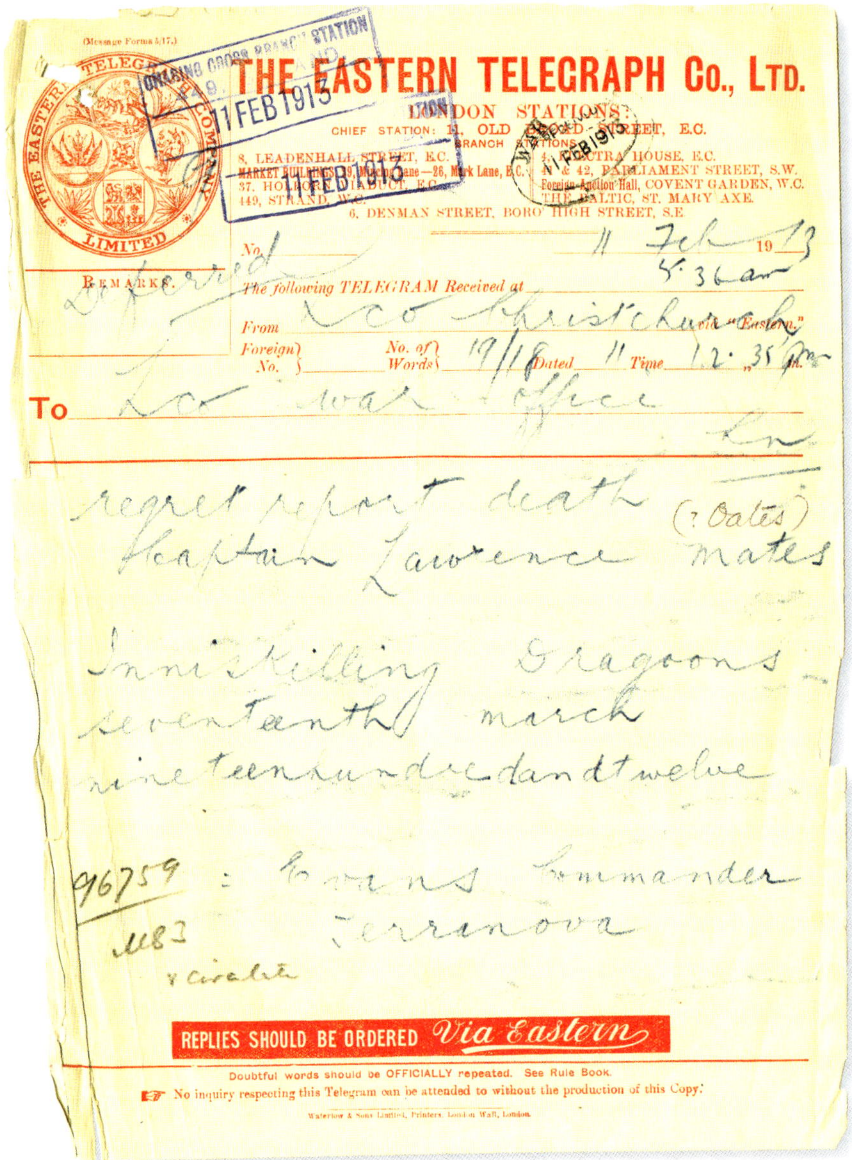
(Message Forms 5/17.)

THE EASTERN TELEGRAPH Co., LTD.

LONDON STATIONS:

CHIEF STATION: 11, OLD BROAD STREET, E.C.

BRANCH STATIONS:

8, LEADENHALL STREET, E.C.

MARKET BUILDINGS, 29, Mincing Lane—26, Mark Lane, E.C.

37, HOLBORN VIADUCT, E.C.

149, STRAND, W.C.

ELECTRA HOUSE, E.C.

42, PARLIAMENT STREET, S.W.

Foreign Auction Hall, COVENT GARDEN, W.C.

THE BALTIC, ST. MARY AXE.

6, DENMAN STREET, BORO' HIGH STREET, S.E.

CHARING CROSS BRANCH STATION 11 FEB 1913

No. 1 11 Feb 1913

8.36am

REMARKS. Deferred

The following TELEGRAM Received at

From LCO Christchurch via "Eastern."

Foreign No. No. of Words 19/18 Dated 11 Time 12.35 pm.

To LCO War Office Ln

regret report death (? Oates) Captain Lawrence mates Inniskilling Dragoons seventeenth march nineteenhundredandtwelve

96759 : Evans Commander Terranova

REPLIES SHOULD BE ORDERED Via Eastern

Doubtful words should be OFFICIALLY repeated. See Rule Book.

No inquiry respecting this Telegram can be attended to without the production of this Copy.

11 Feb 13

The following TELEGRAM received at 8:36am

From LCO Christchurch To LCO War Office, L[ondo]n

Regret report death
Captain Lawrence Oates
Inniskilling Dragoons
Seventeenth March
Nineteen hundred and twelve

Evans Commander
Terranova

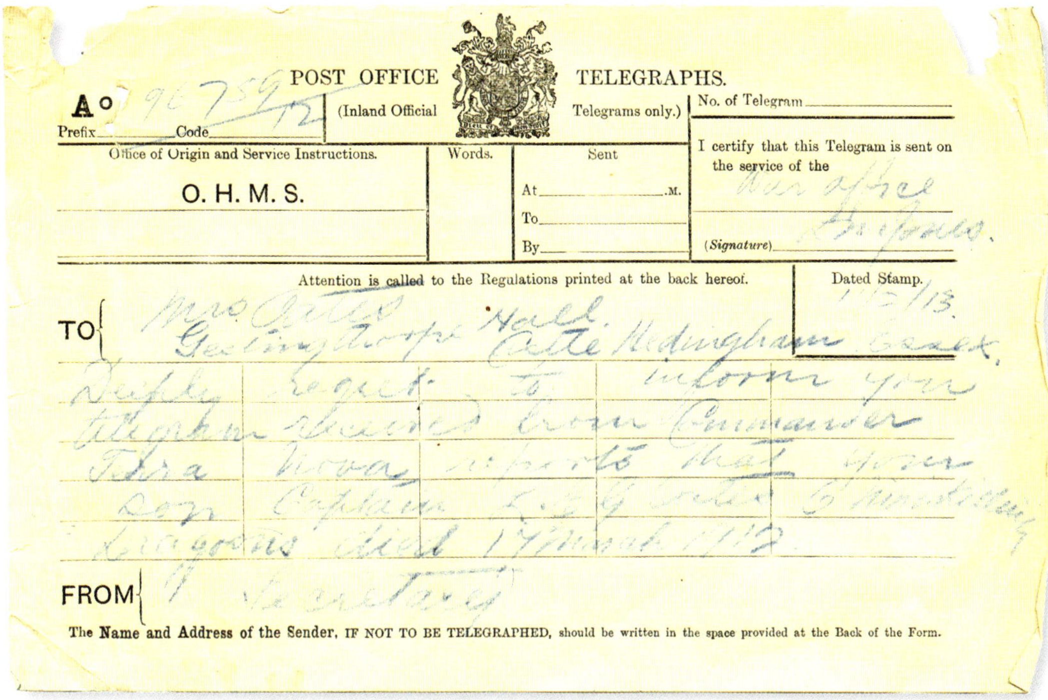
POST OFFICE TELEGRAPHS.

(Inland Official Telegrams only.)

A° 90 759 / 12

Prefix Code

No. of Telegram

Office of Origin and Service Instructions. | Words. | Sent

O. H. M. S.

At .M.

To

By

I certify that this Telegram is sent on the service of the War Office

(Signature) B. Jones.

Attention is called to the Regulations printed at the back hereof.

Dated Stamp. 11/2/13.

TO Mrs Oates Hall. Gestingthorpe Castle Hedingham Essex.

Deeply regret to inform you telegram received from Commander Terra Nova reports that your son Captain L.E.G. Oates 6 Inniskilling Dragoons died 17 March 1912

FROM Secretary

The Name and Address of the Sender, IF NOT TO BE TELEGRAPHED, should be written in the space provided at the Back of the Form.

I certify that this telegram is sent on the service of the War Office.

11/2/13

TO Mrs Oates

Gestingthorpe Hall

Castle Hedingham, Essex.

Deeply regret to inform you telegram received from Commander Terra Nova reports that your son Captain L.E.G. Oates 6 Inniskilling Dragoons died 17 March 1912.

FROM Secretary

Letter from India

KBW Sharland, 26 July 1917, Pashan Camp, Kirkee, India

1914

The Great Western Railway Audit office at Paddington received this letter from Kenneth William Sharland in India. Sharland had joined up in 1914 not long after the start of the war, however this was his first and only letter to the office. He worked in the Agreements Department in a division that was mainly concerned with passenger fares for foreign lines, and worked alongside more regular correspondents to the office, Mark Russell and Edgar Harry Brackenbury, both stationed in France. He describes his long journey to Kirkee, Pashan Camp. Probably it is not surprising that the office had not heard from him before, as he was so far away in India and the postal arrangements were erratic. He was with 1/6 East Surrey Regiment, and other GWR men in the same regiment also made enquiries about him in their letters back to the office.

This battalion carried out garrison duties in the United Provinces and the Punjab in India for two years, then left India to join the Aden Field Force for 12 months and returned to Britain in 1919.

What is unusual about this letter first of all is that it is one of the few written to the Paddington Audit office that does not come from the Western front. Starting out from the training camp in Aldershot, he provided detail about life on board a troop ship, and his contrasting travel experiences on the White Star liner *Suevic* and the Cunard Company's *Laconia* en route to India.

The letter is also interesting because India clearly represented an entirely new cultural experience for Sharland: '*Strange as it may seem to English people native women do most of the work here, and actually act as bricklayers' labourers carrying pans of 'mortar' on their heads, the men do very little indeed. Sunday is the same as any other day to them.*'

Yet in a rather urbane comment, he also seemed satisfied that he had been able to find an Italian restaurant in Poona which was '*very good and is quite the equal of most London restaurants*'. Sharland also observed that in his situation, 6,000 feet above sea level, '*climatic conditions are considered to be ideal*'. One gets the impression that he was very happy with his situation, and had even worked out which were the best-quality cigarettes. This was a topic often commented upon in soldiers' letters home. They often complained about the local brands, or the supplies they were issued by the army as rations. Many men requested cigarettes to be sent out to them. Thus, Sharland's preoccupation with tobacco was not unusual.

Kenneth William Sharland survived the war and returned to the office in November 1919. He retired from the Great Western Railway Paddington Audit office after a further 29 years' service. He died in 1967.

British soldiers on a troopship on their way to India, 1914.

My dear Mr Biggs

The writing mood is on me so I take the opportunity to send you a few lines to let you know how I am getting on, at the same time hoping that at some future date I may have the pleasure of hearing from you. Your letter is bound to be very interesting to me as I have not seen or heard from anybody at Paddington for over six months.

I left Aldershot on March 16th and travelled as far as Durban via Sierra Leone and Cape Town on the White Star Liner Suevic. This part of the journey was delightful, the food and accommodation was very good for a troopship. Of course this is accounted for by the fact that it is an Australian troopship. Everything was done that could be to make the journey enjoyable for the one thousand seven hundred men on board. We stayed just outside Sierre Leone for three days but were not allowed to leave. We arrived at Cape Town on Saturday afternoon four weeks after leaving Keyham and had a route march round the town the same evening. The next day we were allowed to roam about at will all day and a right jolly time we had although it was very hot indeed for winter. Cape Town is a beautiful place and the inhabitants made our visit very enjoyable.

The patriotism of the South African is wonderful to us after the coolness of the English (especially Aldershot). On the Monday we sailed for Durban arriving there on the Thursday evening after a rather rough journey round the Cape. We did not land till the Saturday afternoon and then bid goodbye to the Suevic. She went on to Australia. We had two weeks at Durban and had a glorious time in a rest camp on Ocean Beach. Every day we went bathing and only had parades up to 12 noon each day. The trams were free to us all over the city and invitations were showered upon us by the English residents. You can rest assured that we were very sorry to leave such a delightful spot, still all good things come to an end and we finally had to go on board the Laconia belonging to the Cunard company for four weeks' misery, we lay in the harbour for one week longing to go ashore before we started on the last stage of our journey to India. This ship was actually lousy [infested with lice] and we had to put up with a shirt inspection every day. The food was bad and very little of it and to back it all up the canteen was rotten as well. I was glad to get to Bombay and get off such a rotten ship. I lost a stone in weight during that four weeks.

We arrived in India during the monsoon period and have had plenty of rain more than we like I can assure you.

Kirkee is only about a hundred miles from Bombay and is about six thousand feet above the sea. We will while here never have the extremes of weather as the climatic conditions are considered to be ideal here.

Strange as it may seem to English people native women do most of the work here, and actually act as bricklayers' labourers carrying pans of 'mortar' on their heads, the men do very little indeed. Sunday is the same as any other day to them. As they have their own religious days when they have what they call Ram Jamees. All cartage is done by oxen and is rather slow and cumbersome. Kirkee Bazar is about three quarters of an hour's walk from Pashan Camp and is rather interesting but is very dirty, children run about naked and the drainage and dwellings are very bad indeed. Cigarettes made by the Turkish tobacco company Bandra can be obtained for eleven annas [former unit of Indian currency] per 100 (eleven pence) and are very good indeed, being better than the Nebka. Poona is the nearest city and is about five miles away. I walked there last Thursday to have a look round, this place boasts of one or two hotels and an Italian restaurant but is otherwise an exact counterpart of Kirkee and quite as dirty. The Italian restaurant is very good and is quite the equal of most London restaurants.

We do not receive very many letters out here, as the mail is so uncertain, we never know when the next one will arrive.

When you are writing you must let me know all the news, I wonder whether your section will ever be established again as it was before.

Since I came out here I have taken up signalling and find it very useful, there is just a possibility I might be able to learn wireless, if so I don't doubt that it might be useful to me, when we get back to Blighty if there is half a chance to do so I will cease it.

Our Battalion is at Aden and unless the signalling alters my destination I will eventually find myself there. It is not exactly the place I should choose if I had my own way but of course there is no choice about it.

Well I think I have given you all the news now and am sure you are tired of reading this letter by now, so will close with best wishes to you all from,

yours sincerely,

Kenneth W. Sharland

Medals into munitions

The fight at home: funding the First World War

1917

While civil servants and government ministers undertook the huge task of financing the First World War, ordinary members of the public bore their fair share of the burden too. Fuelled by propaganda, marketing slogans and stories from the front, British citizens were keen to help the war effort in any way possible. Aside from the official funding schemes that people could be part of, such as the War Loan and National War Bonds, some chose to informally aid the war effort through small loans and gifts of money. Documents held at The National Archives include lists of those who sent money to the Treasury, as well as letters that accompanied small material gifts.

This letter is from an injured soldier who was being treated in a London hospital and desperate to aid the war effort. The serviceman didn't send a cheque, he sent something of far greater value: a gallantry medal awarded to him by the President of the United States. To be honoured with this medal McDonald had saved a life, most likely endangering his own in doing so, yet he was prepared to give up his award to further the Allied cause.

Government advertising campaigns fuelled these gifts; Mr McDonald himself acknowledges that he was inspired to help by a government appeal for the war loan. Poster slogans such as 'fight with national war bonds' produced during the First World War suggested that a financial contribution was as valuable as fighting in the trenches. Perhaps this was a small comfort to injured men suffering survivor's guilt, as well as the poster's target female audience. There is no doubt, though, that patriotism was at the heart of Mr McDonald's gift; his phrase '*thrash the Huns out of Existance [sic]*' makes this perfectly clear.

The same tone is not seen in all letters to Sir Andrew Bonar Law, then Chancellor of the Exchequer, offering gifts of jewellery to aid the war effort. 'A. Mother' from Essex wrote that it was 'heartbreaking to read in the *Daily Mail* everyday, a request for money for the War Loan when one has not any to give', to accompany a gift of a bracelet to be turned into a bullet.

You might wonder how the Treasury responded to these letters offering small items of jewellery to aid the war effort. Fortunately, copies of many letters signed by Bonar Law when returning the gifts survive. To the patriotic Mr McDonald, he wrote that it was not yet 'necessary for the Government to call upon the people of this country to make gifts of this kind', and that he did not feel justified in asking the wounded serviceman 'to make so great a sacrifice'.

One might say that Mr McDonald had already sacrificed a lot: he had joined up in the very early stages of the war and most had likely seen some horrific sights, yet for the government it was a step too far to ask him to give up a mark of his honourable character.

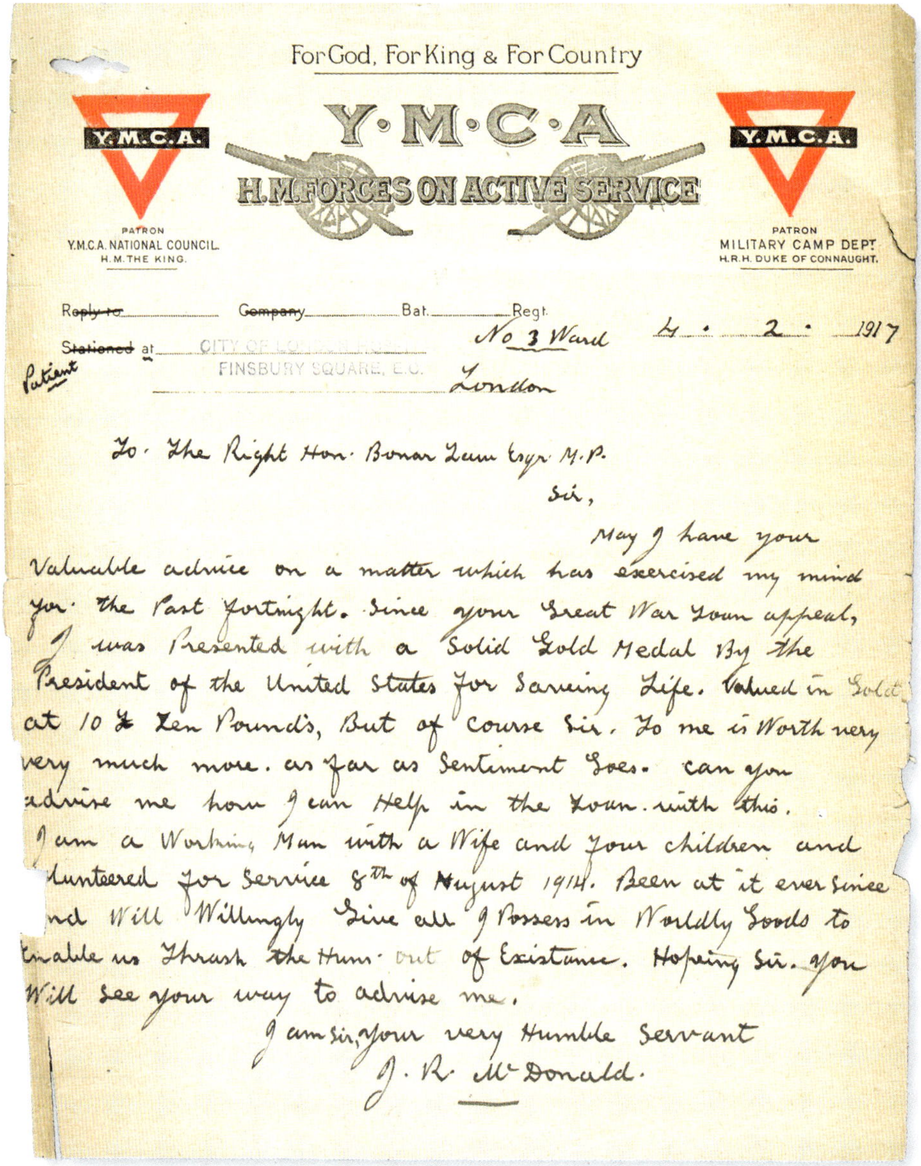

For God, For King & For Country

Y·M·C·A

H.M. FORCES ON ACTIVE SERVICE

Y.M.C.A.

PATRON
Y.M.C.A. NATIONAL COUNCIL
H.M. THE KING.

Y.M.C.A.

PATRON
MILITARY CAMP DEPT.
H.R.H. DUKE OF CONNAUGHT.

~~Reply to~~ ~~Company~~ Bat. Regt.

Patient ~~Stationed~~ at CITY OF LO... FINSBURY SQUARE, E.C. No 3 Ward 4 . 2 . 1917

London

To. The Right Hon. Bonar Law Esqr. M.P.

Sir,

May I have your Valuable advice on a matter which has exercised my mind for. the Past fortnight. Since your Great War Loan appeal, I was Presented with a Solid Gold Medal By the President of the United States for Saveing Life. Valued in Gold at 10 £ Ten Pound's, But of course Sir. To me is Worth very very much more. as far as Sentiment Goes. can you dvise me how I can Help in the Loan. with this. I am a Working Man with a Wife and Four children and lunteered for Service 8th of August 1914. Been at it ever since nd Will Willingly Give all I Posses in Worldly Goods to nable us Thrash the Hun. out of Existance. Hopeing Sir. you Will see your way to advise me.

I am sir, your very Humble Servant
J. R. McDonald.

Patient at No 3 Ward 4.2.1917

City of London Hospital
Finsbury Square, E.C.
London

To the Right Hon. Bonar Law Esq. M.P.

Sir,

May I have your valuable advice on a matter which has exercised my mind for the past fortnight. Since your Great War Loan appeal, I was Presented with a Solid Gold Medal By the President of the United States for Saving Life. Valued in Gold at 10 £ Ten Pounds, But of course Sir, to me is Worth very very much more. as far as Sentiment goes. Can you advise me how I can Help in the loan with this.

I am a Working Man with a Wife and four children and volunteered for service 8th of August 1914. Been at it ever since and Will Willingly give all I Possess in Worldly goods to enable us thrash the Huns out of Existance. Hoping Sir you will see your way to advise me.

I am sir, your very Humble Servant

J. R. McDonald

An appeal from Pioneer Baggs

A tragic attempt to keep a son from war

1918

The passing of the first Military Service Act in January 1916, 18 months after the First World War had begun, meant compulsory military service for every unmarried British male aged between 18 and 41. It was a blunt tool, ignoring the individual circumstances and beliefs of the affected men, but it did allow for exemptions to be made on moral, medical, family or economic grounds. Pioneer Alfred Baggs, himself a veteran of the procedure, addressed this letter to the Middlesex Appeal Tribunal with the hope that his brother, 20-year-old David, would benefit from the last of these exemptions.

David was the youngest of the four Baggs brothers and, with the war having taken its toll, the only one left to help his parents with the family farm. His two eldest brothers had been wounded, while Alfred continued to serve in France, leaving 130 pigs, 300 head of poultry, 4½ acres of fruit trees and an acre of arable land in his hands. With this in mind, David lodged an application with the county tribunal at Middlesex on 15 May 1918, seeking an extension to an exemption he had previously been granted.

As the letter from Alfred makes clear, David's earlier exemption had been approved on the understanding that Alfred would serve in David's place, against the general presumption that a younger, single brother would be called up before an older, married one. Alfred pulls no punches, reminding the tribunal of this arrangement and his continued belief in it: 'I should sooner come out here and be killed and have the consolation of knowing I had done the right thing for my brother than see him come out here'. His words, and his sacrifice, were not in vain. David was granted a three-month exemption on the grounds of his occupation and leave to make further applications beyond this.

This, unfortunately, was not the end of the story. The following August, David applied to the Middlesex Appeal Tribunal to have his exemption extended once again. A bureaucratic shift, however, meant that those seeking exemption with regards to an agricultural occupation now had to apply to their local Agricultural Executive Committee, and so David had to redirect his application to a different body. The delay this caused meant that David's previous exemption lapsed before the new application could be heard, and he was duly called up for training with the Middlesex Motor Volunteer Corps.

If David had to go, his parents, William and Annie, would now be left to care for the farm without their son's assistance, sending William into despair. In early September, David awoke to find the fire unlit and the back door locked from the outside. His mother came downstairs in a panic and showed David a letter from William setting out his intention to kill himself in light of David's conscription. He left in search of his father, but at the top of the lane was met by a girl who told him that there was a man in the river. David soon found him in the Duke of Northumberland's River, face down, drowned in three feet of water. The sense of tragedy was exacerbated by the timing: just two months later the four brothers, William's four sons, returned to the farm. The war was over.

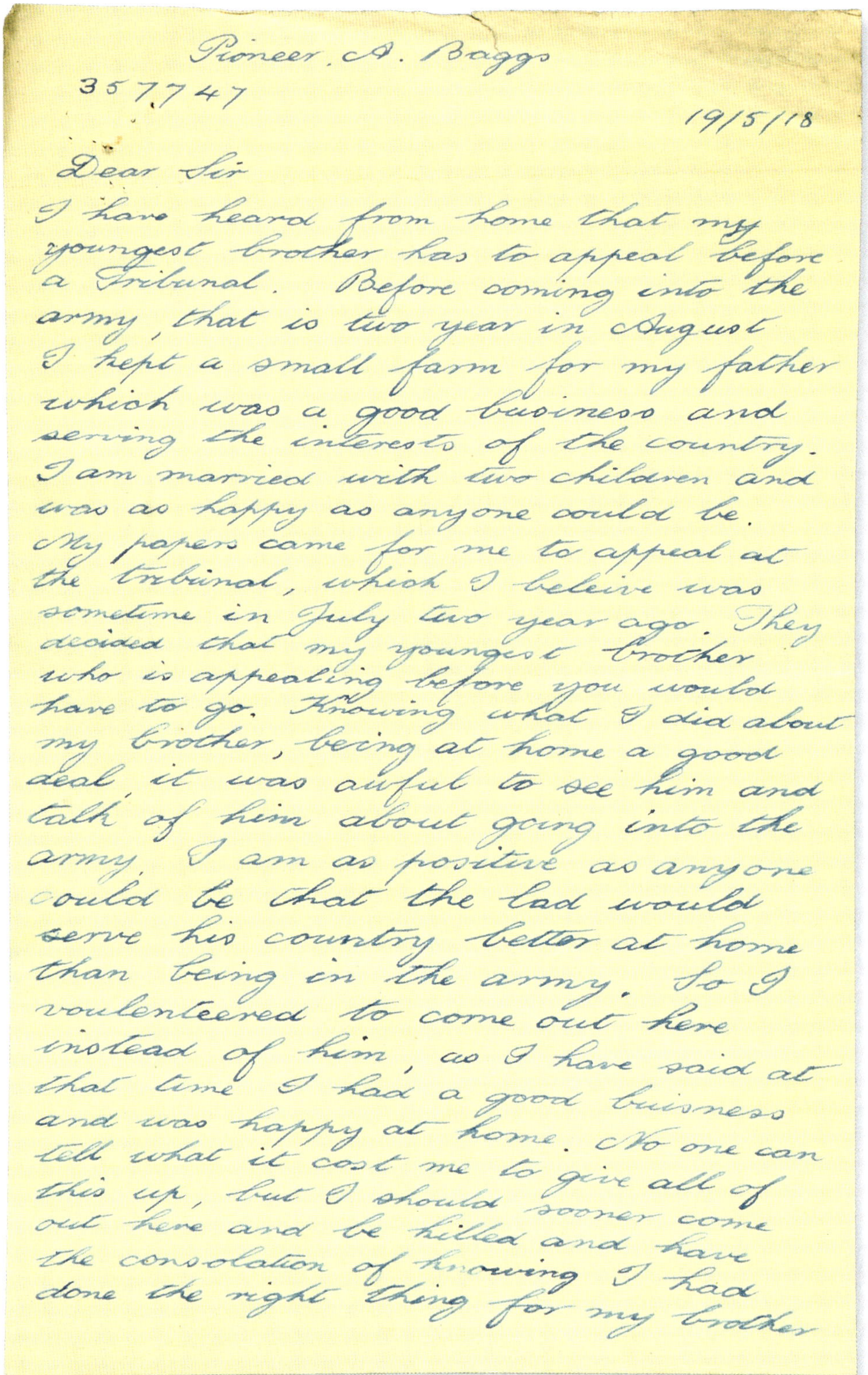

Pioneer. A. Baggs
357747

19/5/18

Dear Sir
I have heard from home that my youngest brother has to appeal before a Tribunal. Before coming into the army, that is two year in August I kept a small farm for my father which was a good business and serving the interests of the country. I am married with two children and was as happy as anyone could be. My papers came for me to appeal at the tribunal, which I beleive was sometime in July two year ago. They decided that my youngest brother who is appealing before you would have to go. Knowing what I did about my brother, being at home a good deal, it was awful to see him and talk of him about going into the army. I am as positive as anyone could be that the lad would serve his country better at home than being in the army. So I voulenteered to come out here instead of him, as I have said at that time I had a good buisness and was happy at home. No one can tell what it cost me to give all of this up, but I should sooner come out here and be killed and have the consolation of knowing I had done the right thing for my brother

than see him come out here. Well Sir
I hope you will give this case your
greatest consideration. Yours Truthfully

Pioneer A. Baggs
R.E. Signals
Attached 1/1st Lowland H.B.
B.E.F. France.

The Caravan Club

Raids on homosexual clubs in the 1930s

1934

What was it like for a man to love a man in 1934?

Two clandestine letters found during a police raid give a unique insight into the relationships between men, not long after the turn-of-the-century hype surrounding the trial of Oscar Wilde.

In the 1930s consensual homosexual sex was still a criminal offence, and it is in this context that we discover this letter within a National Archives Metropolitan Police file.

The date is 24 August 1934, and the atmosphere is described as smoky and claustrophobic. A police officer notes: 'men were dancing with men and women with women as well as mixed couples.' The dance floor was overflowing with people 'only wiggling their posteriors'. The orientally styled room is set up with a series of longue chairs surrounding the packed dance floor; on these chairs men can be seen kissing men.

The members' club provided a space for people to be themselves – frequented by bohemians and outsiders of the era. A police officer later describes the scene as an 'immoral cabaret'.

Central to this scene is an individual going by the exotic pseudonym Cyril Coeur de Leon (Cyril the Lion Heart), also known as the Countess. He is described as an 'effeminate type', with a thickly powdered face and rouged lips. Later, police would use blotting paper to detect make-up on his face.

In the course of the raid, 103 individuals – men and women – were arrested and taken to Bow Street police station.

The most revealing element of the scene comes in the form of two love letters: one found under the seat of Cyril Coeur de Leon, and another discovered in the investigations afterward. In addition to highlighting the social scene possible for gay men in this era, it is revealing of 'queer' identity at this time. The note ends with the honest words, '*Please be a dear boy and destroy this note*'.

The letter to Morris describes Cyril's feelings – '*I only wish that I was going away with you, just you and I to eat sleep and make love together, perhaps when you are away you will think of me sometimes and even write me, I, sincerely hope so*' – this letter was found torn up under the divan with a powder puff, and retyped in the police file.

A further letter found after the raid provides details of Cyril's discovery of his sexual identity, as he notes that he has 'only been queer since I came to London', and that he has a wife and a daughter. It is often hard to trace bisexuality in archival records, or to find an explicit mention of an individual being attracted to more than one gender, but Cyril explicitly notes, 'I still like girls occasionally'. Writing to the seemingly unattainable Billy in this letter, Cyril continues, 'I like you very very much and feel that I can talk this way to you'. This letter speaks of his disappointment in love, feelings long relatable to through time.

The open nature of these letters is revealing of the way gay men themselves spoke about their own sexuality and sense of identity at this time. It also alludes to the social life available to some gay and bisexual men, despite the criminalisation of their love lives.

The interior of the Caravan Club in Endell Street.

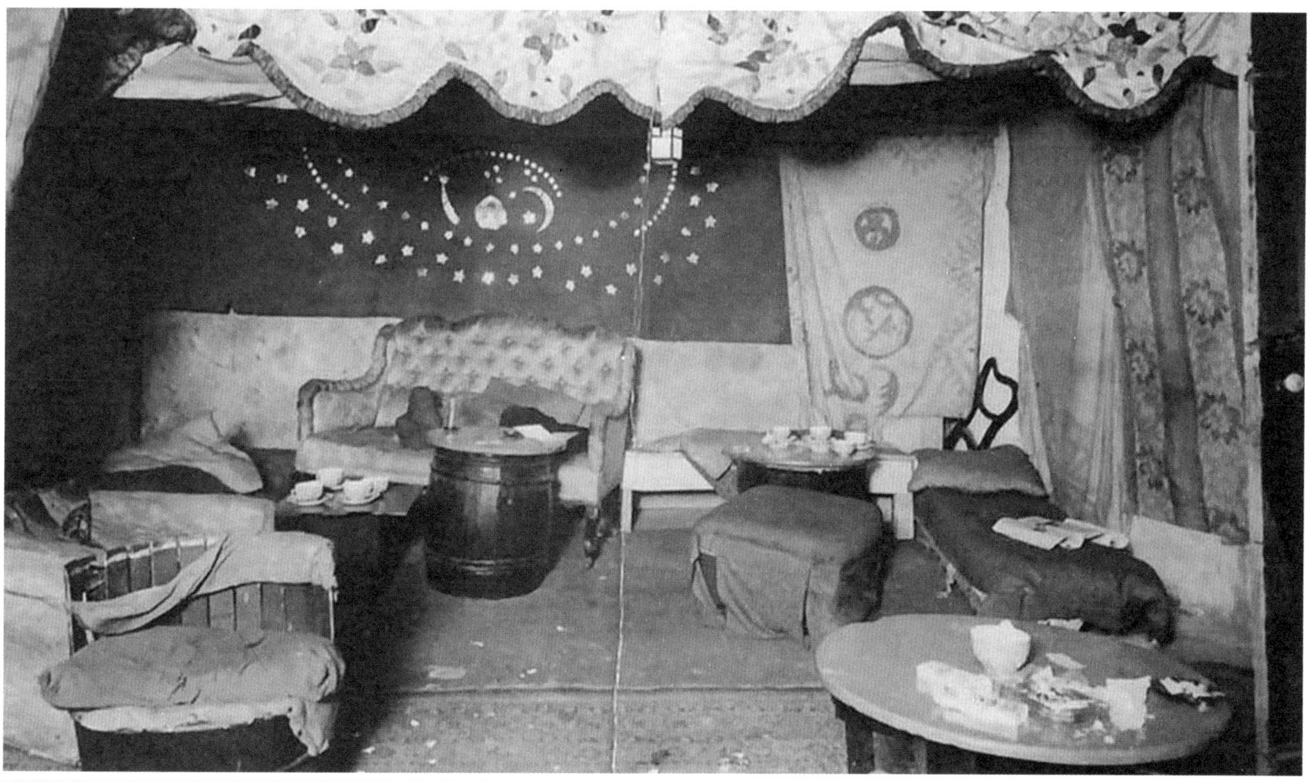

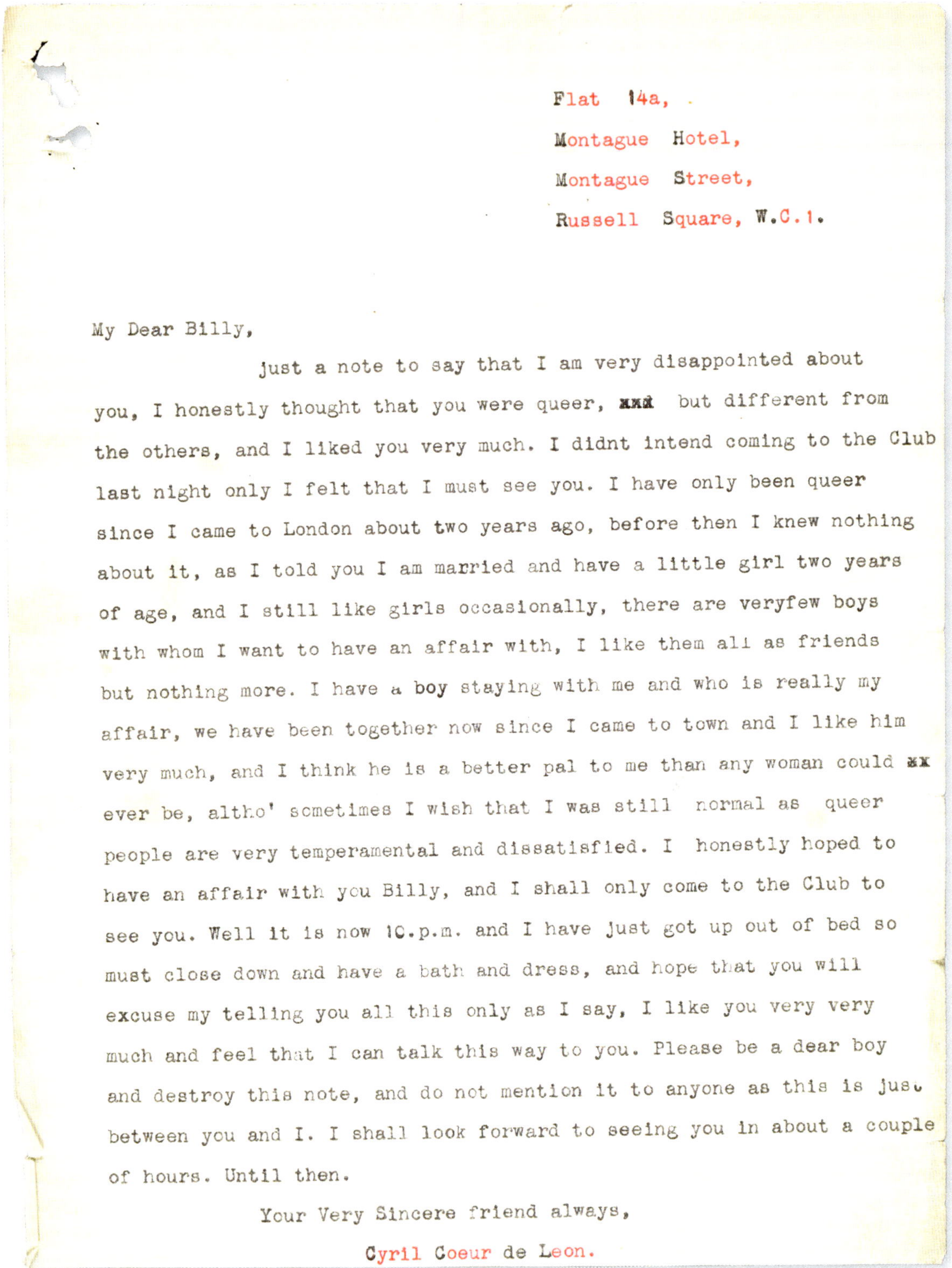

Flat 14a,

Montague Hotel,

Montague Street,

Russell Square, W.C.1.

My Dear Billy,

Just a note to say that I am very disappointed about you, I honestly thought that you were queer, xxx but different from the others, and I liked you very much. I didnt intend coming to the Club last night only I felt that I must see you. I have only been queer since I came to London about two years ago, before then I knew nothing about it, as I told you I am married and have a little girl two years of age, and I still like girls occasionally, there are veryfew boys with whom I want to have an affair with, I like them all as friends but nothing more. I have a boy staying with me and who is really my affair, we have been together now since I came to town and I like him very much, and I think he is a better pal to me than any woman could xx ever be, altho' sometimes I wish that I was still normal as queer people are very temperamental and dissatisfied. I honestly hoped to have an affair with you Billy, and I shall only come to the Club to see you. Well it is now 10.p.m. and I have just got up out of bed so must close down and have a bath and dress, and hope that you will excuse my telling you all this only as I say, I like you very very much and feel that I can talk this way to you. Please be a dear boy and destroy this note, and do not mention it to anyone as this is just between you and I. I shall look forward to seeing you in about a couple of hours. Until then.

Your Very Sincere friend always,

Cyril Coeur de Leon.

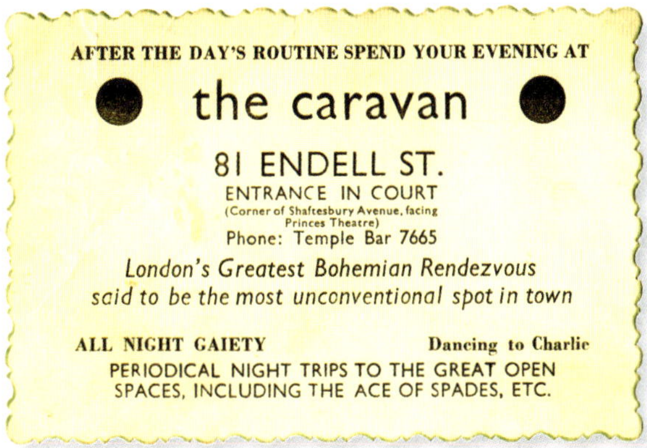
AFTER THE DAY'S ROUTINE SPEND YOUR EVENING AT
the caravan
81 ENDELL ST.
ENTRANCE IN COURT
(Corner of Shaftesbury Avenue, facing Princes Theatre)
Phone: Temple Bar 7665
London's Greatest Bohemian Rendezvous
said to be the most unconventional spot in town
ALL NIGHT GAIETY
Dancing to Charlie
PERIODICAL NIGHT TRIPS TO THE GREAT OPEN SPACES, INCLUDING THE ACE OF SPADES, ETC.

PRIVATE.
''BILLY.''

Children of the Overseas Reception Board

The sinking of the SS *City of Benares*

1940

On the evening of 17 September 1940, just before 10pm, the SS *City of Benares* – packed with 197 passengers, including 90 children – was torpedoed and sunk in the Atlantic.

The torpedo struck the ship on the port side, below the cabins where many of the children were quartered, and it is possible that some of them were instantly killed by the explosion. The rest of the children were immediately mustered by their escorts at their drill stations in an orderly fashion, and 12 boats were launched. The children were being transported as part of a government-sponsored scheme known as the CORB Scheme (Children of the Overseas Reception Board). From information supplied by the four surviving escorts, it was established that repeated searches were made for all surviving CORB children in their cabins before the lifeboats finally drew away from the ship, and it would appear that no children were left behind on the ship. There was a heavy Atlantic swell at the time, with a strong wind blowing. The ship was sinking steadily by the stern and listing slightly, and it was difficult to launch the lifeboats without water being shipped. The wind increased during the night to gale force, accompanied by storms, hail and rain.

Some 113 survivors from this ordeal were picked up by a warship the next day, including 13 children and 18 women. Of these, seven children and two adults were part of the CORB scheme. Subsequently, 46 other survivors were rescued from a lifeboat eight days later and, of these, six were children and two were escorts, again travelling under CORB.

The children were just some of the 2,664 children who were evacuated from Britain in 1940 to embark on new lives in Canada, Australia, New Zealand and South Africa. The CORB scheme was not set up until June 1940, a few years after private schemes had evacuated some 14,000 children from Britain to new lives overseas as war neared.

It was indeed a unique period in British history. In May 1940, the threat to the UK from German air attacks grew and the possibility of invasion heightened, leading to spontaneous offers of hospitality and refuge for British children from overseas governments. These began with Canada on 31 May, when the Canadian government forwarded offers from private households to the UK government. In a few days, similar offers were received from Australia, New Zealand, South Africa and the USA. To coordinate the British response to these offers, CORB was established. Its terms of reference were: 'To consider offers from overseas to house and care for children, whether accompanied, from the European war zone, residing in Great Britain, including children orphaned by the war and to make recommendations thereon.'

Brothers William Cunningham Short and Peter Short from Sunderland were selected for the CORB scheme in June 1940. On their application form, Canada was selected as their preferred destination, with Australia as the second choice. Their parents, John Edward Short and Annie Victoria Short, signed the acceptance and consent form for their evacuation to Canada on 5 August 1940. Nine-year-old William and five-year-old Peter were selected to travel onboard the *City of Benares*.

Following the torpedoing of the vessel, the newspapers reported both boys as missing, but William Short was rescued after eight and a half days at sea. Their father, who had received an offer of financial help from CORB after the disaster sent the following letter in response.

2. Fordwell Cottages

Hylton Road

Sunderland

Nov 19th 1940

Dear Madam,

I am very gratefull [sic] for the cheque you send me today, and I wish to thank you and the gentleman very much for sending it. It will get some of the clothes for my boy who was saved from this tragedy. It would have been grand if I could have had both my boys saved but I thank God for sending one. The homes that have not got any back must be terrible, because I know what is like to miss one.

Again thanking you

I am

Yours sincerely

J. Short

2. Fordwell Cottages
Hylton Road.
Sunderland. 3

3

Nov. 19th. 1940.

Dear Madam,

I am very gratefull for the cheque you send me to-day, & I wish to thank you and the gentleman very much for sending it. It will get some of the cloths for my boy who was saved from this tragedy, It would have been grand if I could have had both my boys saved, but I thank God for sending one. The homes that have not got any back must be terrible, because I know what is like to miss one.

Again thanking you
I am
Yours sincerely
J. Short

'Tell her my grief has no end'

Ken 'Snakehips' Johnson: a life, from Guiana to Soho

1942

Kenrick Johnson was born in 1914 in Georgetown, British Guiana, on the northern coast of South America. His father, Reginald, was a doctor and his mother, Annie, a nurse. As a teenager, Ken was sent to England for his education, spending two years as a pupil at Sir William Borlase's School in Marlow, Buckinghamshire. To the disappointment of his father, who had hoped that he would study medicine, Ken used his musical talent to pursue a career in showbusiness. His dancing ability gave him the nickname 'Snakehips'. By 1938, Ken was the leader of the West Indian Dance Orchestra, an all-black ensemble playing jazz and swing. The band was popular, and was featured in radio broadcasts as well as giving live performances at leading London venues.

Ken 'Snakehips' Johnson in performance.

The band continued to perform after the Second World War broke out. On 8 March 1941 it was playing in the basement at the Café de Paris in Coventry Street, in the West End of London, when a bomb struck. This became one of the most notorious bombing incidents of the London Blitz: at least 34 people were killed, and many others injured. Ken and several fellow musicians were among the dead.

It is rare for records held at The National Archives to include very much information about individual casualties of Second World War bombing, but Ken is an exception: a file from the Colonial Office's Welfare Department contains significant detail about the settlement of his affairs after his death. This file exists for two reasons. Firstly, Ken had no family in Great Britain. His next of kin was his widowed mother, Annie, who was living more than 4,000 miles away in Dutch Guiana (where she had been born), and arrangements had to be made to allow a firm of London solicitors to act on her behalf. Long-distance communication had, of course, become more difficult during the war than it had been during peacetime. Secondly, Ken was found to have been insolvent at the time of his death: his bank account did not contain enough money to cover the amount that he owed in income tax arrears.

Among the papers in the file are four letters written by Annie Johnson to Ivor Cummings, an Assistant Welfare Officer at the Colonial Office. This letter, handwritten on thin, translucent paper, is the last of the four, dated 13 months after Ken's death.

The praise that Annie offers to Ivor for his help and his kindness to her seems to have been well deserved: other papers in the file demonstrate that he had worked diligently to make arrangements that she could not organise for herself. Much of this administrative work related to the memorial service held in the chapel at Ken's old school on the first anniversary of his death. Annie had previously decided that her son's body should be cremated and his ashes remain in England, rather than being sent to her in South America, so they were interred in the school chapel during the service.

Another area where Ivor Cummings proved his worth was in facilitating the licensing of the name 'Ken Johnson Orchestra' to Leon Cassel-Gerard, an agent and manger in the music industry who had been a close associate and supporter of Ken. Just as Annie hopes in the letter, the ten per cent commission that was agreed with Mr Cassel-Gerard was expected to help clear the debts owed by Ken's estate.

Although the rawness of Annie's bereavement is prominent in this letter, she also shows compassion and concern for others. She is deeply touched by the idea that the school might establish a scholarship in Ken's memory for the benefit of other boys and young men from British colonies. As papers elsewhere in the file reveal, a plan was also discussed for Ken's radiogram to be installed in a hostel for colonial students to allow them to enjoy music. We do not know the wider context of the reference to Ivor's mother, who is also mentioned in Annie's other letters (but not in Ivor's replies); it may be that she had also been bereaved.

From her letters, we gain a clear impression of Annie Johnson as a woman made fragile by her grief but capable of maintaining a quiet dignity in the face of loss. The emotion behind her words is compelling. Despite the terrible power of bombs to damage and destroy, this mother's love remained strong and enduring.

Drums and other instruments damaged by the bombing.

14, Stoelmanstraat
Paramaribo Surinam
Dutch Guiana
8th April 1942

44

amd. 47.

Mr L.G. Cummings (Asst Welfare Off)
Colonial Office
2 Park St. W.1.

Dear Mr: Cummings,

The reply of your kind letter seems so long delayed but I am sure you can enter in my position in regards of having to write such sad letters about my dearly beloved son, truly with Ken's passing it seems as if the last bit of light has gone out of my life. You can therefore well realize that your kind help has consoled me very greatly - your kind thought of arranging with his old school for a memorial touched very much. If the scholarship fund can materialize it may thus help some worthy son of the tropics in days to come. Ken's Br: & sisters also I would be only to glad to throw in our help, I sincerely hope this may come to pass.

The Service you arranged for in England and the Scattering of the Ashes at the Grave yard found its duplicate here as the letter arrived the day before, Thus my pastor held a service here at the same hour. It gave me the greatest satisfaction to be able to do this. Again I thank you most sincerely. This will show you the success of your forethought & will surely be of some satisfaction to you. Surely God raised you up to be a friend in the hour of need - thanks are also due to others no doubt & if so kindly be my interpreter to them.

I am sending information regarding a cable received from England as you may be glad to be acquainted with the matter & may give me your kind opinion on the subject — "May I have exclusive right to use name Ken Johnson Orchestra or Johnsonaires. Would appreciate you instructing solicitor to deal with no one else. Willing pay for privilege."

Leon CasselGerard 32 St James St. S.W.1.
27.2.42.

If this is a reliable person? what would be a proper value for such privelege. Seeing Ken's estate has not brought up sufficient to defray the expences if there could be something done wherewith this things could have been paid as he was only for his own recourses & have no other rights anywhere. Please remember me very kindly to your dear Mother, tell her my grief has no end.

With very best Wishes I am Sincerely Yrs.
(Mrs) Annie. F. Johnson

14, Stoelmanstraat
Paramaribo Surinam
Dutch Guiana
8th April 1942

Mr I.G. Cummings (Asst Welfare Off)
Colonial Office
2 Park Str W.1.

Dear Mr: Cummings,

The reply of your kind letter seems so long delayed but I am sure you can enter in my position in regards of having to write such sad letters about my dearly beloved son, truly with Ken's pas-sing it seems as if the last bit of light has gone out of my life[.] You can therefore well realize that your kind help has consoled me very greatly – your kind thought of arranging with his old school for a memorial touched very much. If the scholarship fund can materialize it may thus help some worthy son of the tropics in days to come. Ken's Br: & sisters also I would be only to glad to throw in our help, I sincerly hope this may come to pass.

The Service you arranged for in England and the scattering of the ashes at the Grave yard found its duplicate here as the letter arrived the day before, Thus my pastor held a service here at the same hour. It gave me the greatest satisfaction to be able to do this. Again I thank you most sincerely, This will show you the success of your forethought & will surely be of some satisfaction to you. Surely God raised you up to be a friend in the hour of need – thanks are also due to others no doubt & if so kindly be my interpreter to them.

I am sending information regarding a Cable received from England as you may be glad to be acquanted with the matter & may give me your kind opinion on the subject – "May I have exclusive right to use name Ken Johnson Orchestra or Johnsonaires. Would appreciate you instructing solicitor to deal with no one else. Willing pay for privilege."

Leon Cassel Gerard 32 St James str: S.W. 1.

27.2.42

If this is a reliable person? What would be a proper value for such privelege seeing Ken's estate has not brought up sufficient to defray the expences if there could be something done wherewith this things could have been paid as he was working for his own recourses & have no other rights anywhere. Please remember me very kindly to your dear mother, tell her my grief has no end.

With very best wishes I am Sincerely Yrs.

(Mrs) Annie. F. Johnson

Espionage
and deception

Digging for King and Country

Leonard Woolley and T E Lawrence

1914

Archaeology and espionage have always had close links. Digging is an excellent cover for a bit of spying as it provides agents with a good excuse to snoop around. Archaeologists also know the language, the culture and the country where they excavate quite well. It is therefore not surprising that Leonard Woolley's letter to the Foreign Office, sent about a month after the war broke out, was warmly received.

'I fancy,' he wrote, 'that my name has come before you in connection with work in North Syria'; 'should the present troubles extend in the Near East and the Turkish Empire take sides against us,' he went on, he would be glad to offer his services and those of his 'assistant in Syria, Mr T E Lawrence.' A few years earlier, Woolley and Lawrence, who had yet to become Lawrence of Arabia, had indeed been excavating for the British Museum at Carchemish (Jarabulus, Syria), and although they made a few interesting discoveries, it has often been observed that they were more interested in the progress of the Baghdad Railway.

'And during last winter,' Woolley added, 'I assisted in the survey of South Palestine up to the Egyptian frontier, carried out by Captain Newcombe R E.' In 1913, Woolley and Lawrence were sent to the Sinai on behalf of the Palestine Exploration Fund 'to clarify the history of occupation of this area of the Southern Negev by examining and mapping the archaeological remains from all periods'. Lawrence and Woolley admittedly gathered an impressive quantity of valuable archaeological data, but this survey, 'the wilderness of Zin', was nothing but a smokescreen for a military topographical survey conducted by Captain Stewart Newcombe, of the Royal Engineers, whom Lawrence would meet again in Arabia.

The survey lasted four months and, in June 1914, Lawrence and Woolley, who had made their way back to Baghdad, started off for a summer holiday in England. They travelled the length of the German Baghdad-Damascus railway, gathering information which was later passed on to Newcombe.

'I might perhaps be of some use to the Government,' Woolley ventured. He and Lawrence, along with other fellow archaeologists, such as David Hogarth, the Keeper of the Ashmolean Museum in Oxford, or Gertrude Bell, who had travelled through the Arabian Desert in the spring of 1914, ended up being very useful indeed. They regrouped in the intelligence department of the Egyptian Army in Cairo, and in that of the Indian Expeditionary Force D in Basra, and, in 1916, in the newly created Arab Bureau, whose mission was to harmonise British political activity in the Middle East.

In the Bureau, much emphasis was put on the expertise of the correspondents. That is where archaeologists were useful even though they were sometimes perceived as being freelancers or liabilities – too enthusiastic, maybe, but more likely not used to reporting to anyone.

Incidentally, the Germans were also using archaeologists as spies. Baron Max von Oppenheim, who excavated extensively in northern Syria, and whom Lawrence and Woolley had met there, was appointed at the head of the Nachrichtenstelle für den Orient (Intelligence Bureau for the East), and known to the British as 'The Kaiser's spy'.

Lawrence, appointed in October 1916 as liaison officer with the forces of the Amir Faisal, spent the war creating his own legend, and Leonard Woolley, who had hoped in 1914 that he 'may be called upon in case of need', was recalled during the Second World War to serve as Archaeological Adviser to the War Office.

Lawrence wasn't quite the romantic and highly popular figure portrayed by Peter O'Toole but he and Woolley did their bit for King and Country, paving the way, perhaps, for a romanticised image of archaeologists as bold adventurers.

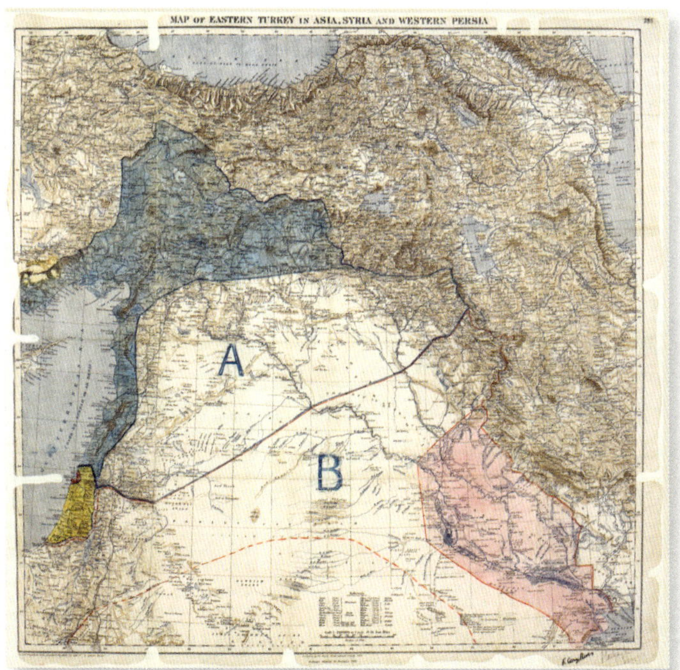

Map showing the Sykes-Picot agreement between the UK and France defining their proposed spheres of influence in south-west Asia in the event that the Ottoman Empire was defeated in the First World War.

Dear Sir,

I fancy that my name has come before you in connection with work in North Syria; and during last winter I assisted in the survey of South Palestine up to the Egyptian frontier, carried out by Captain Newcombe R E. Should the present troubles extend in the Near East and the Turkish Empire take sides against us, I think that, as I know the language, the people and the country, I might perhaps be of some use to the Government. I propose to enlist in the regular army so as to be trained for any such emergency; I do not know whether my enlistment would prevent my being called upon for any special work that might otherwise have been assigned to me.

I may add that, besides Arabic, I know a fair amount of Modern Greek.

My assistant in Syria, Mr T.E. Lawrence, of 2 Polstead Road, Oxford, would also gladly offer his services for any work in that part of the world.

Hoping that I may be called upon in case of need I beg to remain

Yours obediently

Leonard Woolley

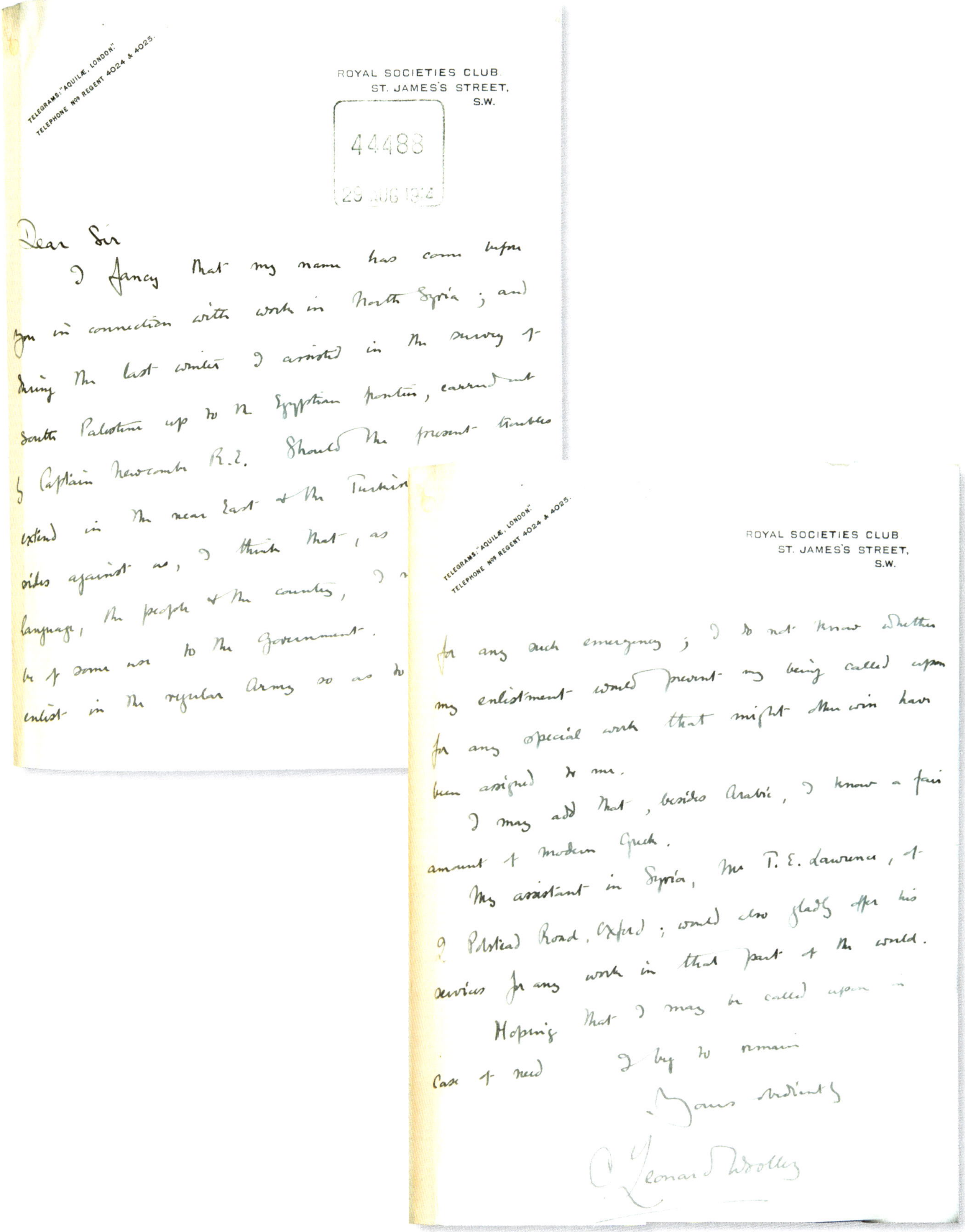

TELEGRAMS: "AQUILÆ, LONDON."
TELEPHONE Nº REGENT 4024 & 4025.

ROYAL SOCIETIES CLUB.
ST. JAMES'S STREET,
S.W.

44488
29 AUG 1914

Dear Sir

I fancy that my name has come before you in connection with work in North Syria; and during the last winter I assisted in the survey of South Palestine up to the Egyptian frontier, carried out by Captain Newcombe R.E. Should the present troubles extend in the near East & the Turkish
sides against us, I think that, as
language, the people & the country, I
be of some use to the Government.
enlist in the regular Army so as to

TELEGRAMS: "AQUILÆ, LONDON."
TELEPHONE Nº REGENT 4024 & 4025.

ROYAL SOCIETIES CLUB.
ST. JAMES'S STREET,
S.W.

for any such emergency; I do not know whether my enlistment would prevent my being called upon for any special work that might otherwise have been assigned to me.

I may add that, besides Arabic, I know a fair amount of modern Greek.

My assistant in Syria, Mr T. E. Lawrence, of 2 Polstead Road, Oxford; would also gladly offer his services for any work in that part of the world.

Hoping that I may be called upon in case of need I beg to remain

Yours obediently

C Leonard Woolley

Carl Lody, the spy in the Tower

Letter from a convicted German on the eve of his execution

1914

Upon the outbreak of the First World War, the people of Britain became sensitive to, and maybe even a little paranoid about, the existence of enemy agents operating on UK shores and aiding the German war effort through acts of espionage and sabotage.

However, despite a lot of these fears being inspired by the national penchant for spy literature produced by the likes of Erskine Childers and William Le Queux, the fact remains that there were spies operating in Britain on behalf of the Germans, following the outbreak of war. Indeed, during the course of hostilities many men and women were arrested and convicted of spying against the British state. Of those arrested, 12 men were executed, and 11 of these men were shot in the formidable surroundings of the Tower of London.

The first man to be shot was Carl Lody, a German national who, following a brief career in the German Imperial Navy, was approached by the German authorities to act as a spy both before the war and, of course, once war had been declared. Lody possessed good spoken English and while posing as an American named 'Charles A Inglis' he began to observe British naval operations and make notes on coastal defences. These observations were sent back to the German military via an address in Stockholm.

Lody had been lying low in Ireland when he was arrested, his un-coded communications proving straightforward for the precursors of MI5 to understand and trace. Following a public trial in London he was convicted of war treason and sentenced to death on 2 November 1914.

Prior to his trial and execution, Carl Lody was held at Wellington Barracks in London under the supervision of the 3rd Battalion Grenadier Guards. This letter, dated the day before his execution, is a curious one. He had already been moved to the Tower of London and was aware he was to be executed. Lody's bravery and frank admissions of his guilt had already been admired by the British press and authorities, and he was keen to display 'good fellowship', as he refers to it in his letter, in the hours preceding his death.

Carl Lody was keen to stress in his letter that it was his 'duty as a German officer' to express his 'thanks and appreciation' towards the guards who had dealt with him since his imprisonment. The letter is addressed to the 'Commanding Officer of the 3rd Battalion Grenadier Guards', and says much about how Lody viewed both the role and conduct expected of an Officer and his individual place in the whole war. He signs the letter under an English translation of his rank and service (Senior Lieutenant German Naval Reserve), and signs off while making note of his profound respect toward the Grenadier Guards who dealt with him so considerately, despite his own acknowledgment that he was 'the enemy'.

The letter exists as a brief insight into a military mind, one that values the display of respect to others regardless of the side one is fighting, or spying, for. As time ticked away, and Carl Lody's execution drew nearer, he took time to say thank you to the men charged with his imprisonment for the way they had treated him.

It should be noted that it was men of the 3rd Battalion Grenadier Guards who would eventually make up the firing squad selected to execute Carl Lody, on 6 November 1914.

36 B

London Nov. 5th 1914.
Tower of London.

To the Commanding Officer of
the 3d Battallion Gren. Guards.
Wellington Barracks

Sir –

I feel it my duty as a German officer to express my sincere thanks and appreciation towards the staff of officers and men who were in charge of my person during my confinement.

Their kind and considered treatment has called my highest esteem and admiration as regards good fellowship even towards the enemy and if I may be permitted, I would thank you for make this known to them.

I am, Sir, with profound respect:

Carl Hans Lody.
Senior Lieutenant Imperial German Naval Res.
II A.

London Nov[ember] 5th 1914.

Tower of London.

To the commanding officer of
the 3rd Battalion Gren[adier] Guards.
Wellington Barracks.

Sir –

I feel it my duty as a German Officer to express my sincere thanks and appreciation towards the staff of officers and men who were in charge of my person during my confinement.

Their kind and considered treatment has called my highest esteem and admiration as regards good fellowship even towards the enemy and if I may be permitted, I would thank you for make [sic] this known to them.

I am, sir, with profound respect.

Carl Hans Lody.

Senior Lieutenant Imperial German Navy Res[erve].

From bank clerk to British spy

The origins of Britain's leading Second World War spy

1940

This unremarkable letter began the career of one of the most successful British spies of the Second World War. The story of Eric Roberts, code-named 'Jack King' has only recently come to light through files released to The National Archives from MI5. It is an extraordinary tale of one man's bravery in exposing the fifth column in British wartime society, those who supported Hitler's fascist policies and would go to any length to help Germany win the war.

When this letter was written in summer 1940, the unassuming figure of Roberts was working at the Euston Road branch of the Westminster Bank. Roberts' past remains something of a mystery, but when MI5 decided to set up an operation to uncover fascist sympathisers in Britain, they quickly selected Roberts as their man. One MI5 official noted that 'Roberts is thoroughly familiar with everything connected with the various pro-Nazi organisations in this country', and that the renowned spycatcher Maxwell Knight 'has the highest opinion of his character and abilities'.

In a wonderful exchange of letters Oswald Allen Harker, Deputy Director General of MI5, wrote to the Westminster Bank stating that he was anxious to 'employ him [Roberts] in my organisation at the earliest possible moment'. Mr RW Jones of Westminster Bank agreed, but wrote cuttingly that 'what we want to know here is – what are the particular and especial qualifications of Mr. Roberts – which we have not been able to perceive'.

Despite this less than ringing endorsement from his former employer, Roberts was swiftly thrust into the dark world of British Nazi sympathisers. He was initially brought in to infiltrate a group of employees of Siemens Schuckert, a British subsidiary of the large German firm, Siemens. One of those who rapidly came to Roberts' attention was Marita Perigoe, a woman of mixed Swedish and German origin, described by MI5 as a 'masterful and somewhat masculine woman. Both in appearance and in mentality she can be described as a typical arrogant Hun.' The security services were so concerned about Perigoe that they changed Roberts' cover, and he went from being a disloyal Englishman to a fully fledged member of the Gestapo.

In part through Perigoe, Roberts managed to build up a large network of Nazi sympathisers who all reported to him any information they came across. While much of this was relatively mundane, there was some extremely sensitive intelligence, including about the early developments of jet fighters and about Operation Window, a technique for blocking German radar. These traitors believed that Roberts was then passing this information on to his superiors in Germany, but in fact it was simply ending up in files at MI5. As such, Roberts managed to channel the subversive activities of many sympathisers into harmless pursuits.

Other intelligence given to Roberts was less sensitive, but lifts the veil on the true nature of those individuals who were desperate for the Nazis to win the war. In 1943 a Nancy Brown from Brighton gave Roberts some information on the air defences of the town, and at their next meeting was 'thrilled at the recent tip and run [German air] raids. She seemed to think that her information was the reason for the German choice of targets and deplored the fact that there had been so many near misses'. Her support for the Nazi cause went beyond a mere callous indifference to the suffering of others. As Roberts reported to his superiors, 'a nearby school was hit and Nancy Brown said with a grin that one expectant mother was killed, two girls badly injured, a clerk and two children killed … Nancy Brown looked a fine, healthy specimen of an Englishwoman, but it is obvious that the deaths of these people meant absolutely nothing to her.'

Through his skill and no little bravery, Roberts expanded the list of those reporting to him into a network that amounted 'certainly to scores, and probably to hundreds' of Nazi sympathisers. According to a report by a very senior MI5 figure at the end of the war, this formed 'the single most valuable source of information' available to those dealing with subversion in Britain. This humorous letter written by a bank manager is the origin of this real-life James Bond story.

Secret. Personal

2a

8th June 1940.

B.

Dear Jones,

I wonder if you would give me your advice on the following matter. There is employed in one of your branches a gentleman who, I understand, is liable to be called up for military service in October. Subject to your being able to give a satisfactory report on his conduct I am anxious to anticipate his call-up and employ him in my organisation at the earliest moment.

Would it be possible for you to arrange for him to be spared to my organisation for the duration of the war without in any way interfering with his prospects in the Bank. As regards salary I would of course see that he was put to no loss financiall by coming to us.

The name of this gentleman is Eric A. ROBERTS, employed at the Euston Road Branch, 2 Hampstead Road, N.W.1.

I am writing to you quite informally on this matter to ask for your advice as to how we should proceed in the event of your being able to release him. Perhaps you would ring me up on Monday and discuss it.

Yours sincerely,

R. W. Jones Esq.,
Westminster Bank Ltd.,
Lothbury.

Extract

WESTMINSTER BANK LIMITED

41 LOTHBURY, LONDON, E.C.2

TELEGRAMS : Fortyone Stock London

TELEGRAPHONE : METropolitan 6600

SECRET AND PERSONAL

Please address reply to
THE MANAGER
quoting

11th June, 1940.

Dear Colonel Harker,

I spoke to our Chief here about Mr. R.A.K. Roberts, whom you mention in your letter of the 8th, and his reply was that if the Bank were satisfied that the release of Mr. Roberts were of real national advantage they would release him at once, but on enquiry at the Branch he found that Mr. Roberts had taken the opportunity yesterday to proceed on his holidays, which seemed to him a peculiar moment to take this step.

However, what we would like to know here is - what are the particular and especial qualifications of Mr. Roberts - which we have not been able to perceive - for some particular work of national importance which would take him away from his normal military call-up in October?

This just confirms my telephone conversation this afternoon, when I was very pleased to hear from you.

Please depend upon my services if I can be of the slightest use to you and believe me always to be,

Yours very sincerely,

R W Jones

Assistant Controller.

Lt. Col. O. Allan Harker,
Box No. 500,
Parliament Street B.O.,
S.W.1.

Operation Mincemeat

How a dead body deceived the Axis in the Second World War

1943

At first glance, this appears to be a love letter from a young woman to her fiancé. Tinged with sadness and emotion, it looks similar to many such letters exchanged between lovers in the midst of war. In fact, neither the sender, 'Pam', nor the recipient of the note, 'Bill', ever even existed. The message formed a key component of Operation Mincemeat, a successful British wartime deception intended to conceal Allied plans for the 1943 invasion of Sicily.

An air crash that took place near the Spanish port of Cádiz in September 1942 provided the inspiration for Mincemeat. The body of the British courier carrying a message to the Governor of Gibraltar was returned to the British authorities, but there was concern about the fate of his cargo, which included the date for the planned invasion of North Africa. While officially neutral, Francisco Franco's Spain was sympathetic to the Axis cause. Nevertheless, the letter apparently remained intact and secure.

Flight Lieutenant Charles Cholmondeley conceived Plan Trojan Horse after reflecting on these events. The essence of his scheme was to use a dead body to carry misinformation, in the hope that Spanish authorities would relay this to the enemy. As the scheme was developed, Lieutenant Commander Ewen Montagu – a King's Counsel and nephew of the former Liberal Cabinet Minister Edwin Montagu – was assigned to help develop the plan.

Glyndwr Michael was an unlikely hero. Unemployed and homeless on the streets of London, the Welshman apparently ended his own life at the age of 34. Having ingested rat poison containing phosphorous, Michael succumbed due to damage to his liver. London coroner Bentley Purchase, an old friend of Montagu's, had already been primed to look for a suitable cadaver. Lacking grieving relatives to mourn him, Michael was ideal.

In death, Glyndwr Michael assumed the identity of Captain (Acting Major) William Martin, Royal Marines. His body was dressed in the appropriate uniform and a briefcase attached to his belt. As part of Martin's backstory, it had been decided that he had met a young woman just five weeks earlier and become engaged after a whirlwind romance. The part of Pam was in fact played by two different women. The letter itself – and another dated Wednesday 21 April – was written by Hester Leggett, head of the secretarial team at MI5. Jean Leslie, a young MI5 secretary, provided the photograph. To further the illusion, a receipt from a New Bond Street jeweller for an engraved engagement ring costing over £53 (a considerable amount of money at the time) was added to Martin's wallet.

Martin also carried fake identification papers and a letter of introduction from Lord Louis Mountbatten, Chief of Combined Operations, to the Commander in Chief in the Mediterranean. The most important document, however, was a 'Personal and Most Secret' letter from Vice Chief of the Imperial General Staff Lieutenant General Sir Archibald Nye to General Sir Harold Alexander, commander of 18th Army Group in Tunisia. Drawn up in the final version by Nye himself, it referred to Operation Husky as an attack on Greece. It also suggested that Sicily was a cover target for another operation (Brimstone). The idea that Greece was the actual target exploited pre-existing German anxieties that the Balkans represented a weak point for the Axis.

In the early hours of 30 April, the decomposing body was released off the coast of Huelva, southern Spain, by the submarine HMS *Seraph*. Operation Barclay, which faked the existence of a British 12th Army, and a campaign against German communications in Greece known as Operation Animals, lent additional weight to the idea that the Eastern Mediterranean was the actual target for Husky. The plan proved to be a great success, helping to ensure that Sicily was captured with far fewer casualties than expected.

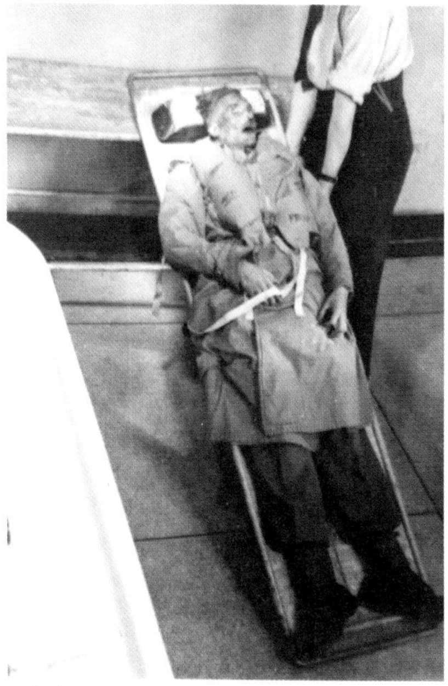

The body (top) and girlfriend of the fictitious Captain (Acting Major) William Martin.

THE MANOR HOUSE
OGBOURNE ST. GEORGE
MARLBOROUGH
WILTSHIRE
TELEPHONE OGBOURNE ST. GEORGE 242

Sunday 18th.

I do think dearest that seeing people like you off at railway stations is one of the poorer forms of sport. A train going out can leave a howling great gap in one's life & one has to try madly — & quite in vain — to fill it with all the things one used to enjoy a whole five weeks <u>ago</u>. That lovely golden day we spent together — oh. I know it's been said before, but if <u>only</u> time could sometimes stand still just for a <u>minute</u> — But that line of thought is too pointless. Pull your socks up Pam & don't be a silly little fool.

Your letter made me feel slightly better — but I shall get horribly conceited if you go on saying things like that about me — they're utterly unlike ME, as I'm

… find out. Here I am
… this divine place
… e being too sweet &
… e whole time, bored
… nting for Monday so
… ck to the old grindstone
… idiotic waste!

… do let me know
… get fixed & can
make some more plans, & don't <u>please</u> let them send you off into the blue the horrible way they do nowadays — now that we've found each other out of the whole world, I don't think I could bear it —

All my love.

Pam

The Manor House
Ogbourne St. George
Marlborough
Wiltshire

Telephone: Ogbourne St. George 242

Sunday 18th

I do think dearest that seeing people like you off at railway stations is one of the poorer forms of sport. A train going out can leave a howling great gap in ones life & one has to try madly – & quits in vain – to fill it with all the things one used to enjoy a whole five weeks ago. That golden day we spent together – oh! I know it's been said before, but if only time could sometimes stand still just for a minute. But this line of thought is too pointless. Pull your socks up Pam & don't be a silly little fool.

Your letter made me feel slightly better – but I shall get horribly conceited if you go on saying things like that about me. They're utterly unlike ME, as I'm afraid you'll soon find out. Here I am for the weekend in this divine place with Mummy & Jane being too sweet & understanding the whole time, bored beyond words and waiting for Monday so that I can get back to the old grindstone again. What an idiotic waste!

Bill darling, do let me know as soon as you get fixed & can make some more plans, & don't please let them send you off into the blue the horrible way they do now a days – now that we've found each other out of the whole world, don't think I could bear it.

All my love,

Pam

Animals and the War effort

GI Joe the hero carrier pigeon

1943

For thousands of years, animals have performed key roles in war. From the elephants used in battles against the early Roman army, to the camels deployed by the Arabs in cavalry charges, to the cats used on ships to keep the rat population down, not to mention the dogs, horses, goats and pigs who have all played their part. GI Joe, the celebrated carrier pigeon discussed in this letter, is part of a greater tradition of animals at war.

Pigeons like GI Joe had a crucial role in conveying important information during both World Wars. They helped crashed bomber crews, supported the Resistance movement in Europe and made lots of journeys to communicate vital messages that often saved lives. Pigeons on duty had a small aluminium tube attached to each leg, where officers could insert their messages. Although it could be difficult to persuade pigeons to fly if the weather was dark, rainy or foggy, generally they were extremely reliable. In the First World War, for example, 100,000 carrier pigeons were used by the British Armed Forces, and they had a 95 per cent success rate for message delivery. Furthermore, unlike messenger dogs, who could only manage about 8km, pigeons had a far greater range. Indeed, in the Second World War there are birds on record that were dropped far into Germany and flew over 480km in 48 hours.

But as GI Joe's story shows, pigeons did not have to fly a long way to make a huge impact. Though he only travelled 20 miles, the successful delivery of his timely message on 18 October 1943 saved the lives of 100 Allied soldiers. On that day, plans were in motion for Allied XII Air Support to bomb the Italian village of Colvi Vecchia, with the aim of breaking the German defence line, which was heavily reinforced. Unbeknownst to the would-be bombers however, the British 10th Corps HQ actually captured the village mere minutes before the bombing was due to take place. It was only with the help of GI Joe that disaster was avoided. No wonder that the men who looked after him dubbed him 'a hero of this second world conflict', and wanted the story reported to the newspapers.

That same year, the involuntary work of animals in war was officially recognised in the UK with the introduction of the Dickin Medal. Commonly referred to as 'the animal's Victoria Cross', it was a bronze medallion inscribed with the words 'For Gallantry'.

Fifty-one years later, in 2004, a monument was built to honour the millions of animals who had died 'in the cause of human freedom'. Located on the edge of Hyde Park in London, the site consists of a curved stone wall engraved with a group of struggling animals, as well as two heavily loaded bronze mules, a bronze horse and a bronze dog. The inscription on the memorial is a fitting epitaph for animals at war: 'They had no choice'.

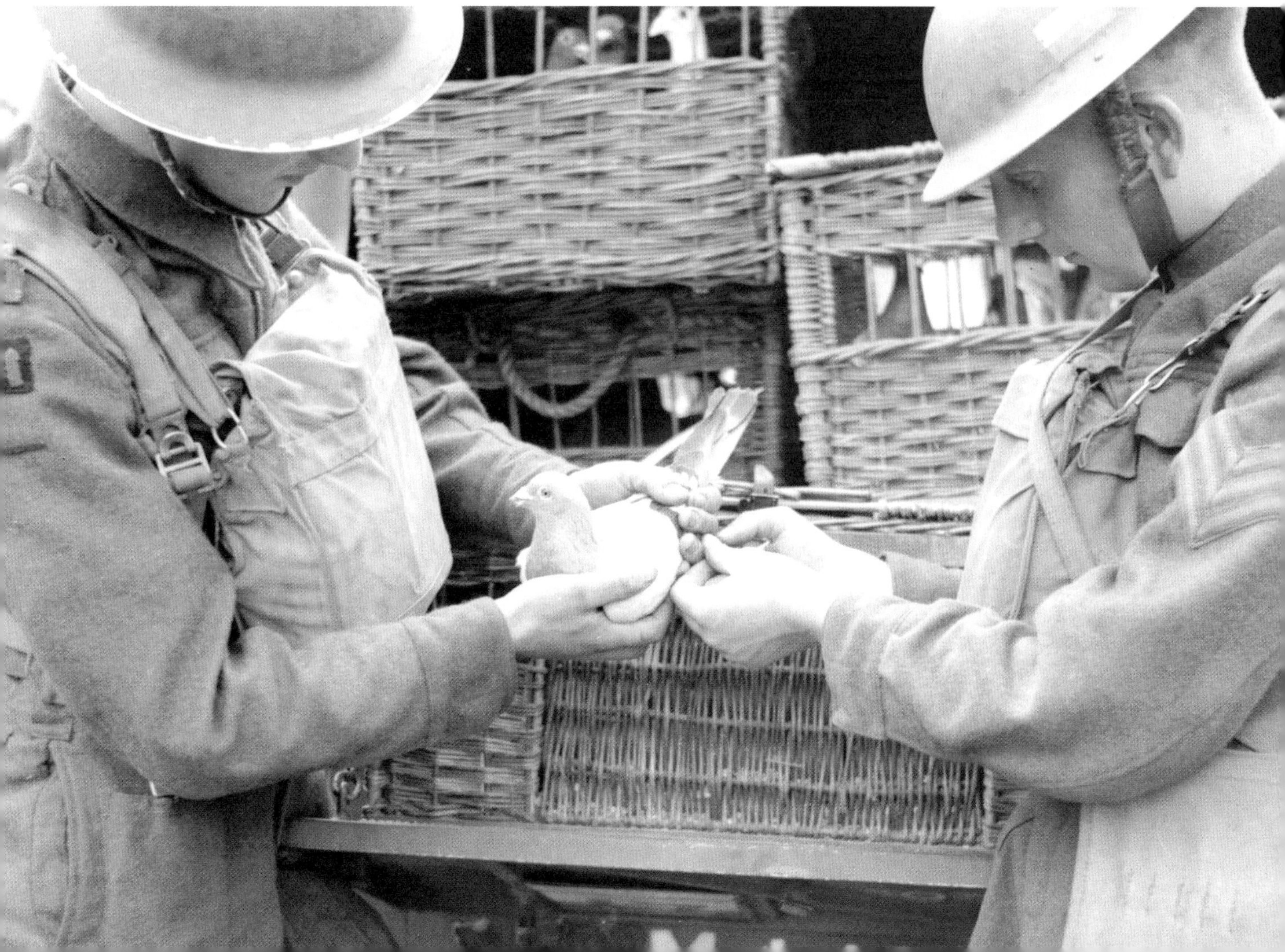

RESTRICTED

AFHQ MESSAGE CENTER

INCOMING MESSAGE

Information Copy to DCSO-Pers

CSO
Exo

Nat
PERS

WAR
NR 248/10
FILED 100531Z

AFSC N392/10
101035A
rth

R O U T I N E

FROM: AGWAR SIGNED MARSHALL (CITE SPSOT)

TO : FREEDOM

REF NO THIS MESSAGE: 2165 10 NOVEMBER 43

Please return to Personnel Div Signal Section

Economy of effort demands consideration of value being derived from Homing Pigeons in actual combat, and expenditure in effort being devoted thereto. Request following information if available and recommendations based on experience in use of Pigeons in your Theater by Ground, Air, and Naval forces. (1) In how many combat actions were pigeons used? (2) How many lofts were employed in each? (3) Were Pigeons reasonably well handled and used? (4) In how many cases were Pigeons the only means of communication available to Air, Ground or Naval Units or individuals. (5) Were there any cases in which delivery of messages by Pigeons actually saved lives, ships, aircraft, or afforded opportunity for favorable combat action to be taken which would have been lost without Pigeons? (6) Could any such losses have been avoided if Pigeons had been available as a reliable emergency means of communication? To permit greatest economy in USA will your needs during next year for Pigeons, equipment, feed and personnel probably increase, decrease or remain at present level?

ACTION: SIGNALS

INFORMATION: SGS MAC SUMMARY
G-3 AG RECORDS

MC IN 5816 10 NOV 43 1347A NO 2165 et/Van

RECEIVED
10 NOV P.M.
Signal Section
A.F. H.Q.

2

RESTRICTED

COPY No.

THE MAKING OF AN EXACT COPY OF THIS MESSAGE IS FORBIDDEN

The Gerson Secret Writing Case

JO Peet and coded correspondence in the Second World War

1943

This letter looks like an ordinary missive from one friend to another. However, it conceals a purpose somewhat different to the list of book recommendations and general chit-chat that the text outwardly portrayed.

In actual fact, this letter was one of many that were intercepted by the Federal Bureau of Investigation (FBI) in New York during the Second World War, on suspicion of betraying US military intelligence to the Germans.

It formed part of a series known as the Gerson Secret Writing Case, and was sent to an address in Portugal – a neutral country – from where it was presumably forwarded on to Germany.

The fact that the message was signed JO Peet was significant in itself. It revealed – as previous intercepted letters suggest – that a secret message would be on the reverse of the letter. Secret ink was just one form of writing missives used for the purposes of espionage, but it was incredibly effective – particularly if the message was intercepted – since it could be written in between the lines or on the reverse of seemingly mundane text. This reverse of this particular letter reveals one such covert message. This message, however, wasn't written in lemon juice (unlike many other messages written in secret ink). Rather, as the technical note that accompanied this intercepted letter confirmed, it was written in something that 'cannot be detected chemically', unlike other forms of secret ink messages. It was in fact created using a method 'strikingly brought out by wetting the paper with water', an indicator that this letter was actually written in urine!

The culprit, 'J.O. Peet' was one of several coded names used by Wilhelm Albrecht von Rautter, a naturalised American with a German father and an English mother. He was the third son of the couple, but given that his elder brothers had died, he was heir to the title and property of his father, Baron Wilhelm Rautter of Wilkam, and mother, Baroness Bertha Bayly Fisher Rautter-Willkam.

Von Rautter himself refused to fight for the German Army in the First World War, and was very close to his English mother, who divorced her husband due to her pro-British sympathies. However, he succumbed to the attempts of the Abwehr (German military intelligence organisation) to recruit him to act as a spy and gather military intelligence in America to help the Nazi cause. His suitability as a spy was immeasurably helped by the fact that he spoke perfect English as well as German.

He was placed on the Most Secret Watch List in late 1943, and was only removed from the list as a result of his arrest in January 1944. He admitted writing the letters of the Gerson Secret Writing Case, although he claimed to have acted only on 'pistol point', ignoring the fact that he was financially remunerated for his endeavours to assist the Nazi state. The American judge, Judge Moscowitz, remained unsympathetic to von Rautter's pleas for leniency and sentenced him to serve 29 years in prison. He was spared the death sentence only due to fears that it could lead to acts of revenge against American citizens living and working in Germany.

The letter, one of many examples, can be seen as either a great example of human ingenuity or perhaps as a prime indicator of the craft and guile required to operate as a wartime spy in the heart of enemy territory.

Transcription of the secret writing follows:

#15 - DIESEL ENGINES
STILL GREATEST BOT-
TLENECK+THE USE O
F COMPRESSED AIR FOR
PROJECTILE PROPU-
LSION APPLICABLE
TO MACHINE AND OTH-
ER GUNS IN SERIOUS
STUDY STAGE+RUM-
OR SAYS RUSSIA ABO-
UT EXHAUSTED AND
UNABLE CONTINUE IN-
TO 1944+ - 120- TAN-
KERS PROPOSED FOR
1943 OUTPUT MORE
THAN DOUBLING 19-
42 PRODUCTION (1942)
AVERAGING 15 to 18
THOUSAND D.W.T.+ WIL-
L WRITE WHEN POSSIBLE.

S E C R E T.

120 Broadway

New York City

Fifth of May 1943

Dear Esteves:

Many thanks for your letter and greetings. It was nice of you to remember me upon this occasion and I sincerely appreciate your thoughtfulness.

Glad to hear that you are wåll and that your business is progressing satisfactorily even though it is connected with many headaches.I am sure everybody has those to contend with, so you should not feel lonesome on that score.

You ask me if I have any good books to recommend.Well, frankly, I have not had much time to devote to books for the past year and I am afraid I have been limiting my reading matter to such weeklies as Time, Life and Readers Digest. That is about all I would claim to be an expert on for the time being. I am ashamed to admit this to you, but it is only the truth.

However, upon inquiry and upon higher advice from a friend of the family who is up to date on all bookish matters, here are his suggestions:

"The Human Comedy" by William Saroyan
(This book is one of the best sellers in the fiction field and promises to become another American epis like Mark Twain's "Huckleberry Finn"

Other good fiction books are:"The Robe" by Lloyd C. Douglass and"Mrs. Parkington" by Louis Brom field.

In the non-fiction field at the present time everybody seems to be reading Wendell L.Willkie's "One World". It is a narrative of his globe encircling trip to Russia and the Far East coupled with his sincere thoughts on the post-war world.This book is a popular seller brief in text, only costs $1., and I am told is very fine reading.

As regards war books, there are of course many on the market these days. Howevem,interest ing books from this standpoint would be;
"Seven came Through" by Captain Eddie V.Rickenbacker
"Dress Rehearsal" by Quentin Reynolds
"We cannot escape History" by John T Whitaker
All three are highly recommended for thei clear matter of fact reporting and interesting reading matter.

I hope I have given yousomething to go on for the time being and I am sure Brentano's will be glad to handle any order for you.

It was nice to have heard from you and with all my best of wishes and regards

always sincerely

J.O. Reed

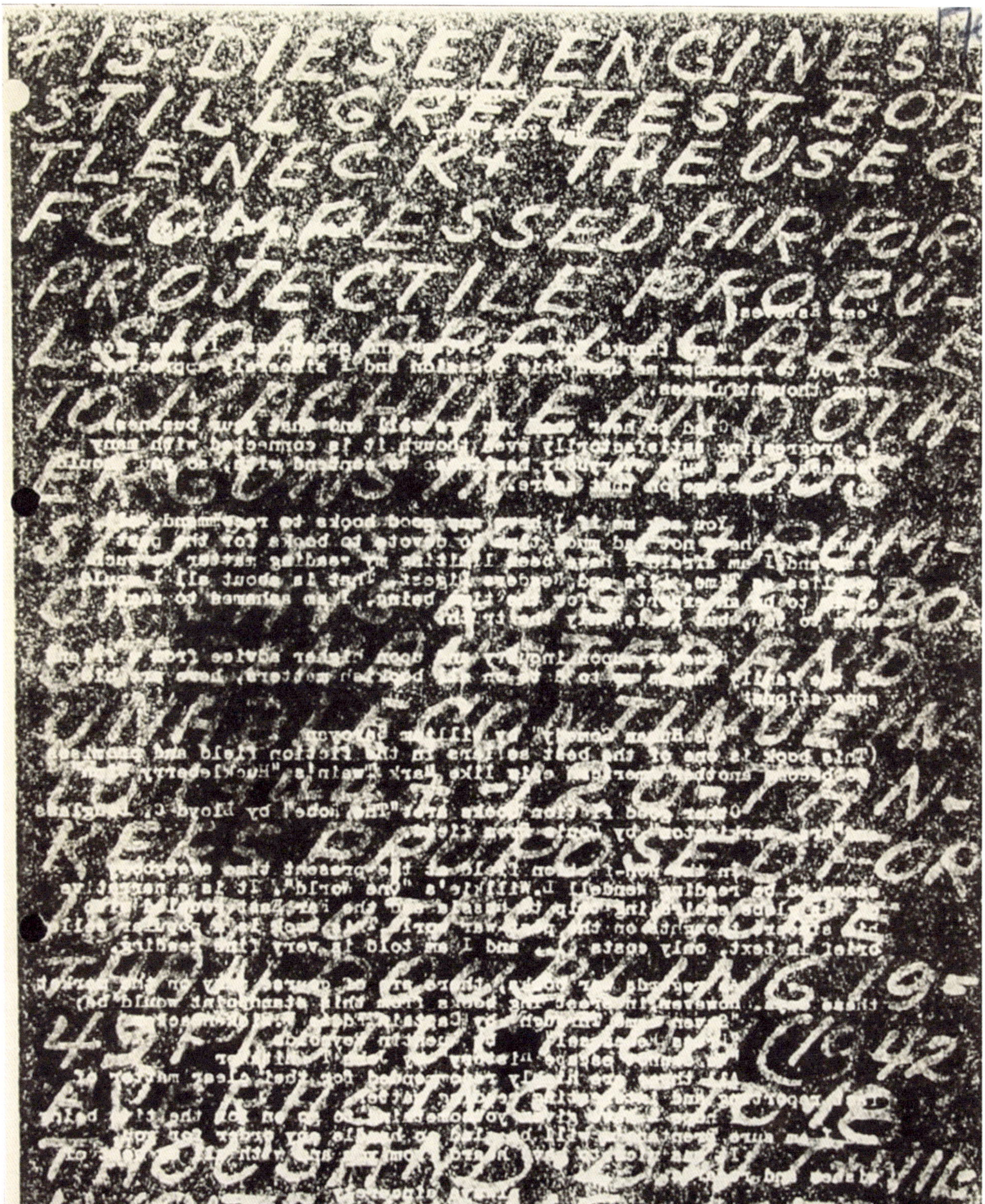
#15-DIESELENGINES
STILLGREATESTBOT
TLENECK-THEUSEO
FCOMPRESSEDAIRFOR
PROJECTILEPROPU-
LSIONAPPLICABLE
TOMACHINEANDOTH
KERSPROPOSEDFOR
LWRITEWHENPOSSIBLE

The first female British spy

Christine Granville: a female Second World War agent

1945

Christine Granville (Krystyna Gizycka) was not only the first female agent recruited by the British intelligence agencies during the Second World War; she was also Winston Churchill's favourite spy. A well-connected Polish countess and former beauty queen, Christine began her war work when Germany and its allies had the upper hand in the war. Struggling against German forces, Churchill had founded the so-called Special Operations Executive (SOE) in July 1940, with the aim of sending intelligence agents into German-occupied countries to spread propaganda, collect information and attack strategic targets. A brave and intelligent woman who spoke several languages, Christine was among the early recruits to SOE.

When Christine wrote this letter, she had worked for SOE for five years, operating behind enemy lines in North Africa, Hungary, Turkey and Italy, as well as in Nazi-occupied Poland and France, at huge personal risk. She had been arrested by the Germans on several occasions, yet had always managed to evade danger. In August 1944 she even secured the release of three Allied officers who had been captured and condemned to death by the Gestapo for being enemy agents. This astonishing reversal of fortunes was achieved through Christine's talent for weaving a good story, and it earned her a George Cross, the second-highest honour in the UK after the Victoria Cross.

Writing to her SOE boss Harold Perkins, Christine opens the letter addressing him as 'Perks Kochany', a Polish term of endearment. In March 1945, as the war came to a close, Christine was living within the safe confines of the British base in Cairo. In this letter, she is desperately volunteering for another mission: *'For God's sake do not strike my name from the firm [SOE] … remember that I am always too pleased to go and do anything for it. Maybe you find out that I could be usefull [sic] getting people out from camps and prisons in Germany – just before they get shot. I should love to do it and I like to jump out of a plane even every day.'*

Despite Christine's eagerness, however, no female agents were being sent into Germany at that juncture, so her suggested mission was not possible. And indeed, at the end of the war her employment with the British intelligence agency came to an end.

Nevertheless, this letter gives us a rare insight into the courage and determination of this remarkable woman, as well as the context in which she operated. As a spy, Christine had been trained to destroy potentially incriminating evidence, and as such, the paper trail about her that remains is relatively scant.

A mere seven years later, Christine was brutally killed by a man named Dennis Muldowney, who took the rejection of his romantic advances badly. Muldowney was tried for Christine's murder and sentenced to death on 30 September 1952, thereby bringing to an end the story of one of the longest-serving of all Britain's wartime women agents.

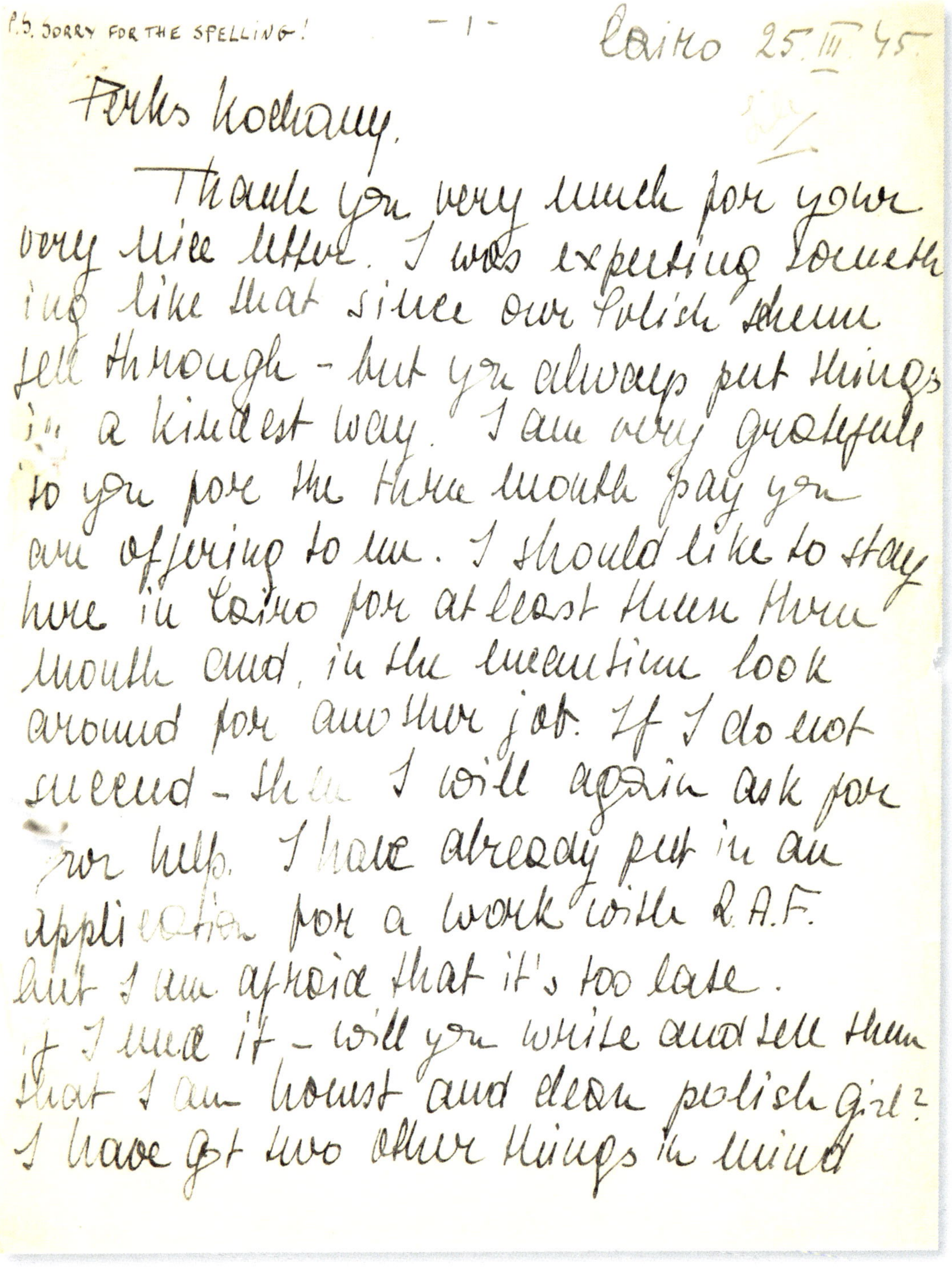
P.S. SORRY FOR THE SPELLING!

-1-

Cairo 25.III.45.

Perks kochany.

Thank you very much for your very nice letter. I was expecting something like that since our Polish scheme fell through – but you always put things in a kindest way. I am very gratefull to you for the three month pay you are offering to me. I should like to stay here in Cairo for at least these three month and, in the meantime look around for another job. If I do not succeed – then I will again ask for your help. I have already put in an application for a work with R.A.F. but I am afraid that it's too late. If I need it – will you write and tell them that I am honest and clean polish girl? I have got two other things in mind

en I maybe one of 2 items will come off.
Anyway I should like to keep in touch with you and for God's sake do not strike my name from the firm till it exist – remember that I am always too pleased to go and do anything for it. Maybe you find out that I could be usefull getting people out from camps and prisons in Germany – just before they get shot. I should love to do it and I like to jump out of a plane even every day. Please Perks, if it's not for your section – maybe somebody's else.

Thank you for the news about my brother I have sent a parcel to him. Did you ever heard something about my husband? Please do look after Andrew and don't

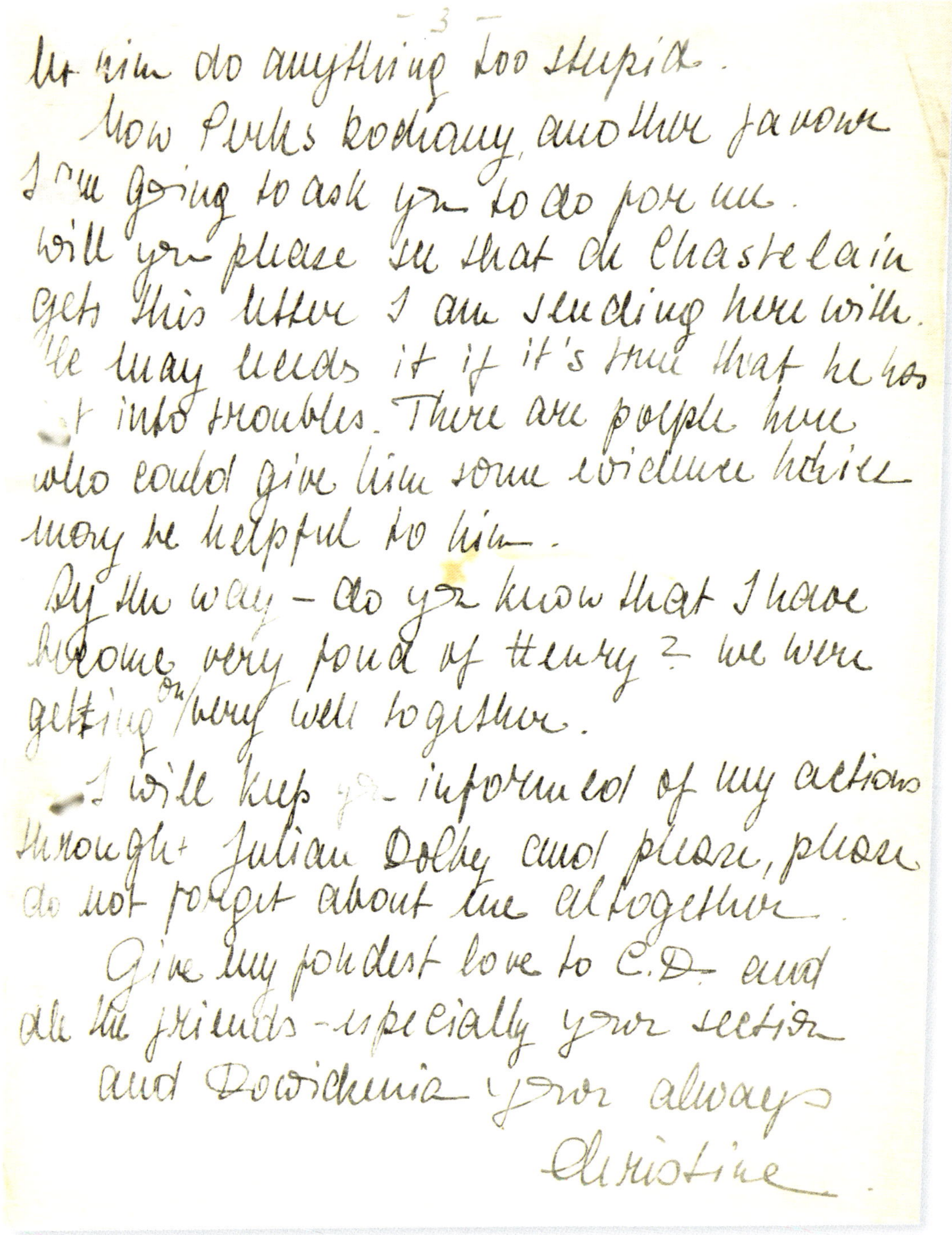

– 3 –

let him do anything too stupid.

Now Perks kochany, another favour I'm going to ask you to do for me. Will you please see that de Chastelain gets this letter I am sending herewith. He may needs it if it's true that he has got into troubles. There are people here who could give him some evidence which may be helpful to him.

By the way – do you know that I have become very fond of Henry? We were getting on very well together.

I will keep you informed of my actions through Julian Dolbey and please, please do not forget about me altogether.

Give my fondest love to C.D. and all the friends – specially your section and Dowidchenia. Yours always

Christine.

Ps. Sorry for the spelling! Cairo 25.III.45

Perks Kochany,

Thank you very much for your very nice offer. I was expecting something like that since our Polish scheme fell through – but you always put things in a kindest way. I am very grateful to you for the three month pay you are offering to me. I should like to stay here in Cairo for at least these three months and, in the meantime, look around for another job. If I do not succeed – then I will again ask for your help. I have already put in an application for a work with R.A.F but I am afraid that it's too late. If I make it – will you write and tell them that I am honest and clean Polish girl?

I have got two other things in mind and maybe one or two of them will come off. Anyway I should like to keep in touch with you and for God's sake do not strike my name from the firm till it exist – remember that I am always too pleased to go and do anything for it. Maybe you find out that I could be usefull [sic] getting people out from camps and prisons in Germany – just before they get shot. I should love to do it. And I like to jump out of a plane even every day. Please Perks. If it's not for your section – may be somebody else.

Thank you for the news about my brother. I have sent a parcel to him. Did you ever heard [sic] something about my husband? Please do look after Andrew and don't let him do anything too stupid.

Now Perks Kochany, another favour I am going to ask you to do for me. Will you please see that de Chastelain gets this letter I am sending here with. He may needs [sic] it if it's true that he has got into troubles [sic]. There are people here who could give him some evidence which may be helpful to him.

By the way – do you know that I have become very fond of Henry? We were getting on very well together.

I will keep you informed of my actions through Julian Dolby and please, please do not forget about me altogether.

Give my fondest love to C.D and all the friends – especially your section and Dowidzenia. Yours always,

Christine

Double agents and the Cold War

The disappearance of Guy Burgess and Donald Maclean

1951

When two British diplomats, Guy Burgess and Donald Maclean, disappeared in May 1951, the news made national headlines. The whereabouts of Burgess and Maclean became a topic of conversation, with many members of the public contacting the Foreign Office with sightings and explanations as to their possible location. This particular letter is from a clairvoyant who offered her services in tracking down the diplomats.

Unbeknownst to the public at the time, Maclean had been suspected of passing information to the Soviet Union. He had been unmasked by the discovery that Foreign Office telegrams had been sent to Moscow from its embassy in 1945. The investigation relied on material uncovered by a secret US project called Venona, which had managed to break a number of Soviet ciphers because of a Russian blunder: the normally impregnable code was broken as a result of a Soviet cipher clerk reusing a one-time pad to transmit intelligence traffic.

Details of the investigation were shared with the British, and as a result Maclean – who was working at the Foreign Office in London – was placed under observation. One of those privy to the investigation was Kim Philby, the head of MI6's operations in America, who also happened to be a Soviet agent recruited in Cambridge in the 1930s. In order to warn Maclean, Philby ordered Burgess, his fellow conspirator who was staying at his house in Washington, to return home. On his return to London, Burgess made contact with Maclean. Alarm bells began to ring when both Burgess and Maclean failed to return to work following a ferry trip to St Malo in France. It soon became clear that Maclean had been tipped off, and due to his close relationship with Burgess, Philby quickly became the prime suspect. Although no conclusive proof could be found, Philby was eventually dismissed by MI6. The fact that Burgess and Maclean had defected to Moscow was not made public until 1956, when the two appeared at a press conference there. In 1962, Philby also defected to Moscow.

Donald Maclean

Guy Burgess

Nothing to be Written in this Margin.

Minutes.

I fear that clairvoyancy is not included in our repertoire of technical subjects - perhaps you have someone qualified !!

E. F. Maltby

(E.F. Maltby).
15th June, 1951.

Mr. Turner.

Mr. Carey-Foster.

We have no establishment for clairvoyants as yet, but if this suggestion meets with support, we could well use the part-time services of one for decyphering Tokyo telegrams.

G. A. T. 16.6

11.6.51

[redacted]

Ilford

Essex

Dear Sir,

I think perhaps I could help you, in the mystery of the two diplomats. If you can let me have the telegrams & cables, handed in, I can in the quiet of my own room, rest with the writing under my head, read the thoughts of the writer; and sometimes, the features will also rise before me. The telegrams also cables, may have passed through too many hands, and the personality of the writer, faded. In that case, of course I shall <u>fail</u> to catch up his thoughts; but there is the chance that enough of his personality, still lingers in it. If you care to accept my offer, send them to me, by a bearer; to hand to me personally. Do not post. The woman living on the ground floor, is not to be trusted, where I am concerned. She is a

Communist also her husband.
I rent two rooms, upper floor.
If the bearer calls at seven in the evening, I will look for him, through my window.
I will return the telegrams & cables to the Foreign Office, the next day. Calling personally. I am British; and offering to help you, as a Daughter of Britannia.
Just number the telegrams & cables, in the corners; and on a sheet of writing paper, state where each telegram & cable, came from.
This is if you care for me, to try it out.

Yours Faithfully

[redacted] (Mrs)

[redacted]

Ilford

Essex

11.6.51

Dear Sir,

I think perhaps I could help you, in the mystery of the two diplomats. If you can let me have the telegrams and cables, handed in, I can in the quiet of my own room, rest with the writing under my head, read the thoughts of the writer; and sometimes, the features will also rise before me. The telegrams also cables, may have passed through too many hands, and the personality of the writer, faded. In that case, of course I shall <u>fail</u> to catch up his thoughts; but there is the chance that enough of his personality, still lingers in it. If you care to accept my offer, send them to me, by a bearer; to hand to me personally. Do not post. The woman living on the ground floor, is not to be trusted, where I am concerned, she is a Communist also her husband. I rent two rooms, upper floor. If the bearer calls at seven in the evening, I will look for him, through my window. I will return the telegrams and cables to the Foreign Office, the next day. Calling personally. I am British; and offering to help you, as a daughter of Britannia. Just number the telegrams and cables, in the corners; and on a sheet of writing paper, state where each telegram and cable, came from. This is if you care for me, to try it out.

Yours faithfully

[redacted] (Mrs)

Allies, diplomacy and foreign relations

Reburying the hatchet

The return of Napolen Bonaparte's remains to France

1840

Napoleon Bonaparte. The name alone was enough to send a shiver down the spine of any true born Englishman. One of the greatest military commanders in history, he almost single-handedly brought Europe under French hegemony and represented one of the most dangerous enemies Britain ever had to face. This letter, written nearly 20 years after Bonaparte's death, records a little-known postscript to these momentous events and helps to signify a burying of the hatchet between Europe's two greatest powers.

For almost two decades Napoleon Bonaparte was a central figure in one of the most turbulent periods of European history. He was hugely influential in providing the military success that prevented the French Revolution from being crushed and exported the revolutionary ideals to the rest of Europe. In time Napoleon became increasingly powerful, taking the position of First Consul and eventually Emperor of the French. There were a series of European coalitions put together in opposition to the aggressive policies of France, and although Napoleon was able to defeat these he was never able to attack his most persistent enemy, Britain. In the end it was attempts to enforce economic warfare against Britain that led to Napoleon's downfall through his ill-fated invasion of Russia. He was initially exiled to the Mediterranean island of Elba, but after his return and eventual defeat at the hands of the Duke of Wellington at Waterloo he was sent to the remote Atlantic island of St Helena.

Napoleon died on St Helena in 1821 and had recorded in his will that he wished his remains to be returned to Paris. For a number of years the French government resisted calls for this to take place because they were worried about the impact of the mass outpouring of public support which would naturally accompany any such move. By 1840 the French government felt that the nationalist fervour which would be unleashed by the return of Napoleon's remains would be beneficial to them politically, and so in May they sent a request to the British government.

This letter is a draft, preserved in the records of the British Foreign Office, of the response of Lord Palmerston to the French desire to *'remove from St Helena to France the Remains of Napoleon Buonaparte*'. He wrote that '*H. M. Gov[enmen]t will with great pleasure accede to this request.*' As a result of this, the French government, with much fanfare, sent a warship to St Helena to collect Napoleon's remains. These were then returned to Paris where, in front of a vast Parisian crowd, they were reinterred at Les Invalides on 15 December 1840.

In his letter Palmerston makes a point of not merely allowing the French request, but directly linking it to the relations between the two countries. Indeed he expressed his wish that 'the readiness with which this answer is given, will be looked upon in France as a Proof of the Desire of H.M. Gov[enmen]t to extinguish every Remnant of those national animosities which during the life of the Emperor arrayed the French and English People in arms against each other; and H.M. Gov[enmen]t trust that if any such Feelings still continue anywhere to exist, they may be buried in the Grave to which these Remains are about to be consigned.'

Napoleon in exile on St Helena.

Foreign Office
May 9. 1840

Draft
Lord Granville
No. 177

My Lord,

HM. Govt having taken into consideration the Request made by the Govt of France for permission to remove from St Helena to France the Remains of Napoleon Buonaparte, your Exly is instructed to assure Monsr Thiers that HM Govt will with great pleasure accede to this Request.

HM. Govt hope that the readiness with which this answer is given, will be looked up in France as a Proof of the Desire of HM Govt to extinguish every Remnant of those national animosities which during the life of the Emperor arrayed the French and English People in arms against each other; and HM. Govt trust that if any such Feelings still continue anywhere to exist, they may be buried in the Grave to which these Remains are about to be consigned.

HM. Govt will concert with that of France the arrangements necessary for carrying this Removal into effect.

I am Sir.

(signed) Palmerston

Draft

Lord Granville

No. 177.

Foreign Office,

May 9. 1840.

My Lord,

H.M. Govt. having taken into consideration the Request made by the Govt. of France for permission to remove from St. Helena to France the Remains of Napoleon Buonaparte, Your Exy. is instructed to assure Monsr. Thiers that H.M. Govt. will with great pleasure accede to this Request.

H.M. Govt.

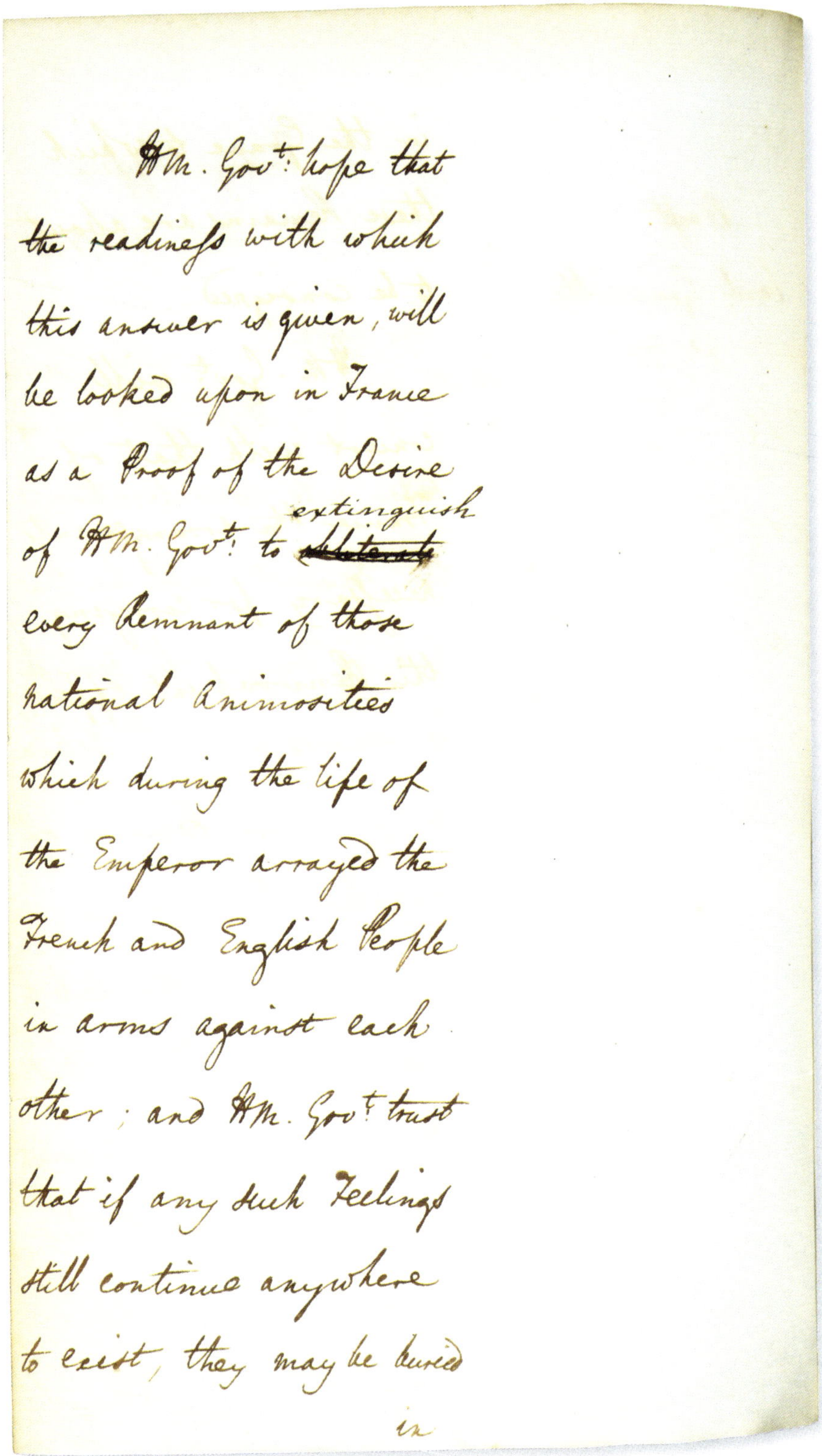

H.M. Govt. hope that
the readiness with which
this answer is given, will
be looked upon in France
as a Proof of the Desire
of H.M. Govt. to ~~obliterate~~ extinguish
every Remnant of those
national Animosities
which during the life of
the Emperor arrayed the
French and English People
in arms against each
other; and H.M. Govt. trust
that if any such Feelings
still continue anywhere
to exist, they may be buried
in

in the Grave to which
these Remains are about
to be consigned.

H.M. Govt. will
concert with that of
France the arrangements
necessary for carrying
this Removal into effect.

I am &c.

(signed) Palmerston.

Nationality and naturalisation

Karl Marx's application to become a British citizen is refused

1874

This letter consists of Karl Marx's application to be naturalised as a British citizen in 1874. Unfortunately for Marx, from 1873 the practice of obtaining a Metropolitan Police report on the respectability of the applicant and referees was established. This was in part due to the activities of certain Belgians and Germans who had committed offences in their respective countries and attempted to apply for naturalisation so as to avoid extradition from the United Kingdom. Clearly, this disloyalty to Marx's native Germany is very much on the report from Scotland Yard pertaining to Marx's application.

Marx was 66 when he applied for British citizenship. He had already written many of his revolutionary works, including *The Communist Manifesto* in 1848. He never became British, but remained in Britain until his death on 14 March 1883. He died a stateless person and is buried in Highgate Cemetery.

Metropolitan Police Office

Scotland Yard

17th August 1874

Carl Marx – Naturalization

With reference to the above I beg to report that he is the notorious German agitator, the head of the International Society, and an advocate of Communistic principles. This man has not been loyal to his own King and country.

The referees Messers, "Seton", "Matheren" "Manning" and "Adcock" are all British born subjects, and respectable house-holders. The statements made by them, with reference to the time they have known the applicant are correct.

W. Reiners,

Sergeant

36228

3000 12 | 73—McC. —P. 2058) 413

Detective Officer's Special Report

Metropolitan Police Office,

SCOTLAND YARD.

17th August 1874.

Carl Marx, – Naturalization.

With reference to the above I beg to report that he is the notorious German agitator, the head of the International Society, and an advocate of Communistic principles. This man has not been loyal to his own King and Country.

The referees Messrs "Seton," "Mathesen," "Manning," and "Adcock" are all British born subjects, and respectable householders. The statements made by them with reference to the time they have known the applicant are correct.

W. Reimers,

Sergeant.

F. Williamson

Supt.

'Wonderful things'
Discovering Tutankhamun's tomb

1924

'Would it not be a gracious, a kindly thing and a very diplomatic thing to do for the British Government and the Egyptian Government,' American citizen G W Chance wrote to the Foreign Office on 7 January 1924, 'to salute with Military honors, the remains and tomb of one of Egypt's Rulers just discovered'. The Eastern Department of the Foreign Office dismissed the suggestion with a casual 'external evidence would point out to his being the possessor of a weak mind,' but the American's idea was actually quite in line with the spirit of his time.

It all started in the Valley of the Kings, on the West Bank of the Nile in the south of Egypt. The Valley, which pharaohs chose as their place of eternity from the 16th century BC, is a fascinating place; among the most desolate, scorching hot spots on the planet, it is also one of the most truly magical. British archaeologist Howard Carter and his sponsor George Herbert, 5th Earl of Carnarvon, were given permission to dig in the Valley of the Kings in 1915. They went from one frustrating, fruitless season to the other until, on 4 November 1922, they discovered the entrance of a tomb with intact seals – that of 18th Dynasty Pharaoh Tutankhamun.

It would take Howard Carter and his team about 10 years to excavate the tomb properly, partly because after the discovery of the first virtually intact tomb of the Valley, a wave of Tutmania swept the entire planet, firing the imagination of the world. Heaps of gold, a boy king, mysterious deaths... The story of King Tut (which became his affectionate nickname) was perfect to put the grim years of the First World War behind for the general public. It was also perfect to become the focus of esoteric theories and very strange suggestions such as the one made by Chance.

'*The reverence that all people of the world have for the abiding places of the dead, may be sneered at by some, but this sentiment is not to be brushed lightly aside*,' Chance wrote, adding: '*Shakespeare felt its possible lack, when he protected his last resting place by a curse on him who moved his bones.*' Indeed, many of the numerous visitors the archaeologists had to contend with were animated by a decidedly morbid curiosity fuelled by the increasingly strong rumours of an ancient curse leading to the death of anyone getting too close to the young pharaoh. Now, as disappointing as it may sound, curses were, at best, infrequent in Ancient Egypt; Lord Carnarvon did die on 5 April 1923 in Cairo (the story says that the lights flickered, and that his hound in Highclere Castle howled at the precise moment of his death), but the medical report attested his unfortunate demise was due to septicaemia following an insect bite rather than to an ancient spell cast by a long-dead king. Besides, one cannot help but notice that Carter died in 1939, 17 years after disturbing Tut's rest.

Everyone, however, is sensitive to the fantastic, and Chance, who thought it was vital to 'think a little seriously of these things, instead of considering the discoveries recently made in Egypt only as a source of cheap jokes and shallow witticisms,' shouldn't be blamed too much. '*While some may say that it is a far cry from that generation to that of Ancient Egypt*,' as he put it, Tutankhamun is still one of the most widely known pharaohs in the world; his famous solid gold death mask adorns many cheap T-shirts, pens and snow globes. He has truly achieved eternity – albeit a tacky one.

The Valley of the Kings in 1922.

To the Secretary for the Colonies,

E

2

(Republication rights reserved).

It was a gracious and kindly thing for the King to do, to request that the body of Tut-Ankh-Amen remain undisturbed, Now how would a military salute appeal?

TUT - ANKH - AMEN

"Requiescat in Pace"

E 796

25 JAN 1924

New York, Jan. 7th, 1924.

While archaeology has rendered services to man in adding to our store of the knowledge of peoples of the past, it is well to pause in these things and not carry the actions at the old tombs to the point of the removal of the remains from the places of the dead's burial.

The reverence that all people of the world have for the abiding places of the dead, may be sneered at by some, but this sentiment is not to be brushed lightly aside.

Shakespeare felt its possible lack, when he protected his last resting place by a curse on him who moved his bones.

This sentiment, very strong among people of our race, has been lately aroused in the case of the proposed removal of Oglethorpes remains to America.

If we conceive, as is taught in some religious, that the ancestor's spirits approve and disapprove of the acts of their descendants, how reverent should be the conduct of such descendants towards their earthly memorials!

While some may say that it is a far cry from this generation to that of Ancient Egypt, and that the characters of the ancient Kings of that land may not merit reverence, yet as to this we have no certain knowledge.

Would it not be a gracious, a kindly thing and a very diplomatic thing to do for the British Government and the Egyptian Government, to salute with Military honors, the remains and tomb of one of Egypt's Rulers just discovered, that nation which has given so much to advance civilization. No matter what may be said as to her persecution of the Jews, for which she has long ago paid in her shorn glory. Let us try to think a little seriously of these things, instead of considering the discoveries recently ~~recently~~ made in Egypt only as a source of cheap jokes and shallow witticisms.

Salute to Old Egyptian Civilization and let her ancient dead rest among their ancestors, and their descendants.

One who believes in Honor to the Dead's Burial Place.

George Whitefield [illegible]
4 W. 34th St.
New York City.

SHEET C-3

THE THEBAN NECROPOLIS

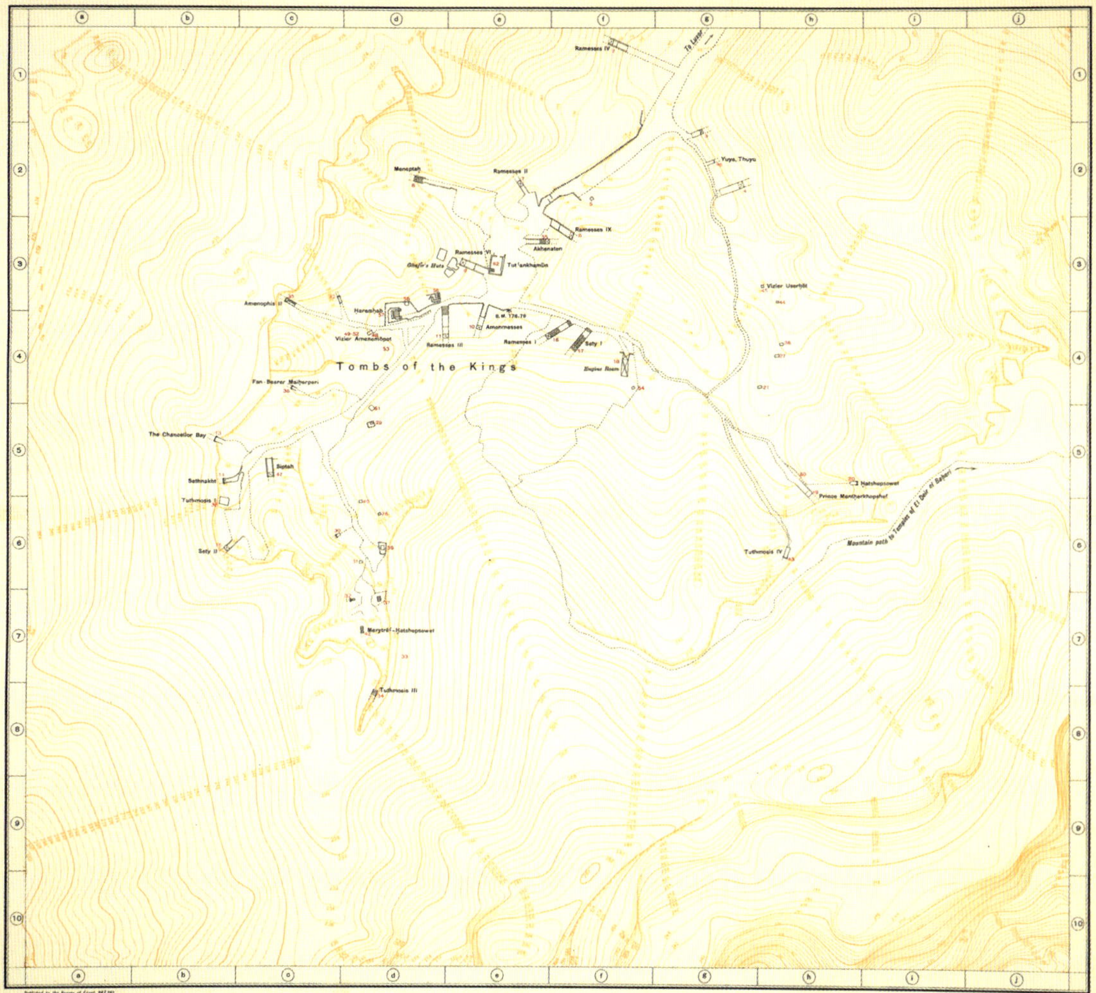

Tomb No.	NAME OF OWNER	Position on sheet	Threshold height in metres above M.S.L.
K 2	Rameses IV ([illegible])	f - 1	167.63
K 3	A late Rameses ([illegible])	e - 2	—
K 4	" " "	d - 2	166.21
K 5	Not identified	f - 2	—
K 6	Rameses IX ([illegible])	f - 2	170.92
K 7	Rameses II ([illegible])	e - 2	169.68
K 8	Menoptah ([illegible])	d - 2	179.15
K 9	Rameses VI ([illegible])	e - 3	173.61
K 10	Amonmesses ([illegible])	e - 4	171.61
K 11	Rameses III ([illegible])	d - 4	174.74
K 12	Not identified	c - 3	—
K 13	The Chancellor Bay ([illegible])	b - 5	165.25
K 14	Sethnakht ([illegible])	b - 5	166.95
K 15	Sety II ([illegible])	b - 6	—
K 16	Rameses I ([illegible])	f - 4	176.41
K 17	Sety I ([illegible])	f - 4	178.07
K 18	A late Rameses ([illegible])	f - 4	—
K 19	Prince Mentherkhopshef ([illegible])	h - 5	167.00
K 20	Hatshepsowet ([illegible])	h - 5	—
K 21	Not identified	h - 4	—
K 26	" "	d - 6	—
K 27	" "	h - 4	—
K 28	" "	h - 4	—
K 29	" "	d - 5	—
K 30	" "	c - 6	—
K 31	" "	d - 6	—
K 32	" "	d - 7	—
* K 33	" "	d - 7	—
K 34	Tuthmosis III ([illegible])	d - 8	—
K 35	Amenophis II ([illegible])	c - 3	166.12
K 36	Fan-Bearer Maiherperi ([illegible])	d - 4	179.70
K 37	Not identified	d - 7	—
K 38	Tuthmosis I ([illegible])	b - 6	—
K 40	Not identified	d - 6	—
† K 42	Merytrē' Hatshepsowet ([illegible])	d - 7	—
K 43	Tuthmosis IV ([illegible])	h - 6	—
* K 44	Not identified	h - 3	—
K 45	Vizier Userḥēt ([illegible])	h - 3	—
K 46	Yuya, Thuyu ([illegible])	g - 3	—
K 47	Siptah ([illegible])	c - 5	165.14
K 48	Vizier Amenemipet ([illegible])	d - 4	—
* § K 49	Not identified	d - 4	—
* § K 50	" "	d - 4	—
* § K 51	" "	d - 4	—
* § K 52	" "	d - 4	—
* K 53	" "	d - 4	—
‡ K 54	" "	f - 4	—
K 55	Akhenaten ([illegible])	e - 3	169.98
* K 56	Not identified	d - 3	—
K 57	Haremhab ([illegible])	d - 4	173.10
‡ K 58	Not identified	e - 3	—
K 59	" "	d - 5	—
* † K 60	" "	h - 5	—
K 61	" "	e - 5	—
K 62	Tut'ankhamūn ([illegible])	e - 3	170.44

* The positions of these tombs are approximate as they have been reburied.
† Contained intrusive burial of [illegible]
ø Contained intrusive burial of [illegible]
§ Contained remains of royal pets.
* Contained jewellery of Twosret and Sety II.
‡ Contained seals of Tut'ankhamūn and Ay.
† Contained royal names of Tuthmosis IV.

Published by the Survey of Egypt, 1927.
In collaboration with the Antiquities Department.

Surveyed in 1926.

REFERENCE

Contour figures in Metres ....
Bench Marks .... B.M. 96.71
Tomb Numbers 26

Scale 1:1,000

Metres 10 0 10 20 30 40 50 60 70 80 90 100 Metres

PRICE { 150 Mill. on linen backed paper; 100 " " paper

Dimensions of Sheet { North-South 550-50 Millimetres; East-West 651-50

The end of 'peace in our time'

Lord Halifax and the declaration of war

1939

'A state of war exists between the two countries as from 11 a.m. today, September 3rd.' This understated, almost bland phrase written by the British Foreign Secretary, Lord Halifax, set in motion one of the most destructive and deadly chains of events in human history, the Second World War in Europe.

Since the mid-1930s, Britain and France had pursued a policy of Appeasement towards Germany under its new National Socialist (Nazi) government. Many in Britain felt that the terms meted out to Germany at the end of the First World War were too harsh, and were willing to let Germany work to return to its position as a strong Central European power. As such, the British government looked on as the Germans asserted control in the Rhineland, the Sudetenland and Austria. Memories of the horror of the First World War remained fresh in the minds of British politicians, and it was hoped that these concessions would be enough to satisfy the demands of Adolf Hitler and his newly assertive Germany. It was this that inspired the Prime Minister Neville Chamberlain's infamous declaration of 'peace in our time' following the 1938 Munich Agreement. This dream was shattered in March 1939 when the Germans tore up the agreement and their army marched into Czechoslovakia. In response, the British government offered Poland, widely acknowledged as Hitler's next target, a guarantee against German aggression.

On 1 September, Hitler put this British commitment to the test, invading Poland on a trumped-up claim of self-defence. The attack on Poland was a step too far for the British government, and in combination with the French, they issued an ultimatum to the Germans that unless they received 'satisfactory assurances that the German government had suspended all aggressive action against Poland', they would 'fulfil their obligations'. Lord Halifax's letter, echoing the famous speech made by Neville Chamberlain, at the same time, states that '*No such assurance having been received I have the honour to inform you that a state of war exists between the two countries*'.

This understated letter began a conflict that ended six years later in the ruined shell of Berlin. What began as a European conflict rapidly spread, drawing in the USSR and the USA, and connecting up with the ongoing war in the Far East. In the European theatre alone tens of millions died, and many more were left homeless, displaced and bereaved. Out of the wreckage of the continent a new Europe was born, divided by what Winston Churchill described as an 'iron curtain' and, while freed from one totalitarian ideology, was directly faced with another, communism. In this respect, these 18 lines mark one of the most significant events in 20th-century history.

Foreign Policy 40

FOREIGN OFFICE, S.W.1.
3rd September, 1939.

Sir,

On September 1st His Majesty's Ambassador in Berlin, acting upon my instructions, informed the German Government that unless they were prepared to give His Majesty's Government in the United Kingdom satisfactory assurances that the German Government had suspended all aggressive action against Poland and were prepared promptly to withdraw their forces from Polish territory, His Majesty's Government in the United Kingdom would, without hesitation, fulfil their obligations to Poland.

2. At 9 a.m. this morning His Majesty's Ambassador in Berlin, acting upon my instructions, informed the German Government that unless not later than 11 a.m., British Summer Time, today September 3rd, satisfactory assurances to the above effect had been given by the German Government and had reached His Majesty's Government in London, a state of war would exist between the two countries as from that hour.

3. No such assurance having been received, I have the honour to inform you that a state of war exists between the two countries as from 11 a.m. today, September 3rd.

I have the honour to be
With high consideration,
Your obedient Servant,
HALIFAX.

The German Chargé d'Affaires
Etc., etc., etc.

Operation Pied Piper: what to feed the children?

Government guidelines for caring for evacuated children

1939

In February 1939, a mere five months after British Prime Minister Neville Chamberlain returned from negotiations with Hitler in Munich declaring that he had secured 'peace for our time', the British government was making preparations for war with Germany. As this letter shows, in what we now know as an interwar rather than a 'peaceful' time, discussions were going on behind the scenes between the Food Department and the Ministry of Health about how British children would be fed if German attacks from the air forced mass evacuation from towns and cities to the countryside. Six months later, the evacuation plan, codenamed Operation Pied Piper, swung into action on 1 September, moving schoolchildren, pregnant women, mothers with young babies, and the disabled to areas less threatened by bombing.

As the evacuees assembled for departure at railway stations across the country, often clutching gas masks and suitcases containing a spare set of clothes and food for the journey, most had little idea of what would greet them upon arrival. Some would be staying with family or friends, but many were sent to live with total strangers.

Government guidelines stated that hosts should treat evacuated children as members of the family, giving them the same diet as they would their own children. To this end, the state provided a weekly allowance of ten shillings and six pence (around £15 in today's money) in the hope that this would guarantee children away from home a decent standard of living. But right from the start, experiences of evacuation varied enormously. Upon arrival at their destination, the children were lined up and one by one picked by their would-be hosts. An evacuee from Bethnal Green later recalled: 'I noticed a woman looking at evacuees' hair and opening their mouths, but one of the helpers said: "They might come from the East End, but they're children, not animals." Nonetheless, the smartest and cleanest evacuees were usually picked first, and girls tended to be preferred over boys, since it was thought that they would cause less trouble.'

Concerned to ensure the welfare of young evacuees who were often billeted with people who had no experience of looking after children, the government issued hosts with guidelines. 'Baths should be given as often as possible', the advice intoned. 'It should be remembered that young children need 11 hours' sleep', it warned. And furthermore, 'a well-balanced diet with plenty of changes' was considered key to having a happy and healthy child. State-recommended 'specimen meals for a child of school age' included a lot of bread and butter, washed down with weak tea, and despite predictions back in February 1939 that bacon would be hard to come by in wartime, it too featured among the suggested fare for breakfast.

By the end of the war, 3.5 million Brits had been relocated to rural areas. Thanks to the careful planning six years earlier, only 5,000 of the 60,000 British civilians killed during the Second World War were children. A similar number of children, 5,200, had settled in so successfully with their host families during the war that they stayed there permanently once it was over.

SECRETARY: C. C. ANDERSON, M.D., LL.D. DEPUTY SECRETARY: C. HILL, M.A., M.D., D.P.H. ASSISTANT SECRETARIES: A. MACRAE, M.A., M.B., CH.B. L. S. POTTER, M.B., CH.B.

TELEGRAMS: MEDISECRA, WESTCENT, LONDON

TELEPHONE: EUSTON 2111 (SIX LINES)

British Medical Association

93446/4/7.

BRITISH MEDICAL ASSOCIATION HOUSE
TAVISTOCK SQUARE
LONDON · W·C·1

SCOTLAND
7 · DRUMSHEUGH GARDENS
EDINBURGH
EIRE
18 · KILDARE STREET
DUBLIN
AUSTRALIA
B · M · A · BUILDING
135 · MACQUARIE STREET
SYDNEY · N · S · W
SOUTH AFRICA
BOX 643 · CAPETOWN
NEW ZEALAND
BOX 156 · WELLINGTON
AFFILIATED TO B · M · A
CANADIAN MEDICAL ASSOC.
184 · COLLEGE STREET · TORONTO

PLEASE ADDRESS ALL COMMUNICATIONS TO THE SECRETARY

YOUR REF | OUR REF CH/EK. | DATE 31st January, 1939.

Sir,

Correspondence received by this Association shows that there is a desire for information on the part of some householders as to the appropriate diet which should be provided by them for children in the event of evacuation schemes being carried out. This would not appear to be a matter on which this Association could properly offer guidance, in view of the fact that to be of practical value any such advice given would require to be related to the anticipated conditions of food supply. I feel, however, that you may wish to have this aspect of the matter brought to your attention.

And this equally applies to the Ministry of Health RAC.

Should it be felt that any action can usefully be taken, you can count on this Association for any co-operation which it was in its power to give.

Yours faithfully,

Charles Hill

Deputy Secretary.

The Secretary,
Ministry of Health,
Whitehall,
S.W. 1.

TELEPHONE:
VICTORIA 8585

Food (Defence Plans) Department,
Great Westminster House,
Horseferry Road,
London, S.W. 1.

27th February, 1939.

Dear Peete,

In reply to your official letter of 18th instant (IVB/93446/4/7), the answer to the B.M.A. seems to be that householders should endeavour to give children who are evacuated the normal diet which they would give to children of their own. If they need any further advice, either the B.M.A. or your Department will, no doubt, be able to give it.

We cannot, of course, prophesy the conditions of food supply and the degree of shortage, if any, that there will be in any particular food. But you can take it as fairly certain that there will be a shortage of bacon - which is not, I imagine, an essential food for children.

Our main object will be to see that additional supplies of the normal staple foods, including milk, are sent to the shops in the areas to which children and other persons are evacuated and, for this purpose, we are counting on being advised beforehand of the numbers to be evacuated to particular places. We are not responsible for what householders in reception areas buy or how they cook it, or what they give to evacuated children.

Yours sincerely,

E. M. H. Lloyd

W.J. Peete, Esq.,
Ministry of Health,
Whitehall, S.W.1.

Mr Hudson, Pl. speak
(to the f.p.) WJP 28/2

The most unsordid act in history

The origins of Lend-Lease

1940

In December 1940, Britain stood alone against Nazi Germany. The French had surrendered to German forces in June 1940, while the USA remained neutral and unwilling to be drawn into another European war. Forced to fight on alone, Britain stood on the verge of bankruptcy, with financial collapse only months away. In a stark attempt to bring home the existential dangers facing Britain, Churchill wrote to the US President Franklin Roosevelt, who had been re-elected for an unprecedented third term in November 1940. The letter, which was dated 8 December 1940, painted a bleak assessment of the British position, stressing that democracy and civilisation were in peril from Nazi oppression and that the fates of both countries were intimately linked. At its most basic it was a heartfelt plea from Churchill to Roosevelt asking for help, from one friend to another.

The letter pulled no punches with its assessment of the war to date: the first half of 1940 was a disaster for the Allies and for Europe, with German domination spreading to Africa and Asia. While Britain could endure the destruction of its buildings and the slaughter of its population, it could not do so alone. Churchill then set out the minimum requirements needed for victory, which included not less than three million tons of additional merchant shipping backed up by the protection of the United States Navy. How a bankrupt Britain intended to pay was also addressed, with Churchill conceding that the moment was fast approaching when Britain would no longer be able to meet the costs of shipping and other supplies. The letter concluded with the plea that the fate of Britain was in the hand of the President and the American people.

Roosevelt never formally responded to Churchill's letter, but at a press conference on 17 December 1940 he employed a telling metaphor that if his neighbour's house was on fire, he would lend him a hosepipe to put out the fire rather than selling it to him. The concept of Lend-Lease was quickly established, with a Bill sent to congress in early January 1941. In a thinly veiled assertion of American dominance, the Bill was given the number 1776 – the year of the declaration of American independence. The legislation was entitled 'An Act to Promote the Defence of the United States', and provided Britain with a financial lifeline enabling the country to continue the war without bankrupting the nation. Churchill later described lend-lease as the most unsordid act in the history of any nation. Britain eventually received $31.4 billion dollars, with repayment spread out over 50 years. The last payment made by the British Treasury to the US Federal Reserve was on 29 December 2006.

Franklin D Roosevelt signing the Lend-Lease agreement.

THIS DOCUMENT IS THE PROPERTY OF HIS BRITANNIC MAJESTY'S GOVERNMENT 225

Printed for the War Cabinet. December 1940.

MOST SECRET. **Copy No.** 25

W.P. (40) 466 (Final Revise).

December 8, 1940.

TO BE KEPT UNDER LOCK AND KEY.

It is requested that special care may be taken to ensure the secrecy of this document.

WAR CABINET.

10 *Downing Street, Whitehall,*
December 8, 1940.

My dear Mr. President,

AS we reach the end of this year, I feel you will expect me to lay before you the prospects for 1941. I do so with candour and confidence, because it seems to me that the vast majority of American citizens have recorded their conviction that the safety of the United States as well as the future of our two democracies and the kind of civilization for which they stand, are bound up with the survival and independence of the British Commonwealth of Nations. Only thus can those bastions of sea power, upon which the control of the Atlantic and Indian Oceans depend, be preserved in faithful and friendly hands. The control of the Pacific by the United States Navy and of the Atlantic by the British Navy, is indispensable to the security and the trade routes of both our countries, and the surest means of preventing war from reaching the shores of the United States.

2. There is another aspect. It takes between three and four years to convert the industries of a modern state to war purposes. Saturation point is reached when the maximum industrial effort that can be spared from civil needs has been applied to war production. Germany certainly reached this point by the end of 1939. We in the British Empire are now only about half-way through the second year. The United States, I should suppose, was by no means so far advanced as we. Moreover, I understand that immense programmes of naval, military and air defence are now on foot in the United States, to complete which certainly two years are needed. It is our British duty in the common interest, as also for our own survival, to hold the front and grapple with the Nazi power until the preparations of the United States are complete. Victory may come before two years are out; but we have no right to count upon it to the extent of relaxing any effort that is humanly possible. Therefore, I submit with very great respect for your good and friendly consideration that there is a solid identity of interest between the British Empire and the United States while these conditions last. It is upon this footing that I venture to address you.

3. The form which this war has taken, and seems likely to hold, does not enable us to match the immense armies of Germany in any theatre where their main power can be brought to bear. We can, however, by the use of sea power and air power, meet the German armies in regions where only comparativly small forces can be brought into action. We must do our best to prevent the German domination of Europe spreading into Africa and into Southern Asia. We have also to

[21964] B

maintain in constant readiness in this Island, armies strong enough to make the problem of an oversea invasion insoluble. For these purposes we are forming as fast as possible, as you are already aware, between 50 and 60 divisions. Even if the United States were our Ally, instead of our friend and indispensable partner, we should not ask for a large American expeditionary army. Shipping, not men, is the limiting factor, and the power to transport munitions and supplies, claims priority over the movement by sea of large numbers of soldiers.

4. The first half of 1940 was a period of disaster for the Allies and for Europe. The last five months have witnessed a strong and perhaps unexpected recovery by Great Britain fighting alone, but with the invaluable aid in munitions and in destroyers placed at our disposal by the great Republic of which you are for the third time the chosen chief.

5. The danger of Great Britain being destroyed by a swift, overwhelming blow, has for the time being very greatly receded. In its place, there is a long, gradually-maturing danger, less sudden and less spectacular, but equally deadly. This mortal danger is the steady and increasing diminution of sea tonnage. We can endure the shattering of our dwellings, and the slaughter of our civil population by indiscriminate air attacks, and we hope to parry these increasingly as our science develops, and to repay them upon military objectives in Germany as our Air Force more nearly approaches the strength of the enemy. The decision for 1941 lies upon the seas. Unless we can establish our ability to feed this Island, to import the munitions of all kinds which we need, unless we can move our armies to the various theatres where Hitler and his confederate, Mussolini, must be met, and maintain them there, and do all this with the asurance of being able to carry it on till the spirit of the Continental Dictators is broken, we may fall by the way, and the time needed by the United States to complete her defensive preparations may not be forthcoming. It is therefore in shipping and in the power to transport across the oceans, particularly the Atlantic Ocean, that in 1941 the crunch of the whole war will be found. If, on the other hand, we are able to move the necessary tonnage to and fro across salt water indefinitely, it may well be that the application of superior air power to the German homeland and the rising anger of the German and other Nazi-gripped populations, will bring the agony of civilization to a merciful and glorious end.

But do not let us underrate the task.

6. Our shipping losses, the figures for which in recent months are appended, have been on a scale almost comparable to that of the worst year of the last war. In the five weeks ending the 3rd November losses reached a total of 420,300 tons. Our estimate of annual tonnage which ought to be imported in order to maintain our effort at full strength is 43 million tons; the tonnage entering in September was only at the rate of 37 million tons and in October at 38 million tons. Were they to continue at this rate they would be fatal, unless indeed immensely greater replenishment than anything at present in sight could be achieved in time. Although we are doing all we can to meet this situation by new methods, the difficulty of limiting losses is obviously much greater than in the last war. We lack the assistance of the French Navy, the Italian Navy and the Japanese Navy, and above all of the United States Navy, which was of such vital help to us during the culminating years. The enemy commands the ports all around the north and western coast of France. He is increasingly basing his submarines, flying-boats and combat planes on these ports and on the islands off the French coast. We are denied the use of the ports or territory of Eire in which to organize our coastal patrols by Air and sea. In fact, we have now only one effective route of entry to the British Isles, namely, the Northern approaches, against which the enemy is increasingly concentrating, reaching ever farther out by U-Boat action and long-distance aircraft bombing. In addition, there have for some months been merchant ship raiders, both in the Atlantic and Indian Oceans. And now we have the powerful warship-raider to contend with as well. We need ships both to hunt down and to escort. Large as are our resources and preparations, we do not possess enough.

7. The next six or seven months bring relative battleship strength in home waters to a smaller margin than is satisfactory. *Bismarck* and *Tirpitz* will

certainly be in service in January. We have already *King George V*, and hope to have *Prince of Wales* in the line at the same time. These modern ships are of course far better armoured especially against Air attack, than vessels like *Rodney* and *Nelson* designed twenty years ago. We have recently had to use *Rodney* on Transatlantic escort, and at any time when numbers are so small, a mine or a torpedo may alter decisively the strength of the line of battle. We get relief in June, when *Duke of York* will be ready, and will be still better off at the end of 1941, when *Anson* also will have joined. But these two first-class modern 35,000-tons 15-in.-gun German battleships force us to maintain a concentration never previously necessary in this war.

8. We hope that the two Italian *Littorios* will be out of action for a while, and anyway they are not so dangerous as if they were manned by Germans. Perhaps they might be! We are indebted to you for your help about the *Richelieu* and *Jean Bart*, and I dare say that will be all right. But, Mr. President, as no one will see more clearly than you, we have during these months to consider for the first time in this war a fleet action, in which the enemy will have two ships at least as good as our two best and only two modern ones. It will be impossible to reduce our strength in the Mediterranean, because the attitude of Turkey, and indeed the whole position in the Eastern basin depends upon our having a strong fleet there. The older, unmodernized battleships will have to go for convoy. Thus even in the battleship class we are at full extension.

9. There is a second field of danger: the Vichy Government may either by joining Hitler's New Order in Europe or through some manœuvre, such as forcing us to attack an expedition dispatched by sea against the Free French Colonies, find an excuse for ranging with the Axis Powers the very considerable undamaged naval forces still under its control. If the French Navy were to join the Axis, the control of West Africa would pass immediately into their hands, with the gravest consequences to our communications between the Northern and Southern Atlantic, and also affecting Dakar and, of course, thereafter South America.

10. A third sphere of danger is in the Far East. Here it seems clear that Japan is thrusting southward through Indo-China to Saigon and other naval and air bases, thus bringing them within a comparatively short distance of Singapore and the Dutch East Indies. It is reported that the Japanese are preparing five good Divisions for possible use as an overseas expeditionary force. We have to-day no forces in the Far East capable of dealing with this situation should it develop.

11. In the face of these dangers we must try to use the year 1941 to build up such a supply of weapons, particularly of aircraft, both by increased output at home in spite of bombardment, and through ocean-borne supplies, as will lay the foundations of victory. In view of the difficulty and magnitude of this task, as outlined by all the facts I have set forth, to which many others could be added I feel entitled, nay bound, to lay before you the various ways in which the United States could give supreme and decisive help to what is, in certain aspects, the common cause.

12. The prime need is to check or limit the loss of tonnage on the Atlantic approaches to our island. This may be achieved both by increasing the naval forces which cope with the attacks, and by adding to the number of merchant ships on which we depend. For the first purpose there would seem to be the following alternatives:—

(1) The reassertion by the United States of the doctrine of the freedom of the seas from illegal and barbarous methods of warfare, in accordance with the decisions reached after the late Great War, and as freely accepted and defined by Germany in 1935. From this, United States ships should be free to trade with countries against which there is not an effective legal blockade.

(2) It would, I suggest, follow that protection should be given to this lawful trading by United States forces, *i.e.*, escorting battleships, cruisers, destroyers and air flotillas. The protection would be immensely more effective if you were able to obtain bases in Eire for the duration of

the war. I think it is improbable that such protection would provoke a declaration of war by Germany upon the United States, though probably sea incidents of a dangerous character would from time to time occur. Herr Hitler has shown himself inclined to avoid the Kaiser's mistake. He does not wish to be drawn into war with the United States until he has gravely undermined the power of Great Britain. His maxim is "One at a time."

The policy I have ventured to outline, or something like it, would constitute a decisive act of constructive non-belligerency by the United States, and more than any other measure, would make it certain that British resistance could be effectually prolonged for the desired period and victory gained.

(3) Failing the above, the gift, loan, or supply of a large number of American vessels of war, above all destroyers, already in the Atlantic is indispensable to the maintenance of the Atlantic route. Further, could not the United States Naval Forces extend their sea control of the American side of the Atlantic, so as to prevent the molestation by enemy vessels of the approaches to the new line of naval and air bases which the United States is establishing in British islands in the Western Hemisphere. The strength of the United States Naval Forces is such that the assistance in the Atlantic that they could afford us, as described above, would not jeopardize the control of the Pacific.

(4) We should also then need the good offices of the United States and the whole influence of its Government, continually exerted, to procure for Great Britain the necessary facilities upon the Southern and Western shores of Eire for our flotillas, and still more important, for our aircraft, working to the westward into the Atlantic. If it were proclaimed an American interest that the resistance of Great Britain should be prolonged and the Atlantic route kept open for the important armaments now being prepared for Great Britain in North America, the Irish in the United States might be willing to point out to the Government of Eire the dangers which its present policy is creating for the United States itself.

His Majesty's Government would of course take the most effective measures beforehand to protect Ireland if Irish action exposed it to German attack. It is not possible for us to compel the people of Northern Ireland against their will to leave the United Kingdom and join Southern Ireland. But I do not doubt that if the Government of Eire would show its solidarity with the democracies of the English-speaking world at this crisis, a Council for Defence of all Ireland could be set up out of which the unity of the Island would probably in some form or other emerge after the war.

13. The object of the foregoing measures is to reduce to manageable proportions the present destructive losses at sea. In addition, it is indispensable that the merchant tonnage available for supplying Great Britain and for the waging of the war by Great Britain with all vigour, should be substantially increased beyond the 1¼ million tons per annum which is the utmost we can now build. The convoy system, the detours, the zig-zags, the great distances from which we now have to bring our imports, and the congestion of our Western harbours, have reduced by about one-third the fruitfulness of our existing tonnage. To ensure final victory, not less than 3 million tons of additional merchant shipbuilding capacity will be required. Only the United States can supply this need. Looking to the future it would seem that production on a scale comparable to that of the Hog Island scheme of the last War ought to be faced for 1942. In the meanwhile, we ask that in 1941 the United States should make available to us every ton of merchant shipping, surplus to its own requirements, which it possesses or controls, and to find some means of putting into our service a large proportion of merchant shipping now under construction for the National Maritime Board.

14. Moreover, we look to the industrial energy of the Republic for a reinforcement of our domestic capacity to manufacture combat aircraft. Without that reinforcement reaching us in substantial measure, we shall not achieve the

massive preponderance in the air on which we must rely to loosen and disintegrate the German grip on Europe. We are at present engaged in a programme designed to increase our strength to 7,000 first-line aircraft by the Spring of 1942. But it is abundantly clear that this programme will not suffice to give us the weight of superiority which will force open the doors of victory. In order to achieve such superiority it is plain that we shall need the greatest production of aircraft which the United States of America are capable of sending us. It is our anxious hope that in the teeth of continuous bombardment we shall realise the greater part of the production which we have planned in this country. But not even with the addition to our squadrons of all the aircraft which, under present arrangements, we may derive from planned output in the United States can we hope to achieve the necessary ascendancy. May I invite you then, Mr. President, to give earnest consideration to an immediate order on joint account for a further 2,000 combat aircraft a month? Of these aircraft, I would submit, the highest possible proportion should be heavy bombers, the weapon on which, above all others, we depend to shatter the foundations of German military power. I am aware of the formidable task that this would impose upon the industrial organisation of the United States. Yet, in our heavy need, we call with confidence to the most resourceful and ingenious technicians in the world. We ask for an unexampled effort, believing that it can be made.

15. You have also received information about the needs of our Armies. In the munitions sphere, in spite of enemy bombing, we are making steady progress here. Without your continued assistance in the supply of machine tools and in further releases from stock of certain articles, we could not hope to equip as many as 50 Divisions in 1941. I am grateful for the arrangements, already practically completed, for your aid in the equipment of the army which we have already planned, and for the provision of the American type of weapons for an additional 10 Divisions in time for the campaign of 1942. But when the tide of Dictatorship begins to recede, many countries trying to regain their freedom may be asking for arms, and there is no source to which they can look except to the factories of the United States. I must therefore also urge the importance of expanding to the utmost American productive capacity for small arms, artillery and Tanks.

16. I am arranging to present you with a complete programme of the munitions of all kinds which we seek to obtain from you, the greater part of which is, of course, already agreed. An important economy of time and effort will be produced if the types selected for the United States Services should, whenever possible, conform to those which have proved their merit in our hands under the actual conditions of war. In this way reserves of guns and ammunition and of airplanes, become interchangeable, and are by that very fact augmented. This is, however, a sphere so highly technical that I do not enlarge upon it.

17. Last of all, I come to the question of Finance. The more rapid and abundant the flow of munitions and ships which you are able to send us, the sooner will our dollar credits be exhausted. They are already, as you know, very heavily drawn upon by the payments we have made to date. Indeed, as you know the orders already placed or under negotiation, including the expenditure settled or pending for creating munition factories in the United States, many times exceed the total exchange resources remaining at the disposal of Great Britain. The moment approaches when we shall no longer be able to pay cash for shipping and other supplies. While we will do our utmost, and shrink from no proper sacrifice to make payments across the Exchange, I believe you will agree that it would be wrong in principle and mutually disadvantageous in effect if, at the height of this struggle, Great Britain were to be divested of all saleable assets, so that after the victory was won with our blood, civilization saved, and the time gained for the United States to be fully armed against all eventualities, we should stand stripped to the bone. Such a course would not be in the moral or economic interests of either of our countries. We here, would be unable, after the war, to purchase the large balance of imports from the United States over and above the volume of our exports which is agreeable to your tariffs and industrial economy. Not only should we in Great Britain suffer cruel privations but widespread unemployment in the United States would follow the curtailment of American exporting power.

18. Moreover, I do not believe that the Government and people of the United States would find it in accordance with the principles which guide them, to confine the help which they have so generously promised only to such munitions of war and commodities as could be immediately paid for. You may be certain that we shall prove ourselves ready to suffer and sacrifice to the utmost for the Cause, and that we glory in being its champions. The rest we leave with confidence to you and to your people, being sure that ways and means will be found which future generations on both sides of the Atlantic will approve and admire.

19. If, as I believe, you are convinced Mr. President, that the defeat of the Nazi and Fascist tyranny is a matter of high consequence to the people of the United States and to the Western Hemisphere, you will regard this letter not as an appeal for aid, but as a statement of the minimum action necessary to achieve our common purpose.

I remain,
Yours very sincerely,
WINSTON S. CHURCHILL.

Nuclear weapons and the new world order

Letter from Attlee to Truman

1945

The possibility of producing an atomic bomb was suggested in 1940 by two refugee scientists, Otto Frisch and Rudolf Peierls, then working at the University of Birmingham, and led to the formation of the so-called MAUD (Military Application of Uranium Detonation) Committee. Reporting in June 1941, the Committee concluded that a bomb was feasible and that every effort should be made to develop the weapon. The findings were subsequently shared with the Americans and helped facilitate the Manhattan Project, a research and development programme designed to produce the world's first nuclear weapons during the Second World War.

In August 1943, Churchill and Roosevelt signed the Quebec Agreement, which governed Anglo-America atomic relations until the end of the war. Under the terms of this agreement, Britain and America could not use the bomb against a third country without the other's consent. In short, the agreement granted the British a veto over the use of the atomic bomb in which its scientists played a limited though significant role. By the end of 1944, it was apparent that a Nazi atomic bomb, feared by many of the Allied scientists, would not be realised. When Roosevelt met Churchill in September 1944 they agreed that when the bomb was ready it might be used against the Japanese, who should be warned that the bombardment would be repeated until they surrendered.

Operational planning for the use of atomic weapons against Japan began in October 1944. The knowledge that the USA was now in the final stages of preparation prompted Churchill to consider how British consent to the operation should be given. On 1 July, the Prime Minister gave his consent to drop the atomic bomb against Japan, with the decision recorded in the minutes of the Combined Policy Committee that managed the joint programme. Defeated in the General Election of July 1945, Churchill was replaced as Prime Minister by Clement Attlee, the leader of the Labour Party. Although he held the position of Deputy Prime Minister in the wartime coalition, Attlee knew virtually nothing of the atomic bomb project. President Truman informed Attlee of the decision to drop the bomb on 1 August, at the Potsdam Conference. Attlee later recalled that the agreement for using nuclear weapons against Japan had been given by Churchill, but if he had been asked he would have agreed.

The atomic destruction of the Japanese cities of Hiroshima and Nagasaki in August 1945 raised profound questions concerning the control and ownership of nuclear weapons and the very survival of civilisation. Majority opinion in the US Congress favoured keeping nuclear technology a closely guarded American secret. A significant minority, however, were in favour of sharing the peaceful benefits of nuclear energy within the context of the United Nations, provided there was 'absolute and effective agreement for worldwide inspection and control'. In September 1945, Clement Attlee wrote to the American President, Harry Truman, outlining his thoughts on the question of international control. Attlee was a strong advocate of international control, and argued that the United Nations should play a major role in maintaining peace and security in the nuclear age. How this was to be achieved in practice, however, proved more problematic. On the one hand, Attlee believed that the only hope for the world was an international system in which war was entirely ruled out. On the other, he maintained that atomic weapons should be available to the UN to restrain aggression, and that the establishment of better relations with the Soviet Union should precede the exchange of technical information. In short, Attlee sought to reconcile realist and utopian visions, which would characterise international control of nuclear weapons for the next 20 years.

ANNEX I

25th September, 1945.

Dear Mr. President,

Ever since the U.S.A. demonstrated to the world the terrible effectiveness of the atomic bomb I have been increasingly aware of the fact that the world is now facing entirely new conditions. Never before has there been a weapon which can suddenly and without warning be employed to destroy utterly the nerve centre of a great nation. The destruction wrought by the Germans through their air fleet on Warsaw and Rotterdam was startling enough, but subsequent attempts to do the same to London were defeated though without much to spare. Our own attacks on Berlin and the Ruhr resulted in the virtual destruction of great centres of industry. In Europe the accumulated material wealth of decades has been dissipated in a year or two, but all this is not different in kind from what was done in previous wars in Europe during the Dark Ages and the Thirty Years War, in America by your own civil war. Despite these losses civilisation continued and the general framework of human society and of relations between peoples remained. The emergence of this new weapon has meant, taking account of its potentialities, not a quantitative but a qualitative change in the nature of warfare.

Before its advent military experts still thought and planned on assumptions not essentially different from those of their predecessors. It is true that the conservative (with a small c!) mentality tended to maintain some of these although they were already out of date. For instance we found at Potsdam that we had to discuss a decision taken at the Crimea Conference as to the boundaries of Poland. These were delimited by rivers although the idea of a river as a strategic frontier has been out of date ever since the advent of air warfare. Nevertheless it was before the coming of the atomic bomb not unreasonable to think in terms of strategic areas and bases although here again it has seemed to me that too little account had been taken of the air weapon.

Now, however, there is in existence a weapon of small bulk capable of being conveyed on to a distant target with inevitable catastrophic results. We can set no bounds to the possibilities of airplanes flying through the stratosphere dropping atomic bombs on great cities. There are possible developments of the rocket for a similar purpose. I understand that the power of the bombs delivered on Nagasaki may be multiplied many times as the invention develops. I have so far heard no suggestion of any possible means of defence. The only deterrent is the possibility of the victim of such an attack being able to retort on the victor. In

-1-

many discussions on bombing in the days before the war it was demonstrated that the only answer to the bomber was the bomber. The war proved this to be correct. This obvious fact did not prevent bombing but resulted in the destruction of many great centres of civilisation. Similarly if mankind continues to make the atomic bomb without changing the political relationships of States sooner or later these bombs will be used for mutual annihilation.

The present position is that whilst the fundamental scientific discoveries which made possible the production of the atomic bomb are now common knowledge, the experience of the actual processes of manufacture and knowledge of the solutions which were found to the many technical problems which arose, are confined to our two countries and the actual capacity for production exists only in the United States. But the very speed and completeness of our joint achievement seems to indicate that any other country possessing the necessary scientific and industrial resources could also produce atomic bombs within a few years if it decided now to make the effort. Again, our two Governments have gone a long way in securing control of all the main known sources of uranium and thorium, the two materials at present believed to be of importance for the process. But new sources are continually coming to light and it would not be surprising if it were found that large deposits existed in parts of the world outside our direct or indirect control. Nor may it be altogether easy to defend the measures which we have already taken in this matter when they become known and are considered in the light of such principles as that of the freedom of access to raw maetrials.

It would thus appear that the lead which has been gained as a result of the past effort put forth in the United States may only be temporary and that we have not much time in which to decide what use is to be made of that lead. It is true that other countries, even if they succeed in producing atomic bombs, may not, at any rate at first, be able to produce them on the same scale. I am told, however, that, in future, it may be possible for the process to be developed at a far smaller cost in industrial resources than has inevitably been demanded by your pioneer production enterprise, carried through in time of war when speed was the first essential; and in any case, with a weapon of such tremendous destructive power, it is perhaps doubtful whether the advantage would lie with the possessor of the greatest number of bombs rather than with the most unscrupulous.

A further consideration which I have had in mind is that the successful manufacture of bombs from plutonium shows that the harnessing of atomic energy as a source of power cannot be achieved without the simultaneous production of material capable of being used in a bomb. This means that the possible industrial uses of atomic energy cannot be considered separately from its military and security implications.

It is clear to me, therefore, that, as never before, the responsible statesmen of the great Powers are faced with decisions vital not merely to the increase of human happiness but to the very survival of civilisation. Until decisions are taken on this vital matter, it is very difficult for any of us to plan for the future. Take the case of this country. During the war we had to shift much of our industry to the less exposed parts of our island. We had to provide shelters for our people. Now we have to restart our industries and rebuild our wrecked homes. Am I to plan for a peaceful or a warlike world? If the latter I ought to direct all our people to live like troglodytes underground as being the only hope of survival, and that by no means certain. I have to consider the defence forces required in the future in the light of San Francisco, but San Francisco did not envisage the atomic bomb. Its conceptions of security are based on appreciations of a situation existing in June of this year. We considered regional security and a policing of the world by the Powers with the greatest resources in the interests of all so that there should be available the forces to prevent aggression. I have only mentioned Great Britain as an example; for every Head of Government must, in varying degree, find himself confronted with the same problems.

In these circumstances while realising to the full the importance of devising means to prevent as far as possible the power to produce this new weapon getting into other hands, my mind is increasingly directed to considering the kind of relationship between nations which the existence of such an instrument of destruction demands. In your country and ours resort is not had to violence not just because we have efficient police forces but because the vast majority of our citizens are law abiding and conditions are such that men are not driven to have recourse to desperate measures. Our constitutions allow of peaceful change.

We have it seems to me if we are to rid ourselves of this menace to make very far reaching changes in the relationship between States. We have in fact in the light of this revolutionary development to make a fresh review of world policy and a new valuation of what are called national interests. We are ourselves attempting to undertake such a review. What was done on American initiative at San Francisco was a first step at erecting the framework of a new world society, but necessarily it could have regard only to the requirements imposed by the technical advances in methods of warfare then known. Now it seems to us that the building, the framework of which was erected at San Francisco, must be carried much further if it is to be an affective shelter for humanity. We have to secure that these new developments are turned to the benefit rather than to the destruction of mankind. We must bend our utmost energies to secure that better ordering of human affairs which so great a revolution at once renders necessary and should make possible.

-3-

I am therefore most anxious, before we proceed much further with our own deliberations, to know how your mind is moving; and it is primarily for this reason that I have set before you at such length my tentative views before they have really begun to crystallise.

Mr. Byrnes has had a preliminary talk with Mr. Bevin here on the matter but, later on, I think it may be essential that you and I should discuss this momentous problem together so that we may agree what the next step should be and be in a position to take it before the fears and suspicions which may be developing elsewhere have got such a firm hold as to make even more difficult any solution we may decide to aim at.

Yours sincerely,

(Signed) C.R. ATTLEE

The President of the United States of America.

An invitation to the Queen

Idi Amin invites Elizabeth II to celebrate Ugandan independence

1972

What aspects of a person's character or life make them a suitable subject for a Hollywood biopic? Bravery? Status? Success?

Or perhaps infamy?

At the 79th Academy Awards, held in 2007, Forest Whitaker won the Oscar for Best Actor, for his portrayal of the third President of Uganda, Idi Amin, in the film *The Last King of Scotland*. Amin's notoriety and chaotic tenure as President of Uganda provided the necessary real-life inspiration for the blockbuster film.

Idi Amin's infamy stems from the well-reported nature of his eight-year regime as President and Commander-in-Chief of Uganda's military forces from January 1971 until April 1979. Respected commentators, political scientists and historians agree that his regime was marked by systemic corruption and human rights abuses.

Upon his seizure of power in 1971, Idi Amin's diplomatic outlook was shaped by support that he received from the West and Israel; indeed he was a former officer of the King's African Rifles (a British Army unit), and was one of the first two Ugandan officers in the British Army. This background, and his predecessor President Milton Obote's 'Move to the Left', which would in theory see the government of Uganda embrace wider state control of the economy with a mixture of socialism and nationalism, meant that Amin was seen as a far more preferable leader in the region by any nation fearful of the further extension of socialist ideology in world politics.

This letter, addressed to Queen Elizabeth II herself, indicates that in January 1972 Idi Amin was, most certainly, willing to play the diplomat for the British government and state. The language employed by Amin is extremely respectful and polite. At this stage we can speculate that he is revelling in his new role as an international Head of State, displayed in the tone of this letter, and he is clearly keen for a respected world sovereign to attend Uganda's independence celebrations and further legitimise his role as a world leader.

This diplomatic tact would not last forever. By 1976 Britain was compelled to sever diplomatic ties with Uganda as a response to the behaviour of Idi Amin's regime.

The course of Idi Amin's diplomatic policy would fluctuate from offering invitations to Queen Elizabeth II and her family, to sharing platforms with Muammar Gaddafi of Libya and Mobutu Sese Seko of the Democratic Republic of the Congo (then Zaire). His regime was characterised by great swings in ideology and doctrine, Amin's erratic personality being responsible for driving policies such as the expulsion of Uganda's Asian community, and the commitment to a war with Tanzania that ultimately led to the end of his regime in 1979.

This letter provides a snapshot into the Western-facing nature of Idi Amin's early tenure, and is fascinating when juxtaposed against the internal politics of Uganda under his rule, and the future international relationships he would later cultivate.

It is worth noting that Queen Elizabeth II did not attend the event celebrating the 10th year of Ugandan independence, on 9 October 1972. Later that month she did perform a state visit, but to Yugoslavia as a guest of President Tito instead.

Lieutenant Colonel Idi Amin (left) talking to officers of the British and Kenyan Rifles on his first visit to Britain.

STATE HOUSE
ENTEBBE
UGANDA

CONFIDENTIAL

10th January, 1972.

Your Majesty,

It is with great pleasure that I take the opportunity of writing to you to wish you a Happy New Year and a very successful 1972. The past year has seen a great deal of fruitful cooperation and understanding between your Government and mine, and between the people of Great Britain and of the Republic of Uganda. It is my wish and desire that this good relationship continues with greater strength in the coming year.

I should like here to place on record on behalf of myself, my Government and the people of Uganda our deep appreciation for the good work that your Subjects have been doing in Uganda over the years and for assistance that your Government has rendered to Uganda, especially in 1971. I am confident that with the goodwill and understanding of friendly nations like yours, the big problems that we face in this Country will be overcome successfully.

I should here like to inform Your Majesty that the Republic of Uganda will be celebrating her 10th Anniversary of Independence on 9th October, 1972. It would do my Government and my Country a great honour if Your Majesty could grace these Celebrations, which will be special to us, with your presence, in the company of your husband and the rest of your family. I have no doubt that such a visit would go a long way towards strengthening the bonds of friendship that already exist between your Country and ours.

It is my hope that Your Majesty will be disposed to accept our invitation, in which case we shall be happy to send you a detailed programme for the approval of yourself and your officers.

Allow me, to renew to Your Majesty, the assurances of my highest consideration and esteem.

Yours Very Sincerely,

Idi A Dada.

GENERAL IDI AMIN DADA,
PRESIDENT OF THE REPUBLIC OF UGANDA.

Her Majesty,
Queen Elizabeth II,
Buckingham Palace,
Westminster,
LONDON S.W.

CONFIDENTIAL

UGANDA ARMY

13000 FRAUE

Protest,

revolution

and rebellion

Braveheart

A letter from the King of France regarding William Wallace

1300

The name William Wallace conjures up an image of a swaggering Scottish hero, ready for battle. But William Wallace was also a diplomat. In the letter, just three lines long, the King of France, Philip IV, tells his agents at the court of the Pope in Rome to assist 'William le Walois of Scotland, knight', in the business that he has to carry out. This raises the tantalising possibility that this tiny letter was in Wallace's personal possession more than 700 years ago.

William Wallace was born into a noble Scottish family in the later 13th century. During his childhood, the Scottish kingdom was ruled, largely peacefully, by Alexander III. But at his death in 1286 the sole heir was his infant granddaughter, Margaret, daughter of the King of Norway. Known as the 'Maid of Norway' she died on her journey from Norway to Scotland in 1290, leaving no clear candidate for the succession. The future of Scotland was thrown into confusion as several men from elite families laid claim to the kingship.

A Victorian representation of William Wallace.

Edward I of England took advantage of the Scottish situation to assert ever-greater claims to overlordship in the kingdom until, in 1296, he finally invaded. The early stages of the campaign were a great success, and the Scottish coronation stone, the symbol of its independent kingship, was removed from Scone and taken to Westminster Abbey.

Edward I then turned his attention to France. But all was not over in Scotland. Unrest spread in early 1297 and William Wallace emerged from the shadows of history. In May, he killed William Heselrig, the English sheriff of Lanark, and the symbol of English authority in the region. The killing galvanised the Scots – many more joined the fight against the English, and Wallace became the leader of a full-scale rebellion. He joined forces with another rebel, Andrew Murray, and together they led a Scottish force against the English army at Stirling Bridge in September 1297. The English resistance was superior in numbers and led by an experienced warrior, John de Warenne, Earl of Surrey and Edward I's lieutenant in Scotland. The two armies faced each other from opposite sides of the Forth, separated by a narrow bridge. The Scottish army waited, holding its nerve, until the English forces began to cross the bridge. When enough of the army had crossed, the Scottish charged down, surrounded this vanguard, and took control of the end of the bridge, preventing reinforcements from arriving. The English troops who had crossed the bridge were slaughtered or drowned in the Forth; those who had not beat a hasty retreat, led by de Warenne.

Wallace's triumph at Stirling Bridge cemented his reputation, and the Scottish rebels under his leadership went from strength to strength, driving the English out of Scotland. He led a large-scale raiding party into England in late 1297, plundering and laying waste to tracts of the northern counties. Documents of the time referred to him as the 'guardian of Scotland'.

To counter the rebels, in the summer of 1298 Edward I led an army into Scotland. Wallace was keen to avoid pitched battle, but Edward was determined to take the fight to the Scots and in July tracked the Scottish army to Falkirk where the strength and tactics of Edward's forces won the day and Wallace left the field defeated.

Perhaps because of this defeat, Wallace resigned the guardianship of Scotland, but continued to argue for his country's independence from England, pursuing his aims through diplomacy. By the end of 1299, Wallace was in France, trying to persuade Philip IV to support the Scots against Edward. France and Scotland were old allies, and in November 1300 the French king wrote this letter. It is likely that it was carried by Wallace who perhaps travelled with it to Rome to present the Scottish case against the claims of Edward I. In early 1301 a Scottish delegation was in Rome doing just that, although we cannot say for certain that Wallace was among this group.

By 1303 Wallace was back in Scotland taking a leading role in the military campaign against Edward I. The English King was determined to capture this symbol of Scottish independence, and Wallace was finally taken prisoner in Glasgow in August 1305. He was taken to London and tried at Westminster for treason. Found guilty, he was hanged, disembowelled and cut into quarters. His head was displayed on London Bridge, and four parts of his body were distributed to four different towns in Scotland. Payments to the men who conveyed these quarters were coolly noted in the records of Edward I's Exchequer.

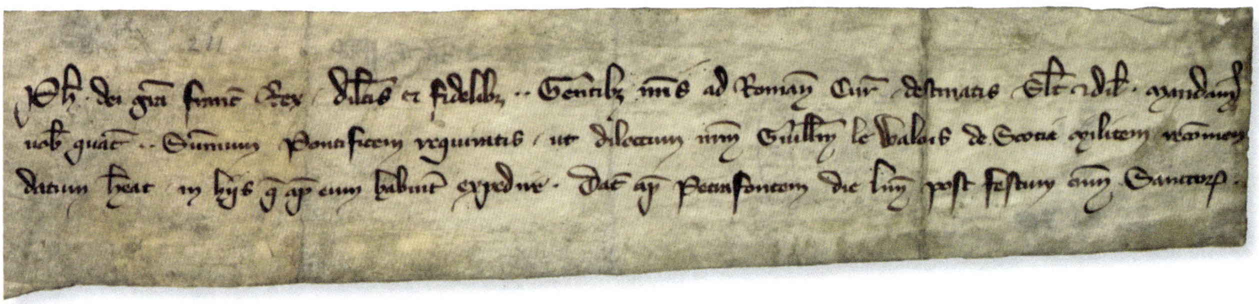

81
SC1/30

Philip by the grace of God King of the French to our loved and faithful our agents appointed to the Roman Court, greetings and love. We command/ you to request the Supreme Pontiff to consider with favour our beloved William le Walois [Wallace] of Scotland, knight/ in those things which he has to transact with him. Given at Pierrefonds on Monday after the feast of All Saints. [7 November 1300]

Endorsement: Fourth letter of the King of France

'Terrible blow this Parliament'

A warning about the Gunpowder Plot

1605

This letter was sent to the Catholic Lord Monteagle, on 26 October 1605. The writer warned him to avoid the state opening of Parliament due in a few days' time and remain at his estate for the purposes of safety. Despite being instructed not to ignore the warning contained in the letter and to burn the evidence, Lord Monteagle gave the letter directly to the Privy Council and King James I in Whitehall. His actions did not prevent the plotters from going ahead with their plan.

During the reign of Elizabeth I, it was extremely difficult for Catholics to practise their religion owing to harsh fines and the risk of imprisonment. Catholic priests were banned and arrested by government spies. When James I of England and James IV of Scotland ascended the throne they hoped for greater freedom to practise their faith, but unfortunately this did not happen. In 1605, a group of discontented Catholic noblemen led by Robert Catesby – including John Wright, Thomas Wintour, Thomas Percy, Guy Fawkes, Robert Keyes, Thomas Bates, Robert Wintour, Christopher Wright, John Grant, Ambrose Rookwood, Sir Everard Digby and Francis Tresham – decided to blow up the King and Parliament. After the explosion, the group planned to lead an uprising in the Midlands. They would kidnap Princess Elizabeth, James's young daughter, at Coombe Abbey with the intention of using her as a figurehead through whom they could rule the country and restore the rights of Catholics. However, their explosives expert, a mercenary called 'John Johnson' (also known as Guy Fawkes) was disturbed in the cellar below the Houses of Parliament with a large quantity of gunpowder.

The plotters escaped from London. Robert Catesby was killed after a shoot-out at Holbeach House in Staffordshire, where they had gone into hiding. The remaining members of the group were captured and tried at Westminster Hall; eight of them were found guilty and executed by January 1606. The plot increased the popularity of James I, and it became even more difficult for Catholics to practise their religion or participate in civil society. Today it remains a myth that Guy Fawkes was the main plotter, an idea perpetuated by the celebrations which take place every year for Bonfire Night on 5 November.

ates
Robert Winter
Christopher Wright
Iohn Wright
Thomas Percy
Guido Fawkes
Robert Catesby
Thomas Winter

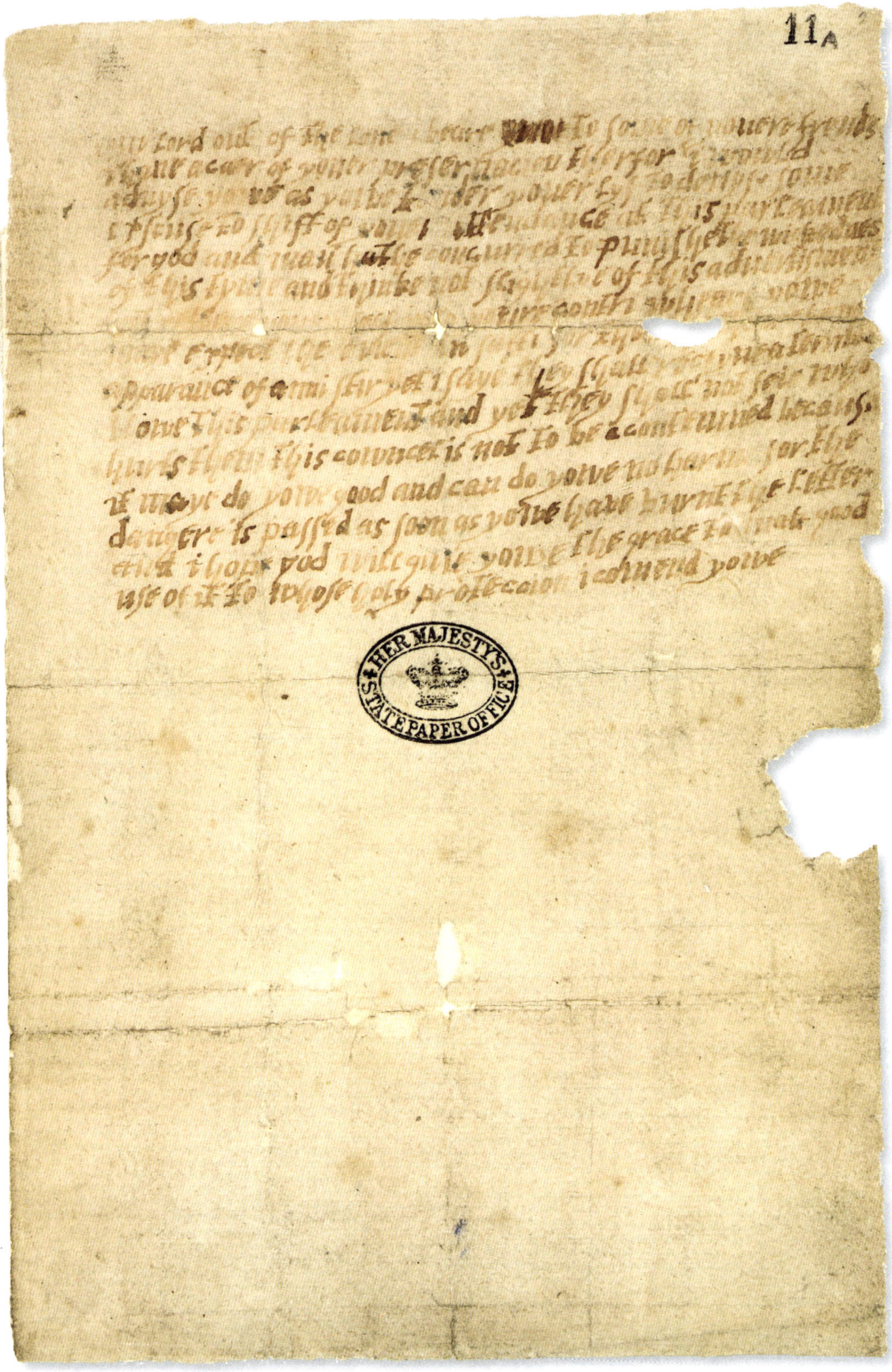
11A
my lord out of the love i beare to some of youere frends
i have a caer of youer preservacion therfor i would
advyse yowe as yowe tender youer lyf to devyse some
exscuse to shift of youer attendance at this parleament
for god and man hath concurred to punishe the wickednes
of this tyme and thinke not slightlye of this advertisment
but retyere youre self into youre contri wheare yowe
maye expect the event in safti for thowghe theare be no
apparance of anni stir yet i saye they shall receyve a terrible
blowe this parleament and yet they shall not seie who
hurts them this cowncel is not to be contemned because
it maye do yowe good and can do yowe no harme for the
dangere is passed as soon as yowe have burnt the letter
and i hope god will give yowe the grace to mak good
use of it to whose holy proteccion i commend yowe
HER MAJESTY'S STATE PAPER OFFICE

My lord, out of the love I beare to some of youere frends, I have a care of youre preservacion, therefore I would aduyse you as you tender your life to devise some excuse to shift youer attendance at this parliament, for God and man hath concurred to punishe the wickedness of this tyme, and thinke not slightly of this advertisement, but retire yourself into your country, where you may expect the event in safety, for though there be no apparance of anni stir, yet I saye they shall receive a terrible blow this parliament and yet they shall not seie who hurts them this cowncel is not to be contemned because it may do yowe good and can do yowe no harme for the dangere is passed as soon as yowe have burnt the letter and i hope God will give yowe the grace to mak good use of it to whose holy proteccion i comend yowe.

'Ye have not yet done as ye ought'

A letter from 'Captain Swing' – the agricultural unrest of 1830

1830

This rather terrifying letter was received by the Reverend M Huntley of Kimbolton in Huntingdonshire, during November 1830, at the height of the 'Swing Riots' – a wave of agricultural unrest that swept over most of southern and eastern England from the winter of 1830 through to 1831, characterised by widespread arson attacks, the intimidation of wealthy locals across the countryside, and threatening letters such as this one.

The years after the end of the Napoleonic Wars in 1815 were grim for England's agricultural labourers. 'Enclosure', the privatisation of common land, deprived them of a way to make ends meet. Wartime food fluctuations saw them facing increasingly hostile and distant farmers, shorter, insecure contracts and ever-decreasing wages. Parish 'poor relief', which was sometimes given as a cash payment but often through a 'dole' of bread to stave off starvation, allowed farmers to pay insufficient wages, knowing the parish would cover the shortfall. However, spiralling relief bills meant many parishes reduced the bread dole to the barest possible minimum, pushing already destitute labourers even closer to the edge.

Matters were further aggravated by extortionate tithes; charges levied on every member of a parish, including the poor, by the Church of England, that were used to pay the wages of the local parson. The increasing introduction of threshing machines, which automated the process of separating husks from grain during harvest and further threatened labourers' livelihoods, can be seen as the straw that broke the agricultural worker's back.

Beginning in East Kent in November 1830 and spreading across East Anglia, the Home Counties and much of southern England throughout the winter of 1830–31, workers rose up, often claiming to take their lead from the non-existent 'Captain Swing' (swing was a reference to a colloquial term for a flail used in harvesting, while captain was a term for a labourer who would take informal charge of his fellow gangmates while working). The riots were characterised by the destruction of threshing machines, barns and haystacks – either by arson or hand and axe, as well as mass gatherings of labourers outside the homes of local farmers and other wealthy individuals, where a collective demand would be made for higher wages and lower tithes and rents, often followed by a 'request' for some money for the men to adjourn to a local ale shop and refresh themselves.

These riotous assemblies of destruction, intimidation and incendiarism were often preceded by a letter forewarning local dignitaries and farmers of the rioters' intended action, often signed as 'Swing'. Often these letters take the form of an ultimatum. For instance, a letter received by Mr Bibble, a farmer from High Wycombe, informs him that unless he destroys his own threshing machines, 'Swing' and his companions will 'commence our labour'.

Huntley's, however, does not seem to offer him a way of pacifying Captain Swing's fury. He is a 'Blackguard' (pronounced 'blaggard', an archaic term for a scoundrel) and an enemy of the people, one of the 'Black Hearts in the Black Book'. Huntley is identified as being a 'Parson [sic] Justasses', the wealthy rural oligarchy of landowners, magistrates and clergy who were seen as ultimately responsible for the workers' high rents and tithes, low wages and starvation rations. Huntley and his like are advised to make their wills (this is probably an empty threat, only one person was killed during the riots, a rioter, by a soldier).

As a result of the riots, wages were in some places raised, and tithes and rents lowered. However, most of those involved only suffered more: 1,976 men were tried for their involvement in the riots; 644 jailed, 7 fined, 1 whipped, 481 transported to Australia, and 19 executed. The riots also contributed to one of the most controversial pieces of legislation of the period; the 1834 Poor Law Amendment Act brought about a far harsher, centrally regulated way of 'relieving' those in poverty with dreaded workhouses spreading across the country.

What makes the Swing letters interesting is that they preserve the thoughts and writing of a class of people of whose inner and intellectual lives we know little – poor agricultural labourers. Often with only rudimentary literacy and little interaction with officialdom, usually the only records of these people are baptisms, marriages and burials, or perhaps a record of trial if they were arrested. During the Swing Riots, these violent shouts against the injustice of their existence were collected by government officials trying to understand an almost spontaneous wave of protest and fire, preserving the words of these angry and alienated people and their uprising for generations to come.

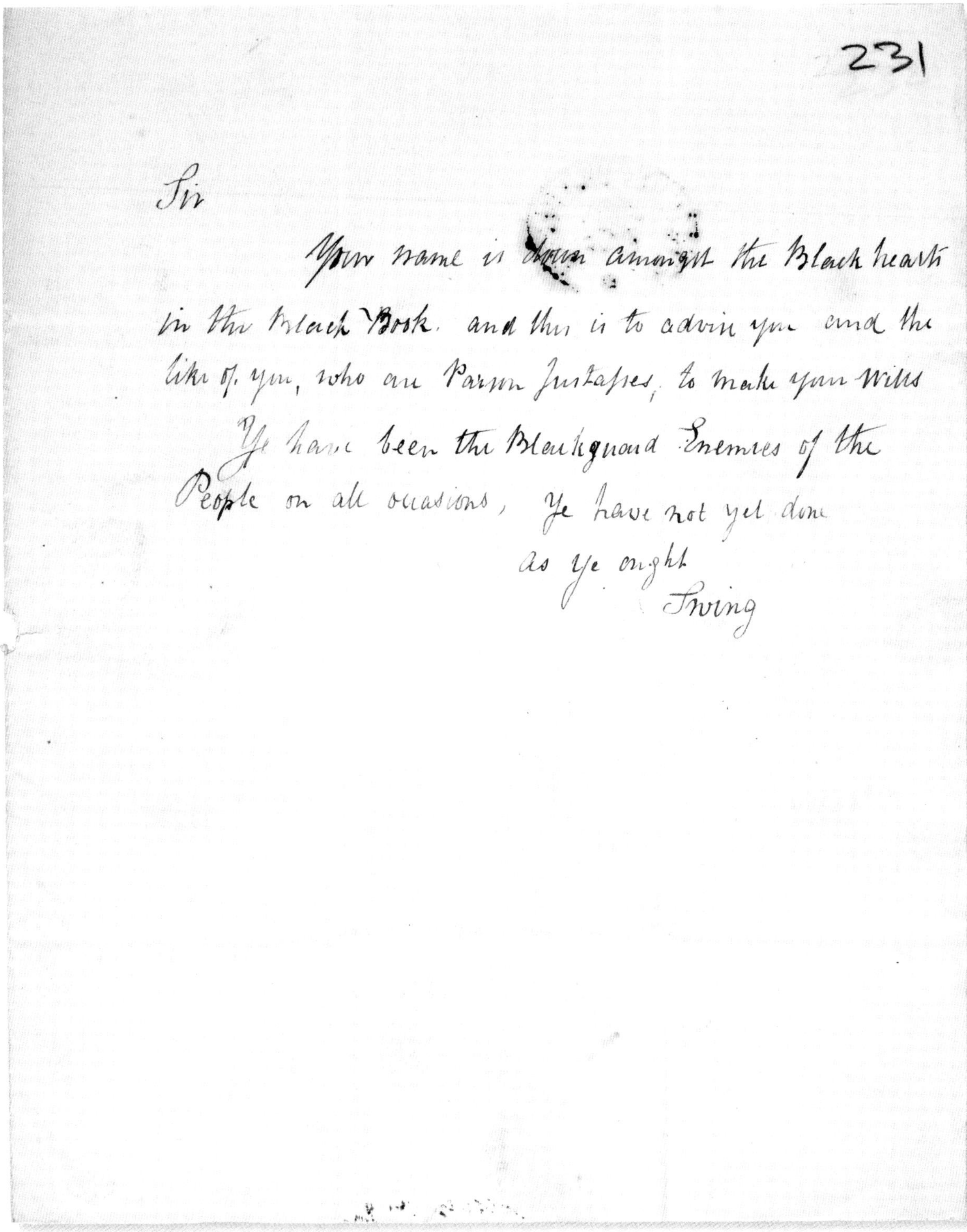

231

Sir

Your name is down amongst the Black hearts in the Black Book. and this is to advise you and the like of you, who are Parson Justasses, to make your Wills

Ye have been the Blackguard Enemies of the People on all occasions, Ye have not yet done as ye ought

Swing

Sir,

Your name is down amongst the Black Hearts in the Black Book and this is to advise you and the like of you, who are Parson Justasses [sic], to make your Wills

Ye have been the Blackguard Enemies of the People on all occasions, ye have not yet done

as ye ought.

Swing

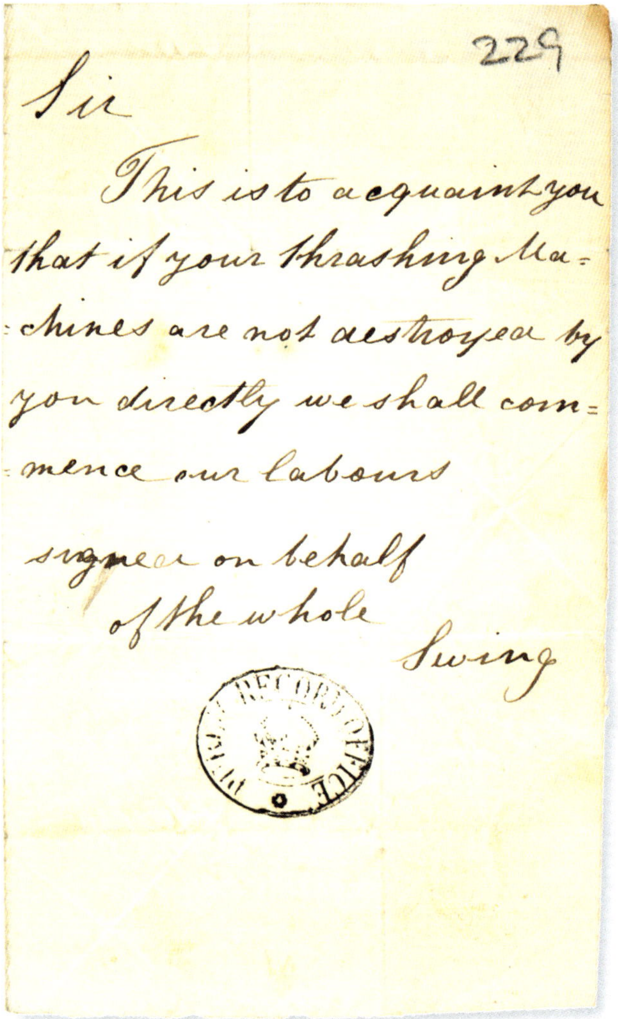
229

Sir

This is to acquaint you that if your thrashing Machines are not destroyed by you directly we shall commence our labours

signed on behalf of the whole

Swing

Sir,

This is to acquaint you that if your thrashing machines are not destroyed by you directly we shall commence our labours

signed on behalf
of the whole
Swing

A farm-worker (centre) explains to a clergyman how he has set fire to a hay-rick in protest at being evicted from both his farm and cottage.

'... we may lie and die in a land of plenty ...'

Thomas Henshaw's demand for redress in the "Hungry 40s"

1841

In early 1841, Thomas Henshaw, who lived in Ilkeston in Derbyshire (part of the Basford Poor Law Union), wrote an uncompromising letter to the Poor Law Commission in London, essentially accusing the local welfare/poor-law officials of leaving him and his family to starve. Thomas was an unemployed framework knitter, a poorly paid trade in decline and an occupational watchword for poverty and desperate living conditions.

The Poor Law Amendment Act 1834 established the Victorian 'workhouse system' and sought to transform welfare by curtailing, or at least restricting, the rights of the able-bodied poor to outdoor relief. It also established a central authority to oversee and 'supervise' poor relief across the country. It is to this 'authority' that Thomas writes.

He sketches out the position of the family and his inability to earn enough to feed them. He sets the scene by stating that he has '*...been for A length of time nearly out of employment and now entirely so...*'. In his brutal introduction he refers to his wife and children who '*...have been completely destitute of food since February the 1st to the present time*'. This would mean the family had gone without food for some four to five days. The root of his complaint is that he has followed the rules as set out by the 1834 Act, but that local officials, in this case Mr Stotten, the relieving officer, and Mr Bennett, the assistant overseer, had refused to help. Undeterred, Thomas then walks some six miles to see a Mr Radford, who was a magistrate at Smalley, who provided a positive order to Bennett to see Thomas and his family; again Thomas was refused. Here things take a legalistic turn and Thomas quotes from the 54th clause of the 1834 Act which should have ensured Thomas and his family relief as they were destitute. Not to be defeated Henshaw challenged those in charge asking whether he and his family '*may lie and die in A land of plenty*' and once again used his knowledge and understanding of the system to remind the Commissioners of their obligations in cases of neglect. His reference to the Chadwick circular showed not only an awareness of the circulars and their content but also of Edwin Chadwick, secretary to the Poor Law Commission and one of the architects of the 1834 Act.

Thomas appears as an articulate, well-informed and confident man. He quotes his rights and the law which gives them to him and his family. Living through the 'Hungry 40s' the background to his letters speaks to us of the political and economic differences between the rich and poor (even the moderately well-off and the poor) which were enormous. 'Rights' were also on the local Basford agenda in the early 1840s – it was a place where active Chartists sought the vote for working men and Henshaw would have been very much aware of this.

What is fascinating here is that it is a letter not about the Victorian poor (which is common) but one written by one of the poorest. He asks for redress not favour, he claims his rights not charity and he is blunt in his assessment of the local authorities whom he finds wanting.

A cartoon mocking the Poor Law from a publication called *The Glorious Working of the Whigs*, published in 1836.

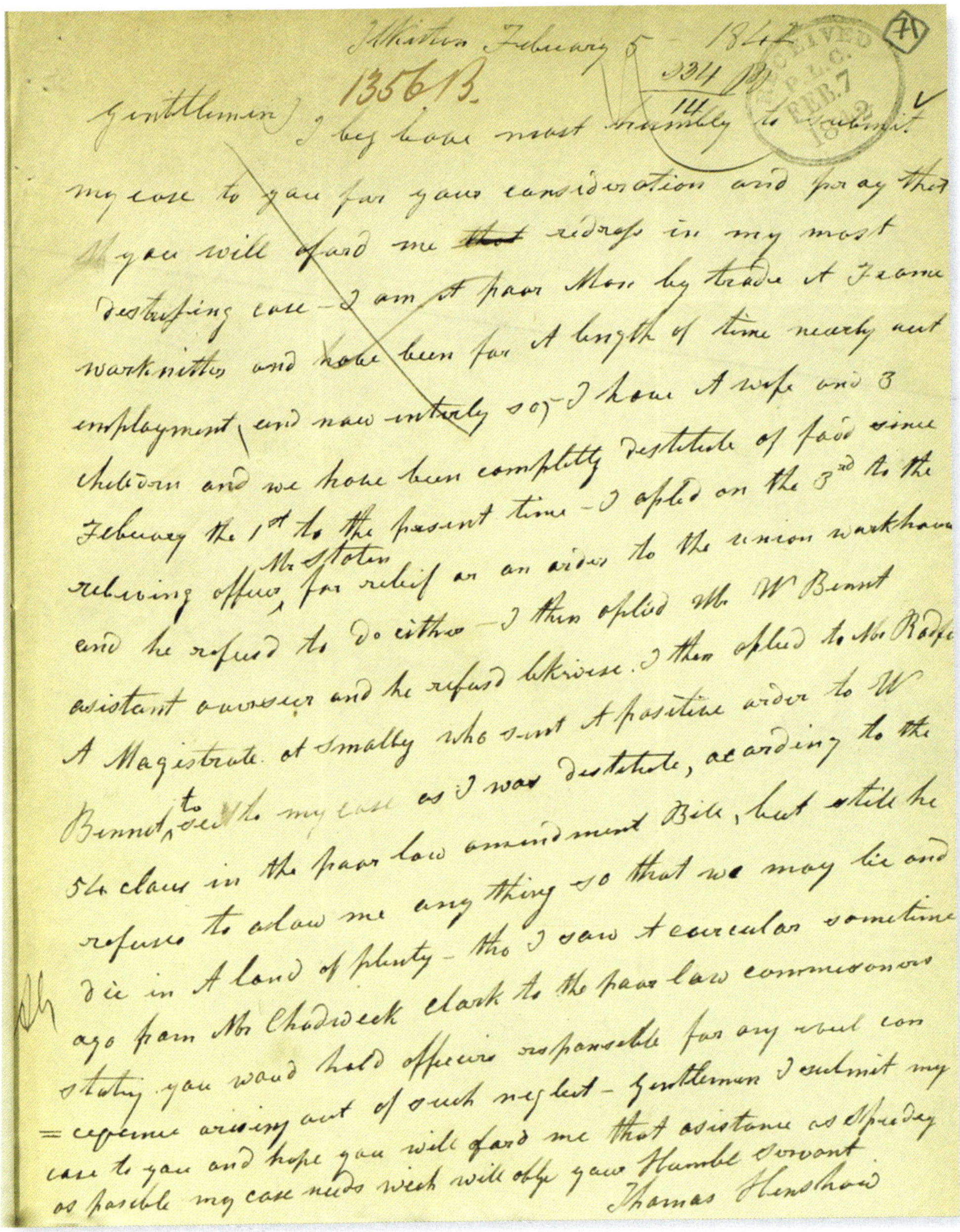

Ilkiston February 5 – 1842

13561B.

334 B

14

RECEIVED P.L.C. FEB.7 1842

Gentlleman I beg have most umbly to submit
my case to you for your consideration and pray that
you will aford me that redress in my most
destresfing case – I am A poor Man by trade A Frame
work nitter and have been for A length of time nearly out
employment and now intirely so – I have A wife and 3
children and we have been completly destitute of food since
Febuary the 1st to the present time – I aplied on the 3rd to the
relieving officer Mr Stoten for relief or an order to the union workhouse
and he refused to do either – I then aplied Mr W Bennt
asistant overseer and he refused likewise. I then aplied to Mr Rodfe
A Magistrate at Smalley who sent A positive order to W
Bennet to see to my case as I was destitute, according to the
54 claus in the poor law amendment Bill, but stile he
refuses to alow me any thing so that we may lie and
die in A land of plenty – tho I saw A circular sometime
ago from Mr Chadwick clark to the poor law commisoners
stating you would hold officers responsible for any evil con
=sequence arising out of such neglect – Gentlemen I submit my
case to you and hope you will aford me that asistance as speeday
as posible my case needs which will oblige your Humbel Servant
Thomas Henshaw

Ilkeston February 5 1841

Gentleman,

I beg leave most humbly to submit my case to you for your consideration and pray that you will aford me redress in my most distresing case - I am a poor Men by trade a frame workknitter and have been for A length of time nearly out of employment and now entirely so,- I have A wife and 3 children and we have been completely destitute of food since February the 1st to the present time – I applied on the 3rd to the relieving officer, Mr Stotten for relief or an order for the union workhouse and he refused to do either – I then applied to Mr Bennett assistant overseer and he refused likewise. I then applied to Mr [Radford] A Magistrate at Smalley who sent A positive order to Mr Bennett to see to my case as I was destitute, according to the 54 clause in the poor law amendment Bill, but still he refuses to allow me any thing so that we may lie and die in A land of plenty – tho I saw A circular sometime ago from Mr Chadwick clark to the poor law commissioners stating you would hold officers responsible for any [bad] consequence arising out of such neglect – Gentlemen I submit my case to you and hope you will aford me that asistance as Speedy as possible my case needs wich will oblige your Humble Servant

Thomas Henshaw.

Class antagonism onboard the *Titanic*

Did your class affect your chances of survival?

1912

When the *Titanic* sank in the early hours of Monday 15 April 1912, many questions were raised. It was one of the largest, most luxurious ships in the world, boasting better facilities than any other liner, and yet it sank on its maiden voyage when it collided with an iceberg. How did it happen? Why did it happen? Why had so few passengers been saved? And why did first-class passengers have a better chance of survival than those travelling in second and third class? More than 1,500 passengers and crew had died in the freezing ocean, and relatives, friends and onlookers alike were looking for answers in the wake of the tragedy.

Among those concerned was Benn Tillett, the author of this letter. A famous trade union leader, he was hugely critical of the allegedly 'vicious class antagonism' that had led to the disproportionate loss of life among third-class passengers. Had the officers loading the life rafts deemed richer passengers more important than poorer ones? Benn Tillett clearly believed this to be the case. And the survival figures do show that the more a passenger had paid for his ticket, the greater his chance of survival. Indeed, fewer than 25 per cent of all third class passengers survived.

Whether these figures can be attributed solely to 'class antagonism' and a 'callous disregard of human life' is debatable, however. Practical factors were at play too. In designing the ship, the architects had ensured that passengers of different classes would not mix, and to this end certain stairways were barred off with metal gateways. In theory, these gateways could be unlocked by a key-holding crew member. In practice, on the night disaster struck, there were no staff available to open the gateways, and as a result, hundreds of passengers were trapped below deck and drowned as water gushed in. Since the third class accommodation was furthest from the boat deck, in many ways this group had the least chance of survival even before class differences were considered.

Tillett's letter outlines some of the key reasons why more lives weren't saved, and petitions the Marine Department to introduce more rigorous safety regulations in future. He complained that higher-class passengers were given priority in the lifeboats, which is definitely true, but more indicative that the loading of the lifeboats in general was completely mismanaged. The first raft launched, for example, took just 28 people, even though it had the capacity for 65. The crux of the issue, however, as Tillett explains, was simply the lack of sufficient lifeboats. Though it had been recommended to the designers that the *Titanic* should have 64 such vessels, the number was reduced to just 20 in order to keep the decks clear and to give the ship a more streamlined appearance. As a result, the *Titanic* ended up with lifeboats that could take only a third of the ship's capacity. Not only this, but ships passing through iceberg-infested waters normally slowed down or stopped entirely when travelling at night. The *Titanic*'s crew had received warnings about icebergs from other nearby ships but, in spite of this, carried on at full tilt – partly to show what a marvellously fast vessel she was. Consequently, the impact on collision with the iceberg was much more severe than it might have been.

Mere weeks after the supposedly 'unsinkable' *Titanic* had been launched, people like Tillett understandably emphasised the need for safety over speed, and the importance of sufficient lifeboats over aesthetic considerations. By the end of April 1912, the draw of being the first ship to have a heated swimming pool and the luxury of 11-course dinners in first class seemed somewhat less appealing if the ship's crew could not safeguard the lives of its passengers.

Titanic on her maiden voyage.

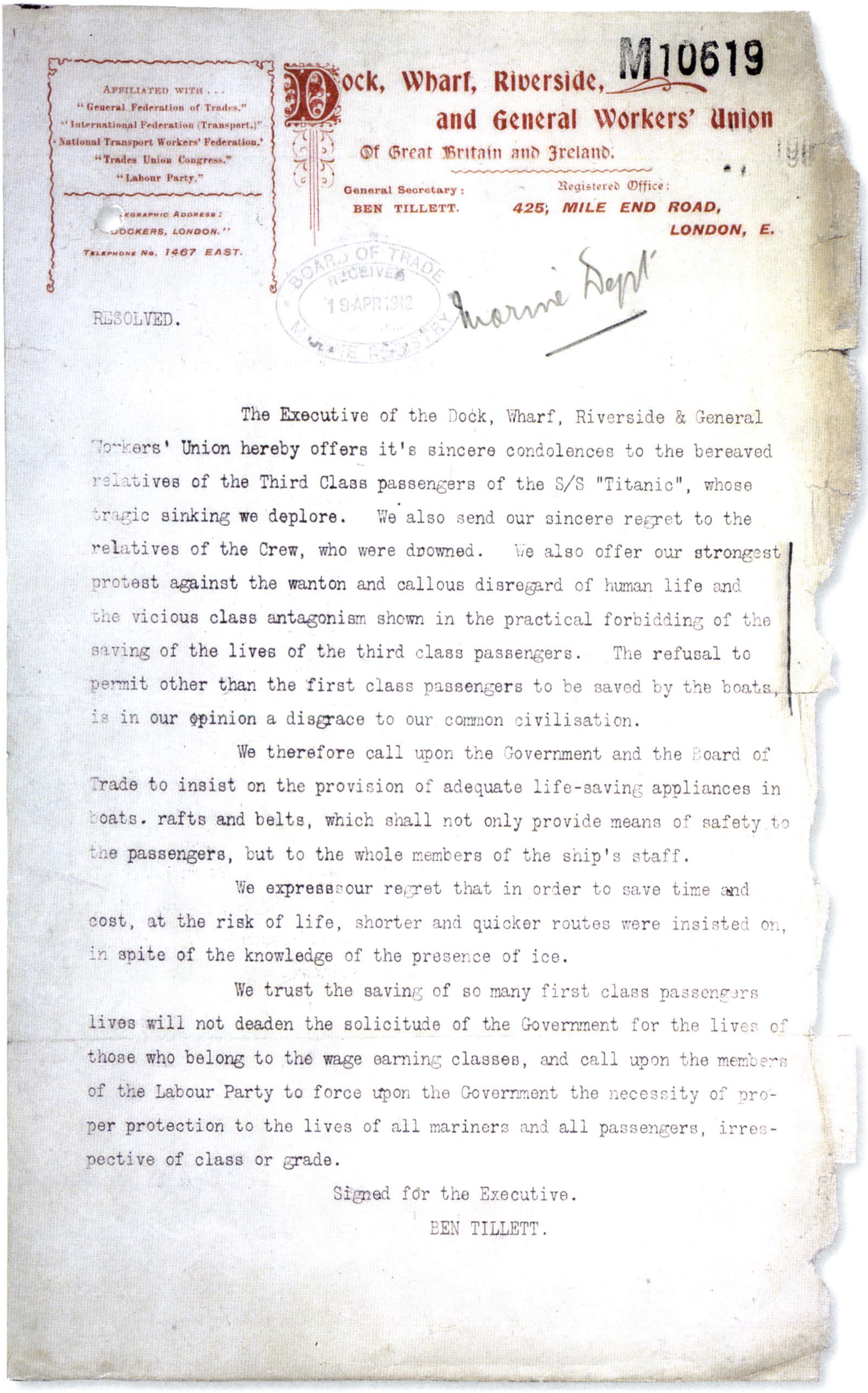

M10619

Dock, Wharf, Riverside, and General Workers' Union Of Great Britain and Ireland.

Affiliated with . . .
"General Federation of Trades."
"International Federation (Transport.)"
"National Transport Workers' Federation."
"Trades Union Congress."
"Labour Party."

Telegraphic Address: "Dockers, London."
Telephone No. 1467 East.

General Secretary: BEN TILLETT.

Registered Office: 425, MILE END ROAD, LONDON, E.

BOARD OF TRADE RECEIVED 19 APR 1912 MARINE REGISTRY

Marine Dept

RESOLVED.

The Executive of the Dock, Wharf, Riverside & General Workers' Union hereby offers it's sincere condolences to the bereaved relatives of the Third Class passengers of the S/S "Titanic", whose tragic sinking we deplore. We also send our sincere regret to the relatives of the Crew, who were drowned. We also offer our strongest protest against the wanton and callous disregard of human life and the vicious class antagonism shown in the practical forbidding of the saving of the lives of the third class passengers. The refusal to permit other than the first class passengers to be saved by the boats, is in our opinion a disgrace to our common civilisation.

We therefore call upon the Government and the Board of Trade to insist on the provision of adequate life-saving appliances in boats. rafts and belts, which shall not only provide means of safety to the passengers, but to the whole members of the ship's staff.

We expresssour regret that in order to save time and cost, at the risk of life, shorter and quicker routes were insisted on, in spite of the knowledge of the presence of ice.

We trust the saving of so many first class passengers lives will not deaden the solicitude of the Government for the lives of those who belong to the wage earning classes, and call upon the members of the Labour Party to force upon the Government the necessity of proper protection to the lives of all mariners and all passengers, irrespective of class or grade.

Signed for the Executive.

BEN TILLETT.

The Russian East Asiatic S.S. Co. Radio-Telegram. 526

S.S. "Birma".

No Words.	Origin. Station.	Time handed in.	Via.	Remarks.
bg to 6.	Titanic	11 H.45M. April 14/15 1912.		Distress call Ligs Loud.

Cgd - Sos. from M. G. Y.

We have struck iceberg sinking fast come to our assistance.

Position Lat. 41.46 n. Lon. 50.14. w.

M.G.Y.

‘Wrong and wicked punishment’

Sir Douglas Haig defends Field Punishment No. 1

1916

In October 1916, an article published in the *Illustrated Sunday Herald* sparked a national debate about the form that military discipline should take during the First World War. Written by retired serviceman Robert Blatchford, it railed specifically against the ominously titled ‘Field Punishment No. 1’, and prompted letters to the War Office, questions in Parliament and, eventually, the letter pictured: a defence of the punishment from the then Commander-in-Chief of the British Armies in France, Sir Douglas Haig.

Field Punishment No. 1, a name derived from the Manual of Military Law that permitted its use, was intended to deal with minor offences in the field as an alternative to imprisonment and as a replacement to flogging, which had been outlawed in 1881. It required that a soldier be tied to a stationary object, often a fence post or the wheel of a wagon, for hourly periods, with the attendant discomfort and shame intended to serve as both a punishment for the soldier and a public deterrent against future misdemeanours. Its apparent similarity to crucifixion, and reports of soldiers being placed within range of enemy shellfire, perhaps even dying following the procedure, made it a controversial form of discipline, and Blatchford’s article struck a chord with a public wearied by two years of war.

The archival file that covers the controversy includes letter after letter imploring the War Office to abolish the punishment. Miss Grieve of Sunderland asked why ‘our brave men’ should be ‘subjected to such wrong and wicked punishment’; Mr Hardy of London called on the Prime Minister Lloyd George to end ‘such terrible punishment’, believing it to be too like the ‘militarism which we so heartily despise in Germany’; while Mr Lucas of Leicester went to the very top, writing to King George V with the request that he ‘use [his] Royal prerogative in this matter’.

The dispute gained momentum during the winter of 1916. Letters pages of newspapers began to fill up with talk of the punishment, trade unions across the country started to pass resolutions against the practice and, soon enough, questions cropped up in Parliament. As such, after a quick survey of opinion within the Army, Haig attempted to draw a line under the issue with this letter to the War Office, written on 4 December, offering both a defence and a compromise.

Haig gave three reasons for Field Punishment No. 1's retention. First, he cited the lack of a suitable alternative. Imprisonment removed men from the fighting line and compared favourably with 'discomfort in the trenches', extra work was meaningless 'when all are hard worked to the fullest extent', while forfeiture of pay was 'little felt when opportunities for spending money are scarce'. Second, he argued that the physical convenience must be sufficiently 'irksome' so as to be a noticeable deterrent in an environment where the conditions are already far from optimal. Lastly, he suggested that abolishing the punishment without replacement would lead to more frequent recourse to the death penalty.

Haig then went on to say that, to allay concerns, he would standardise the punishment to both safeguard the soldier and play down the similarities to crucifixion. These new rules included limitations on the punishment's frequency, its duration and on how tight the straps could be around the soldier's feet and wrists. A sketch was included to illustrate these, which was soon made available through the War Office.

The robust defence of the practice offered by Haig seems to have served its purpose. The new rules were sent out through the War Office in January 1917, and Field Punishment No. 1 continued to be used in this new, standardised form for the remainder of the war. It was eventually abolished with the passing of the Army and Air Force (Annual) Act 1923.

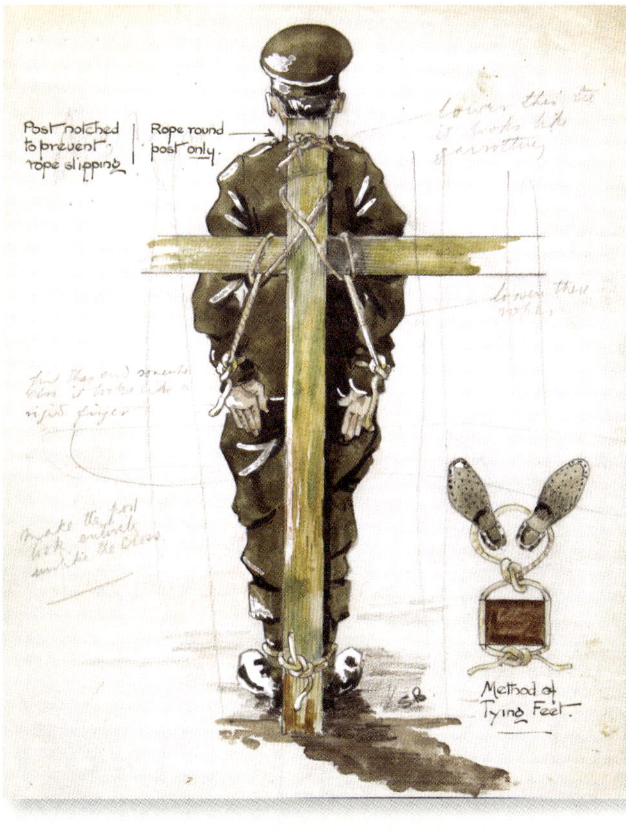

WO.

Health Insurance Office.

Over **700** Branches.

The ...

Workers' Union.

ESTABLISHED 1st MAY, 1898.
REGISTER No. 1,157, T.U.

President: Councillor J. Beard.
Vice-President: Tom Mann.
General Secretary: CHARLES DUNCAN, M.P.
Solicitors: Messrs. Pattinson & Brewer, 30, Great James Street, London, W.C.
Bankers: The Co-operative Wholesale Society.
Auditors: Sidney H. Hossell & Co., Chartered Accountants, Hatherton Chambers, Old Square, Birmingham.

Organisers:
Yorkshire District: Alderman R. Morley.
South Wales District: Matt Giles.
Midland District: Councillor John Beard.
Manchester District: Councillor Geo. Titt.
Scotland: Councillor Geo. Kerr.
London District: George Dallas.

Registered Office: 16, AGINCOURT ROAD, HAMPSTEAD, LONDON, N.W.

Trade Union Office.

Money Orders to be made payable at **Hampstead Heath Station Post Office.**

Telephone: 3023 Hampstead.

Received from Private Secretary

Affiliated to the Labour Party

Branch ST. PANCRAS. *No.* 459 31st January, 1917.

Address 10, Prebend Place, Camden Town. N.W.

140,000—18-10-15

The Right Hon. David Lloyd George., P.C., M.P.,
Prime Minister.
10, Downing Street,
Whitehall. S.W.

WAR OFFICE -2 FEB 1917

AG3

Sir,

With reference to the subject of punishment inflicted by the Army Authorities on our Soldiers in the Field, I am instructed by my Branch to forward you the following resolution which was unanimously passed at its last meeting :-

> "That this Branch of the Workers' Union protests against the continued infliction by the Army Authorities of what is known as 'crucifixion' upon our brothers in the Field, and demands that this degrading and humiliating form of punishment be forthwith abolished."

I trust, Sir, that you will use your power in the direction indicated by the resolution, and am,

Your obedient servant,

G. Bailey

Branch Secretary.

TELEPHONE Nº 63 MUSEUM. TELEGRAPHIC ADDRESS BEWARE, EUSQUARE, LONDON.

National Union of Railwaymen,

UNITY HOUSE, EUSTON ROAD, LONDON, N.W.

In your reply refer to Nº ....

Crewe No. 5. Branch.

Address 37 Underwood Lane, Crewe.

November 25th 1916.

The Rt. Hon. the Secretary of State for War,
Parliament Buildings,
Westminster.

WAR OFFICE RECEIVED 27 NOV 1916

Dear Sir,

At a meeting held on the 18th inst. a resolution was passed and I was instructed to convey the same to you, appealing to you to use your influence so that the matter might receive some consideration.

The resolution is as follows, viz:-

" The Crewe No. 5 Branch National Union of Railwaymen "
" protest by every means in its power against the awful "
" practice of the Field punishment commonly known as "
" CRUCIFICTION, in the British Army, and we call upon the "
" Prime Minister, the Minister for War, and Mr. E. Craig, M.P."
" to use all their energies to get this anomaly abolished.

Signed on behalf of the members,

Yours respectfully,

W. H. Farmer.

Branch Secretary.

A letter of farewell to his mother

Patrick Pearse: executed for being a leader of the Easter Rising

1916

Patrick Pearse, an Irish schoolteacher and writer read the 'Proclamation of the Irish Republic' to the gathered Irish Rebel Forces at the General Post Office in Dublin, on 24 April 1916. What would become known as the Easter Rising had started that morning, and Pearse was spokesperson for the leaders of the attempted revolution.

The General Post Office had been selected as the headquarters of the insurrection, and Patrick Pearse was joined there by other revolutionary leaders such as Tom Clarke, Joseph Plunkett and Seán Mac Diarmada.

Pearse had grown up in a middle-class family, and as a result of his intelligence and opportunity became a leading light in the Gaelic League and Gaelic revival, which placed significant emphasis on the importance of culture to the soul of a nation and, specifically, the importance of saving the Irish language from what he perceived to be the cultural suppression of 'Irishness' by successive British governments.

These politics fed into Patrick Pearse's Irish nationalism, and he became a member of the Irish Volunteers and of the secret underground organisation the Irish Republican Brotherhood (IRB) in 1913. An articulate speaker and gifted writer, fluent in both Irish and English, Pearse was invited to be a part of the IRB's 'Supreme Council'. The IRB was dedicated to the establishment of an Irish Republic, and using a combination of Irishmen from various organisations, but especially the Irish Volunteers and IRB, an armed insurrection was planned and attempted in April 1916. Pearse was a signatory to the 'proclamation of the Irish Republic', and a key leader of this rebellion against British rule, undertaken in the middle of the First World War.

Six days after he read the 'Proclamation of the Irish Republic' outside the GPO, Pearse issued the order to unconditionally surrender, and he was subsequently arrested by the British military authorities.

While in gaol in Arbour Hill Barracks, Dublin, he wrote to his mother, Margaret Pearse, on 1 May 1916. This letter was not the last he would write to Margaret (although she would receive neither), but whereas his final note focused on his goodbyes, this letter dated two days before his execution addresses the rising itself.

Pearce's letter notes that after six days of fighting, the leaders of the rising realised they were surrounded by British forces and were without food. Having been told by the British that they would only accept an unconditional surrender, Pearce duly arranged to do so on 29 April 1916. He notes in his letter that in addition to the lack of food, he and the other leaders wanted to '*prevent further slaughter of the civilian population … in the hope of saving the lives of our followers*'.

Pearce lets his mother know that he was with his brother and fellow revolutionary, Willie, in the Barracks, and attempts to put her mind at ease, stating that although as a leader of an attempted revolution he was certain to be executed, he and the other leaders were '*ready to die and we shall die cheerfully and proudly*'.

Writing to a loved one knowing you are going to die must be extremely difficult, but in Pearse's words his commitment and belief in his politics is clear. He states that his mother '*must not grieve for all this. We have preserved Ireland's honour and our own. Our deeds of last week are the most splendid in Ireland's history*'.

Prophetic words indeed from Patrick Pearse. The Easter Rising is considered one of the, if not *the*, most important events in the history of the Irish Republic. Pearse's execution along with other leaders of the Easter Rising is seen as a contributing factor to the rise in active support for a Republic in Ireland in the years that followed. Pearse stated that, '*People will say hard things of [the Rising's leaders] now, but we shall be remembered by posterity and blessed by unborn generations*'.

The multitude of schools, roads, buildings, stadiums and sports clubs that exist in Ireland today named after Patrick Pearse prove that he was quite right in believing he would be '*remembered by posterity*' in Ireland, as this letter so asserts.

Arbour Hill Barracks,

Dublin, 1st May, 1916.

Dearest Mother,

You will, I know, have been longing to hear from me. I do not know how much you have heard since the last note I sent you from the G.P.O.

On Friday ev[enin]g the Post Office was set on fire, and we had to abandon it. We dashed into Moore Street, and remained in the houses in Moore until Saturday afternoon. We then found that we were surrounded by troops and that we had practically no food.

We decided in order to prevent further slaughter of the civil population and in the hope of saving the lives of our followers, to ask the General Commanding the British Forces to discuss terms. He replied that he would receive me only if I surrendered unconditionally and this I did. I was taken to the Headquarters of the British Command in Ireland, and there I wrote and signed an order to our men to lay down their arms. All this I did in accordance with the decision of our Provisional Gov[ernmen]t who were with us in Moore St. My own opinion was in favour of one more desperate sally before opening negotiations, but I yielded to the majority, and I think now the majority was right, as the sally would have resulted only in losing the lives of perhaps 50 or 100 of our men, and we should have had to surrender in the long run as we were without food.

I was brought here on Saturday ev[enin]g and later on all the men with us in Moore Street were brought here. Those in the other parts of the City have, I understand, been taken to other barracks and prisons. All here are safe and well. Willie and all the St. Enda's boys are here. I have not seen them since Saturday, but I believe they are all well, and that they are not now in any danger. Our hope and belief is that the Gov[ernmen]t will spare the lives of all our followers, but we do not expect that they will spare the lives of the leaders. We are ready to die and we shall die cheerfully and proudly. Personally I do not hope or even desire to live. But I do hope and desire and believe that the lives of all our followers will be saved, including the lives dear to you and me (my own excepted) and this will be a great consolation to me when dying.

You must not grieve for all this. We have preserved Ireland's honour and our own. Our deeds of last week are the most splendid in Ireland's history. People will say hard things of us now, but we shall be remembered by posterity and blessed by unborn generations. You too will be blessed because you were my mother.

If you feel you would like to see me, I think you will be allowed to visit me, by applying to the Headquarters, Irish Command, near the Park. I shall I hope have another opportunity of writing to you.

Love to W.W., M.B.., Miss Byrne, [ILLEGIBLE] and to your own dear self.
P.

P.S. - I understand that the German expedition on which I was counting actually set sail but was defeated by the British.

but we do not expect that they will 6
spare the lives of the leaders. We
are ready to die and we shall
die cheerfully and proudly. Personally
I do not hope or even desire to live.
But I do hope and desire and believe that the lives of all our
followers will be saved, including
the lives dear to you and me (my
own excepted) and this will be
a great consolation ~~to me when dying~~. You must not
grieve for all this. We have pre-
served Ireland's honour and
our own. Our deeds of last week
are the most splendid in Ireland's history. People will say hard
things of us now, but we shall be
remembered by posterity and blessed
by unborn generations. You too will
be blessed because you were my
mother.
[redacted] [illegible] [redacted] would like to see
me, I think you will be allowed to
visit me, by applying to [redacted] headquarters [illegible]. I shall
Irish Com[illegible]
I [redacted] hope, be[illegible]
write to you [illegible]
mind, a[illegible]

P.S. – I understand that the German expedition on which I was ~~counting~~ counting actually set sail – but was defeated by the British. 4

Arbour Hill Barracks,
Dublin, 1st May 1916.

Dearest Mother,

You will, I know, have been longing to hear from me. I don't know how much you have heard since the last note I sent you from the G.P.O.

On Friday evg. the Post Office was set on fire, and we had to abandon it. We dashed into Moore Street, and remained in the houses in Moore Street until Saturday afternoon. We then found that we were surrounded

in order to prevent further slaughter of the civil population and in the hope of saving the lives of our followers, to ask the General commanding the British forces to discuss terms. He replied that he would receive me only if I surrendered unconditionally, and this I did. I was taken to the Headquarters of the British Command in Ireland, and there I ~~wrote~~ wrote and signed an order to our men to lay down their arms. All this I did in accordance with the decision of the members of our Provisional Govt. who were with us in Moore Street. My own ~~idea~~ opinion was in favour of one more desperate sally before

opening ~~terms~~ negotiations, but I yielded to 5
the majority, and I think now the majority were right, as the sally would have resulted only in losing the lives of perhaps 50 or 100 of our men, and we should have had to surrender in the long run, as we were without food.

I was brought here on Saturday evg. and later on all the men with us in Moore Street were brought here. Those in the other parts of the city have, I understand, been taken to other barracks and prisons.

All here are safe and well. Willie and all the St. Enda's boys are here. I have not seen them since Saturday, but I believe that they are all well, and that they are not now in any danger. Our hope and belief is that the Govt. will spare the lives of all our followers,

Animals in a cage

Women's petitions for equal participation in Parliament

1911

In 1911, not only did women not have the vote; the grounds for divorce were still unequal, mothers did not have equal custody rights, and while women could study at more universities they were not entitled to the formal degrees that male students were. Without the Sex Disqualification Act that would follow in 1919, women were legally allowed to be discriminated against for jobs on the basis of gender or marriage.

So if you were a woman in 1911 how would you have been able to interact with parliamentary politics? Before 1834, a limited number of privileged women were able to observe parliamentary debates through a ventilation shaft in the ceiling of the House of Commons. After the 1834 fire in the Palace of Westminster, the Ladies Gallery was created – while less restricted than its predecessor, there were still distinct barriers between women and men in parliament. This was particularly emphasised by the grille that obscured women's view, and hindered their ability to listen to debates. In many ways, this divide represented women's wider position in society.

Women writing into the government complained as early as 1893 about the bad lighting in the Ladies' Gallery, and famously two suffragettes chained themselves to the grille as a protest in 1908. At the height of the suffrage movement in 1911, the grille became a symbolic target to attack. A sign in the gallery alludes to the difficulties, stating 'No demonstration of any kind to be permitted in the Gallery'.

One campaigner noted women were treated like 'Animals in a cage'. AM Tooler wrote in 1911 to the Board of Works 'on behalf of many women', to complain that the Ladies Gallery in the House of Commons be changed, and the 'insulting grid be removed'. Images of the time show the stark contrast of the opulent architecture of the House of Commons' chamber with the minimal furniture in the Ladies Gallery.

Tooler argued that the women contribute to the state, through their work and pay, and therefore should be able to listen to debates in the chamber and 'feel like human beings and not animals in a cage'.

The Ladies Gallery remained through the First World War, despite the workload increasingly carried by women, who were fundamental to the war effort – supporting the home front and the front line in the absences of men – and yet they had no formal way of influencing how the country was run.

The grilles through which female visitors could view proceedings in Parliament.

In 1917, the battle continued against the grille, and a petition was sent by Philippa Strachey on behalf on London Society for Women's Suffrage on 14 May 1917. Along with the Women's Freedom League letter sent in 1916, these items show that contrary to common perception, many suffrage societies did continue to campaign through the war, and many individual women were still active, despite the Women's Social and Political Union (WSPU) ceasing militant action.

The petition opens with the claim: 'We could very easily have obtained many thousands of signatures but we believe that the representative character of those who have signed will convey even more conclusively the overwhelming demand among thinking women for the proposed action.'

Representatives included a vast range of signatories, from Clementina Black, honorary secretary of the Women's Trade Union League and Miss Llewellyn Davies, the General Secretary of the Co-operative Guild, to women listed as being a trained nurse and midwifes.

The grille was eventually removed by a majority vote of MPs in August 1917, just a year before women themselves were able to sit on the other side of it, as participating Members of Parliament.

VOTES FOR WOMEN.

Women's Freedom League

Telephone—Charing Cross, 1285.

Office Hours: 10 till 6.
Saturdays, 10 till 1.

GLASGOW BRANCH:
70 ST. GEORGE'S ROAD,
GLASGOW,

April 6th 1916

To the Right Hon. Mr Harcourt.

Sir,
Our attention has been drawn to your reply to Mr Cowan, re the strangers gallery, when he suggested "that either the men's gallery should have a grille or that the ladies gallery should have its grille removed. You replied "that was a very different matter" & laughter followed. May I ask what the difference is, do you not as Mr Cowan suggested desire the equalization of the conditions of the sexes, or do you desire that insult of the grille placed upon a whole sex should be perpetuated? Now a days in & out of season men prate about services women have rendered the

the state, & of the political men over them.
Have men either in the House or out of it,
taken one opportunity to remove any of the
sex disabilities heaped upon women, or to
remove the many insults which men, time
and convention have placed upon women.
This is the only politics we would accep
It argues badly for the future that even
a question of this kind evokes nothing
but mirth in the House of Commons.

I am yours faithfully

Eunice G Murray

President of the Glasgow Brai

the Women's Free

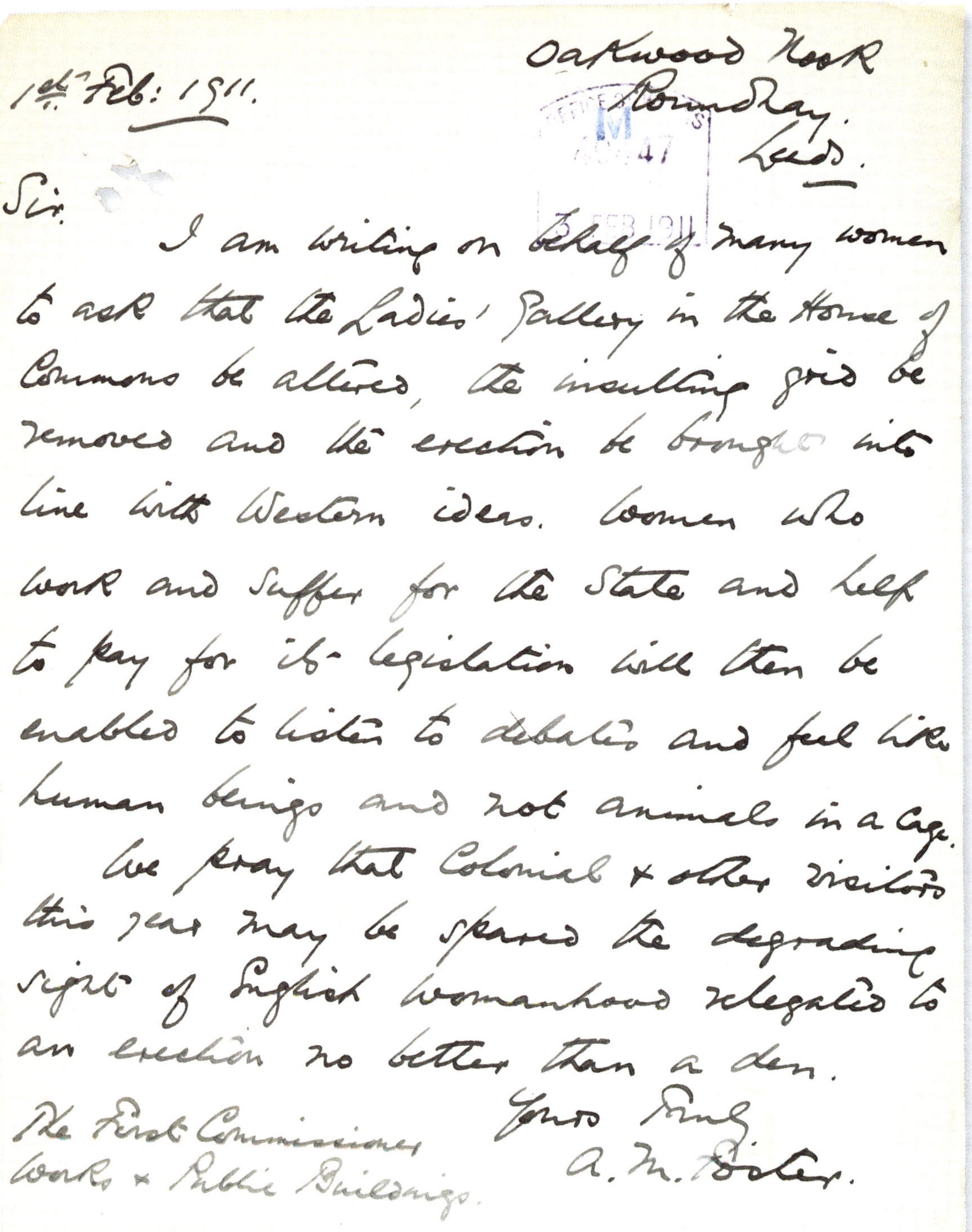
Oakwood Nook
Roundhay.
Leeds.

1st Feb: 1911.

Sir:

I am writing on behalf of many women to ask that the Ladies' Gallery in the House of Commons be altered, the insulting grid be removed and the erection be brought into line with Western ideas. Women who work and suffer for the State and help to pay for its legislation will then be enabled to listen to debates and feel like human beings and not animals in a cage.

We pray that Colonial & other visitors this year may be spared the degrading sight of English womanhood relegated to an erection no better than a den.

Yours truly
A. M. Foster.

The First Commissioner
Works & Public Buildings.

1st Feb 1911

Oakwood Nook
Roundhay
Leeds

Sir,

I am writing on behalf of many women to ask that the Ladies' Gallery in the House of Commons be altered, the insulting grid be removed and the erection be brought into line with Western ideas. Women who work and suffer for the State and help to pay for its legislation will then be enabled to listen to debates and feel like human beings and not animals in a cage.

We pray that Colonial and other visitors this year may be spared the degrading sight of English womanhood relegated to an erection no better than a den.

Yours truly,

A. M. Foster

The First Commissioner
Works and Public Buildings

The Warsaw Ghetto Uprising
Dedicated to the Jewish people of Poland

1943

Between 1939 and the beginning of 1943, the process of ghettoisation, mass shootings and deportations to death camps by the Nazis resulted in the genocide of 75 per cent of European Jewry. In April 1943, the Warsaw Ghetto Uprising was the ultimate show of resistance by the remaining Jews in Warsaw. By May 1943, most of Poland's Jews had been murdered by the Nazis.

Szmul Zygielbojm is a name which deserves its place in Holocaust historiography. There is little published biographical information available about him, despite his prominence in Polish pre-war politics. He was born in Poland and was an active member of the Bund – a Jewish socialist party in Poland. After escaping from Poland and reaching Belgium in December 1939, he fled to France in 1940. From there he travelled to the USA, where he campaigned about the plight of the Jews in Poland. In 1942 he was elected a member of the Polish National Council, a body of the Polish Government in Exile based in London.

In London, he received early reports from sources within Poland about living conditions of Jews, the deportations and mass killings. In January 1943 he met with the Polish courier Jan Karski, who was sent to Warsaw by the Polish Government in Exile to report back on the general situation in Poland. Karski brought back much needed information about the situation of the Jews in Poland, in particular of those Jews living in the Warsaw Ghetto and those waiting to enter the death camp of Belzec. His reports were passed on to the British government, and much of the information was published in December 1942 by the Polish government in Exile, in a pamphlet called *The Mass Extermination of Jews in German Occupied Poland*.

On 28 April, Zygielbojm received a despatch from the fighting units in the Warsaw ghetto: *Only the power of the United Nations can offer immediate and effective help now. On behalf of the millions of Jews burnt and murdered and buried alive, on behalf of those fighting back and all of us condemned to die, we call on the whole world.*

Zygielbojm wanted to do all in his power to provoke a response from the Allies. At a meeting of the Jewish Cadre in Warsaw, during the first few days of Nazi occupation, around 50 people met with Szmul Zygielbojm. None of them were contemplating an insurgency, yet Zygielbojm was already earmarking the front-runners who would lead the uprising in the ghetto. He quoted later on in London: *These are not the same people who we knew before the war – they are intelligent and see dangers ahead and they are not afraid. In London I have met people who cannot see the dangers and are afraid.*

Zygielbojm's last, most desperate, appeal, written on the typewriter on which he wrote so many previous petitions, called for to the world to respond. He was steadfast, courageous, faithful to his ideology and ready to die for his cause.

He chose to use the power of words in the form of a letter addressed to the Prime Minister and the President of Poland. He used his political position to send this final plea to all the Allies to save what remained of the Jews in Poland. Having been very discontented at the lack of Allied response to the Holocaust, he took his own life. His death was a tragic loss not only to Polish Jewry, but also to the whole of Poland. This was a man faithful to his religion and to his nation. He was unable to disconnect his personal tragedy from that of the fate of his countrymen. The evening before his death he met with a friend. 'I am a Pole' he said. Subdued and deeply dispirited, he could not see a future for himself without Polish Jewry.

At his funeral in London, Ignacy Schwarzbart, a Jewish representative on the National Council of Poland, chose these words to describe his legacy: 'His deed was a show of extreme pessimism; his plea was a ray of optimism in defiance of reality.'

Harassment of an elderly Jew in the Warsaw Ghetto.

93

Translation from the Polish.

SZMUL M. ZYGIELBOJM,
Member of the National Council of
the Republic of Poland.

12 Porchester Square,
London, W.2.

11th May 1943.

To the President of the Republic of Poland
Wladyslaw Raczkiewicz

To the Prime Minister
General Wladyslaw Sikorski.

I take the liberty of addressing to you my last words, and through you, to the Polish Government and people, to the Governments and peoples of the Allied States, to the conscience of the world.

From the latest information re ceived from Poland, it is evident without doubt that the Germans, with full ruthless cruelty, are now murdering the few remaining Jews in Poland. Behind the walls of the ghettos the last act of a tragedy unprecedented in history is being performed.

The responsibility for the crime of murdering all Jewish population in Poland falls, in the first instance, on the perpetrators, but indirectly, also weighs on the whole of humanity, the peoples and Governments of the Allied States, which, so far, have made no effort towards a concrete action for the purpose of curtailing this crime. By the passive observation of this murder of defenceless millions and maltreated children, women and men, these countries have become accomplices of the criminals.

I have also to state that although the Polish Government has in a high degree contributed to the stirring of the opinion of the world, yet insufficiently it did not do anything so extraordinary that would correspond to the magnitude of the drama now being enacted in Poland.

From nearly 3 and a half million Polish Jews and about 700,000 Jews deported to Poland from other countries, there still lived in April of this year - according to official information of the Head of the Underground Bund Organisation, sent to us through the Delegate of the Government - about 300,000. And the murder is still going on incessantly.

I cannot be silent and I cannot live while the remnants of the Jewish people in Poland, of whom I am the representative, are perishing.

My comrades in the Warsaw ghetto perished with weapons in their hand in their last heroic impulse.

It was not my destiny to perish as they did, together with them, but I belong to them and to their mass graves.

By my death I wish to express my strongest protest against the inactivity with which the world is looking on and

permitting

permitting the extermination of the Jewish people. I know how little human life is worth, especially to-day. But as I was unable to do anything during my life, perhaps by my death I shall contribute to the breaking of the indifference of those who are able and should act in order to save now, maybe in the last moment, this handful of Polish Jews, who are still alive, from certain annihilation.

My life belongs to the Jewish people in Poland, and therefore I give it to them. I wish that this handful which remained from several millions of Polish Jews, could live to see, with the Polish masses, the liberation, that it could breathe in Poland, and in a world of freedom and in the justice of socialism, for all its tortures and inhuman sufferings. And I believe that such a Poland will arise and that such a world will come.

I trust that the President and the Prime Minister will direct these my words to all those for whom they are destined, and that the Polish Government will immediately begin an appropriate action in the diplomatic and propaganda fields in order to save yet from extermination the remains of the Polish Jews who are still alive.

I bid farewell to all and everything dear to me and loved by me.

S. ZYGIELBOJM.

No.138/V43.

The Polish Consulate General in London hereby certifies that the above is a true and correct translation of the original produced to this Office.

London, the 17th May, 1943.

For Consul General:

A. Filcek.
Acting Secretary.

The League of Coloured Peoples

The mixed-race babies of the Second World War

1945

There is a many a wartime myth about dashing American men wooing British women with stockings and taking them to jitterbug jives to dance the night away, but what was the reality?

In the Second World War there certainly was an influx of American soldiers on British soil, but it wasn't all fun. Ministry of Heath correspondence contains a particularly shocking letter from the campaigning organisation the League of Coloured Peoples, one of the most active organisations on race relations in this period. The letter notes that the conditions of war are leading to a 'large number of unwanted babies', specifically children of African American descent.

The letter claims that, while the white children seem to be dealt with, the authorities are either 'unable or unwilling' to handle the babies of African American parentage. The League of Coloured People claimed a de facto colour bar was in place, affecting the way that mixed-race babies were being treated.

The League of Coloured Peoples, led and founded by Dr Harold Moody, continued to campaign against the colour bar as one of its central issues. The colour bar was a social system in which black people were denied the same rights as white people, affecting job opportunities or even whether people would be served in certain premises. It was never enforced by law in Britain, but racial discrimination was often a de facto reality. At different times this affected multiple areas of public life, with the League protesting the existence of colour bars in British hotels in 1932, and correspondence from all over Africa and the West Indies.

These letters exist in a file concerning conference proceedings about supporting children born illegitimately as a result of the Second World War. At this conference, the children of white women and black men were considered in particular, as there were concerns as to whether these children or their mothers would be discriminated against because of the colour of the children's skin. However, reports at the conference showed that this was not necessarily the case.

This was not a single-organisation issue; many other organisations were also campaigning for change. The conference was attended by the National Council for the Unmarried Mother and her Child, the League of Coloured Peoples and other representatives from around the country. They discussed the scale of the problem in different areas and what was to be done in the best interests of the children, the mothers and the country.

The Second World War was already a time of particular awareness of racial discrimination for the League; agitation peaked again around the limits initially imposed on black men to obtain commissions to serve in the Second World War. The campaign was led through both a deputation and correspondence with the Colonial Office.

The League worked closely with the government to push for progress, however one Home Office file notes that 'Dr Moody, and that is the League, have no extreme views – far from it'. Their methods of campaigning were different from other pressure groups, having a reputation as a moderate Christian organisation. Indeed, despite the discrimination League members faced in Britain, the letter closes by proclaiming they are writing 'both as coloured people and as citizens of a country we love and whose good name we desire to see enriched'.

A table included alongside this letter detailed the 'number of illegitimate children born in this country whose fathers are alleged to be coloured American soldiers', organised by county. It includes the breakdown by married and unmarried mothers, with the highest figure in Devon with 83 babies – showing the impact of change as a result of the war all over the country.

A US serviceman dancing with a girl at Frisco's International Club, Piccadilly, London.

THE LEAGUE OF COLOURED PEOPLES.

FOUNDER AND PRESIDENT - - - - - HAROLD A. MOODY, M.D., B.S. (LOND.)

General & Travelling Secretary: SAMSON U. MORRIS (Grenada).

Assistant Secretary: Mrs. MARGARET FULLER.

Hon. Treasurer: Capt. CHRISTINE O. MOODY, R.A.M.C. *(On Active Service)* *Hon. Acting Treasurer:* Miss JOAN E. MOODY.

President's Address:
164, QUEEN'S ROAD, S.E. 15.
Telephone: NEW Cross 1834.

Monthly Publication:
NEWS LETTER

19, OLD QUEEN STREET,
S.W. 1.
Telephone & Telegrams: WHITEHALL 6591.

HAM/HM/A

16.5.45

MINISTRY OF HEALTH
E17-5-45
No 93216 11/70

93216/2/18

The Rt Hon H.U.Willink M.C.,M.P.,
H.M.Minister of Health,
Whitehall S.W.1

Dear Sir,

I have been instructed to draw your attention to the fact that as a direct result of war conditions there are now emerging a large number of unwanted babies, of which a fair proportion are coloured. Agencies at present at work seem to be able to deal with the white babies, but are either unable or unwilling to deal with the coloured ones. Herein we detect the grave possibilities of an aggravation of the Colour Bar, just at a time when so much is being done to help to abolish this curse.

In our experience the best way in which to deal with such a situation is by some wise action taken by an authoritative person; and we would venture to suggest that inthis case that person should be yourself.

Our Organisation is opposed to the establishing of a Home for coloured babies as such, but we do feel that a Home should be established for these unwanted babies and that they should be admitted thereto in equal proportion of black and white.

One of our members feeling the need for some action tried to establish such a home, but is finding this not so easy as he anticipated. We have had other suggestions and offers made to us from time to time, as to how to deal with this issue, but we do feel that it is a matter for

Government/

Government action and that such action should be taken almost immediately, if we are to anticipate what might develop into a serious and perhaps awkward issue.

We have no doubt, Sir, that your Department has had their attention drawn to this need, but we would like to have your assurance that you feel that you ought to do something about it; and that, in so doing, you will not ignore the help we are able to give in a matter of vital concern to us both as coloured people and as citizens of a country we love and whose good name we desire to see enriched.

Yours very truly,

Harold A. Moody

Harold A.Moody,
Founder & President

'Nkosi Sikelel' iAfrika'

Notes on the trial of Nelson Mandela

1963

This letter marks the start of the trial which led to Nelson Mandela being sentenced to life imprisonment in 1964. Mandela, a key player in the African National Congress (ANC), an organisation campaigning for black liberation from the racial segregation which had been enshrined in South African law in 1948, along with 10 other ANC members, stood accused of forming a detailed plan for waging guerrilla warfare intended to culminate in full-scale revolt against the government of South Africa.

Mandela's trial began on 15 October, and this letter was written the day after, by Lord Dunrossil (John William Morrison), who was a British Foreign Office observer at the trial. In a letter to the Foreign Office in London, Dunrossil reports on the events of the opening day, which took place in the Old Synagogue in Pretoria. He explains that the authorities switched the hearing from Johannesburg to Pretoria at 48 hours' notice, fearing possible demonstrations and violence. He wrote: *'The hearing [was] filled with rows of Africans, some of them in Tembu tribal dress.'*

There were 250 Africans in the crowd, each of whom had come to offer support to Mandela. Like many of his supporters, he too was largely in tribal dress, including a traditional jackal skin. At the end of proceedings, the African crowd, which had maintained order throughout the day burst into harmonious song, singing 'Nkosi Sikelel' iAfrika' (God Bless Africa).

During the trial, Mandela argued that non-violent protest must give way to more violent approaches if the goals of a multi-racial democracy in South Africa were to be achieved. Nonetheless in 1964 Nelson Mandela was sentenced to life imprisonment. He spent 27 years in prison, 18 of these on Robben Island, where he worked in a lime quarry and was allowed only one letter and one visitor every six months.

In February 1990, Mandela was released from prison, and four years later, in May 1994, he took office as the first black President of South Africa.

Nelson Mandela (far right) and Robert Resha walking to the room in which their trial was being held.

copies sent to Durban, C.T., P.E., Joburg & Mr Snelling, S'burg. [illegible] 19/10

British Embassy,
Pretoria.

10136

RESTRICTED

October 16, 1962

Nelson Mandela, the A.N.C. leader, appeared before a magistrate yesterday in Pretoria on the charge of incitement to contravene the laws of the country which he and Walter Sisulu had served on them last August. The case was remanded for another week at Mandela's request. My letters to you of August 10 and 18 refer to Mandela's part in this; but the following account may perhaps serve as 'background'. The trial was expected to be held in Johannesburg, but fearing demonstrations and possible violence arising out of them, the authorities, little more than 48 hours beforehand, switched the hearing to Pretoria, and made it clear for the first time that the two men were not going to be charged jointly. Sisulu was brought before the Magistrate in Johannesburg. He is out on bail, unlike Mandela, and his case has been remanded until December 3 with no evidence being led yesterday. His lawyer, Mr. Joe Slovo, objected to Mandela being removed to Pretoria and Sisulu was cheered by a crowd of Africans who, singing and chanting, carried him away.

2. In Pretoria I attended the hearing of Mandela's case which took place in the Old Synagogue, the main part of whose floor was filled with rows of Africans, some of them in Tembu tribal dress. There were not many white spectators and these were in the galleries above. The proceedings were an hour and a half late in starting and during the wait the few whites were cleared out of one of their two galleries to make way for an orderly and well dressed crowd of Africans. Anywhere else this would be unremarkable, as would be the sight of a white police constable helping a black colleague move extra benches into the crowded African section of the public gallery, but in South Africa it showed how both the court officials and the police were doing their best to appear scrupulously fair and courteous, and in the direction of courtesy, at any rate, it represented a modest advance! By the time the proceedings began there were about 200-250 Africans present.

3. Mandela, at whose entrance most people stood up, appeared wearing largely tribal dress with the traditional jackal skin in which he has appeared before. He at once entered a plea that the case should be remanded for a further two weeks. He based his case on two main grounds: first that he had been deprived of the lawyer of his own choice, Mr. Slovo, who, as a banned person, had been confined by the Minister of Justice to Johannesburg and was therefore not able to be present, and second that being thus deprived of his lawyer he was deprived of access to documents vital to his case. (Slovo was in fact at the time occupied in defending Sisulu.) Mandela, though somewhat tense, spoke clearly and presented his case effectively! He showed a slight tendency to stray off into politics and was interrupted

/ by the

P.M. Foster, Esq.,
Foreign Office,
London, S.W.1.

RESTRICTED

by the magistrate when he tried to make the point that one of the few rights left to an African in South Africa was the freedom to choose his own lawyer in a court of law, but he managed to persist in this by claiming it was relevant. He also alleged that the sudden change from Johannesburg to Pretoria indicated a conspiracy on the part of high persons in the State deliberately to mislead him as to the location of the trial and to deprive him of the proper means to defend himself. As a lawyer himself he carefully dissociated these suggestions from the prosecuting counsel in person.

4. Mandela's pleax was opposed by the State who said that the change from Johannesburg to Pretoria was solely in the interests of public order and was occasioned by the widespread and well-publicised campaigns to hold 'Free Mandela' meetings which had been specifically banned by the Minister of Justice and to produce demonstrations outside courtroom in Johannesburg. Although official notification had only been given on the Saturday, October 13, in the morning to Mandela, the state prosecutor argued that there had still been time for Mr. Slovo to get any documents over to Pretoria; Mr. Slovo had in any case never finally indicated that he would be defending Mandela.

5. After a further exchange between Mandela and the counsel for the prosecution the magistrate, Mr. Van Helsdingen, announced his opinion that Mandala's plea was not a frivolous one, that it was vital to Mandela in the defence of his freedom that he should be given adequate means to defend himself and he agreed that the notice given of the switch to Pretoria was rather short. He therefore got both parties to agree, the prosecution grudgingly, not to the two weeks originally requested, but for a remand of one week, which means that the case will come up again on October 22.

6. Thus Mandela won the first round and the State suffered a minor tactical defeat. I talked afterwards to Mrs. Kantor, the wife of one of the partners in Slovo's firm who appeared for Mandela in August. She said that in fact her husband could perfectly well have come over and taken the case, but that for tactical reasons he was staying away. They wanted to get the best possible value out of the trial.

7. At the end of the proceedings the African crowd, who had been both patient and orderly throughout the long wait and the proceedings themselves, stood up and shouted greetings to Mandela when he left the courtroom. Despite calls for silence by court officials and some of their leaders they then filed out in an orderly manner, singing in powerful African harmony "Nkosi Sikelele Afrika" - "God Bless Africa". Outside the courtroom they hung about singing and laughing amonst themselves for alittle time until two rather worried looking senior police officers addressed them with a portable electronic loud-hailer and told them to disperse within five minutes. To make sure that this had been understood an African constable was made to repeat the message in what sounded like Xhosa.

/ 8.

RESTRICTED

8. After the proceedings I joined a journalist friend and one or two others for a drink nearby with three women who had been present at the hearing. One of them, who had eagerly reported the proceedings, was a Mrs. Hilda Bernstein who is a listed Communist and a banned person. She made no secret of this and said that she had no wish to recant her views for Mr. Vorster. She was incidentally quite interesting on what it was like to be a banned person, saying that one of the current serious controversies among the "banned" is whether to offer the Special Branch tea or not when they come to their houses in the early morningsto do one of their periodical searches from the roof to the floorboards! Another of the women was a Mrs. Wolpe, whose husband is also in the same firm oflawyers as Slovo and isalso a listed person under the Sabotage Act. None of these ladies had much sympathy it seemed for Mrs. Helen Joseph who has recently become the first person to be put under House Arrest under the Sabotage Act. They said she stuck her neck out and rather asked for it. Though we had and amusing talk and much merry laughter, I came away faintly depressed that it is to these fellow-travellers that the defence of such prominent African leaders as Mandela and Sisulu is entrusted, who whatever their relationship with Communism (and it is admittedly fairly close) cannot but become progressively indebted to their legal champions and the political allegiance which motivates them.

(Dunrossil)

RESTRICTED

10136

PRODROME PRETORIA FROM DURBAN TOD 1555/15

BRITISH EMBASSY RECEIVED 18-10-1962 PRETORIA-CAPE TOWN

0651

THREE SABOTAGE ATTEMPTS WERE MADE IN AND NEAR DURBAN LAST NIGHT USING AMATEURISH INCENDIARY BOMBS STOP ONE IGNITED IN A RAILWAY COAXH BETWEEN DURBAN AND VERULAM RESULTONG IN SLIGHT DAMAGE STOP THE SECOND WAS PLACED BETWEEN TWO DOORWAYS OF THE C I D OFFICE IN SMITH STREET AND THE THIRD AGAINST THE BANTU ADMINISTRATION OFFICE IN STANGER STREET STOP A CONSIDERABLE CACHE OF EXPLOSIVES INCLUDING ONE HUNDRED AND SIXTY STICKS OF DYNAMITE AND ONE HUNDRED AND FOUR OF GELIGNITE WAS UNEARTHED YESTERDAY MORNING IN SOME WASTE GROUND ABOUT TEN MILES OUT OF DURBAN N THE PIETERMARITZBURG ROAD STOP THE SABOTAGE ATTEMPTS ARE THOUGHT LIKELY TO BE PART OF THE QUOTE FREE MANDELA UNQUOTE CAMPAIGN

Enter & X D 17/10

EVANS

Sexual Offences Act 1967

The decriminalisation of homosexual acts

1961–1962

Prior to 1967's Sexual Offences Act, it was still illegal for a man to have consensual sex with another man. But what was the public perception? The 1885 Criminal Law Amendment Act had made the prosecution of homosexual acts even stricter, with a wider definition not just including penetrative sex. Many police and Home Office records show the prosecutions of individuals for the associated crimes, labelled by terms from the time, such as 'indecent assault', 'sodomy' or having a 'disorderly house'.

However, 1957 was a watershed year – the Wolfenden Report had been published, radically recommending that 'homosexual behaviour between consenting adults in private be no longer a criminal offence'. The committee was chaired by Sir John Wolfenden, and tasked with investigating the law in relation to homosexuality and prostitution. Conversely, the laws on prostitution as a result of the report became tougher.

Despite the report's recommendations on homosexuality it would take another ten years for the legislation to be passed. Ten years in which individuals were still being prosecuted for consensual acts.

In the interim period, various organisations and individuals wrote to the Home Office. These deputations and letters are contained within a number of Home Office documents that record the transition from the writing of the report to the passing of the law.

In 1962, five years before the passing of the law, Reverend WR Butler, of Stroud Green Baptist Church, London, wrote in to the committee with a poignant plea. He writes, 'possibly only we clergy know the extent of human misery and deaths caused by the application of the law in its present form', urging the government to alter the law. Indeed, maybe this kind of opinion from a reverend should not be surprising; the Homosexual Law Reform Society was founded in 1958 primarily around the need for legal change. The Society's first full-time secretary was Reverend Andrew Hallidie Smith, a married clergyman. The Homosexual Law Reform Society relied strongly on straight allies to help change the law.

Several other letters at this time are from women, such as the two reproduced overleaf. This was an issue many, male and female, were concerned about changing. One wrote strongly in support of the Bill, claiming she '*could not see how it could offend any but the most prejudiced extremist whose views are not worthy of consideration*.'

Organisations such as the Campaign for Homosexual Equality and the Homosexual Law Reform Society (HLRS) were both putting pressure on the government, for example by sending publications by the Albany Trust, the HLRS's charity arm, to ministers.

One particular petition claimed that through the increased awareness created by the report, greater public attention and education had been attained. However, the letter and attached signatories also claimed that homosexuals themselves 'have been frequently told, on the best authority, that the general public is unready to accept them, and that the law must continue to discriminate against them.' Despite this, the law finally changed several years later, at its Third Reading in the Commons on the 4 July.

A National Opinion Poll extracted from the *Daily Mail* in October 1965 stated that 63 per cent of people polled disagreed that homosexual acts in private should be criminal. Although 93 per cent believed that homosexuals were in need of medical or psychiatric treatment (HO 291/127). This represents the framing of the pathology around homosexuality had changed from a language of morality to medicalised opposition.

The impact of the legislation has been debated, with Peter Tatchell arguing that in actuality the law raised public consciousness about the legislation and resulted in an increase in prosecutions. In 1990, Jeremy Corbyn wrote a scathing letter stating that far too many police resources continued to go on 'crimes without a victim'. There continued to be a discrepancy between the decriminalisation of homosexual acts and the continued policing of it, raising the question, how much did the Sexual Offences Act of 1967 really change the lives of gay men?

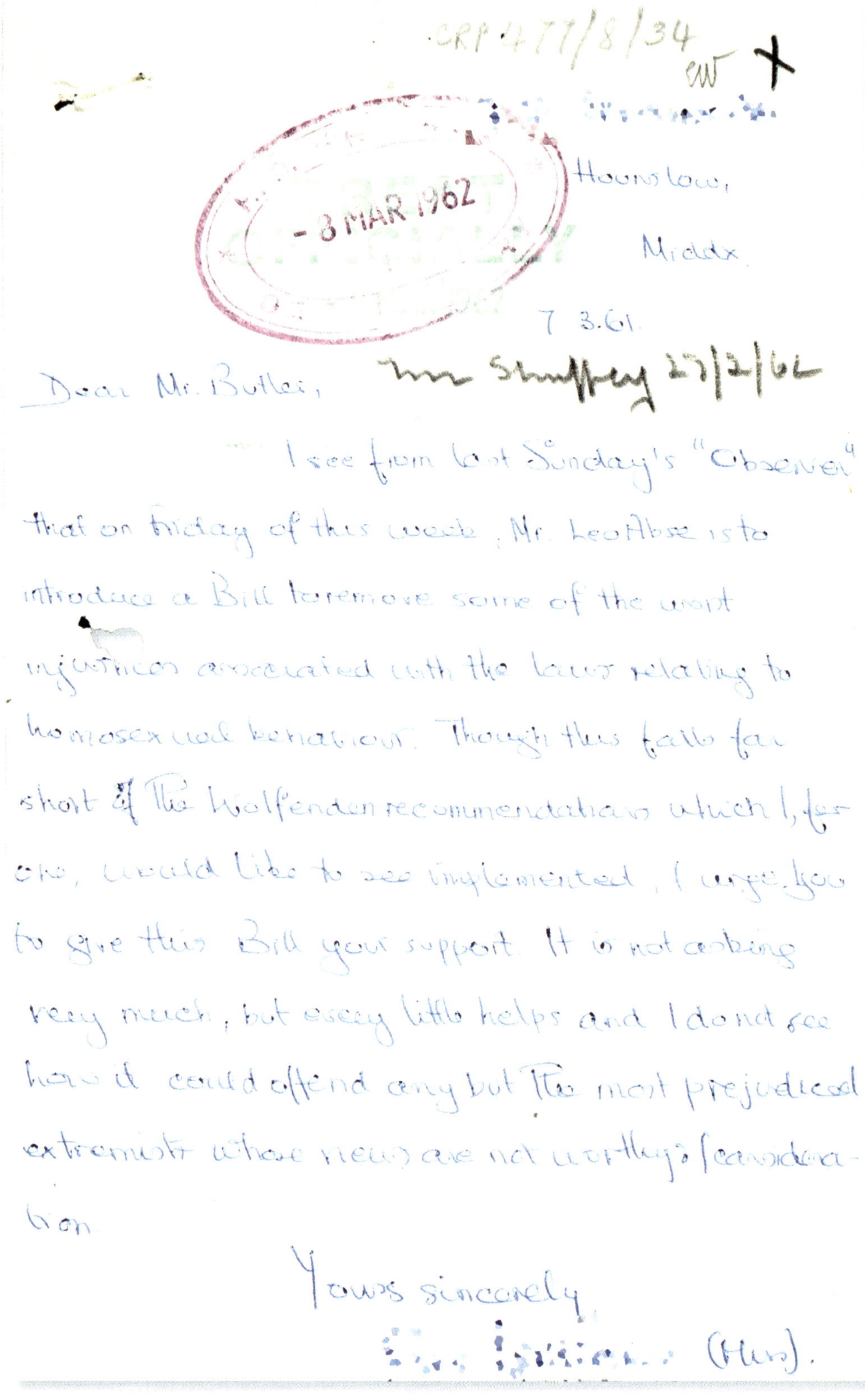

CRP 477/8/34

EW X

[redacted]

Hounslow,

Middx

-8 MAR 1962

7 3.61.

Dear Mr. Butler, Mr Shuffrey 27/2/62

I see from last Sunday's "Observer" that on Friday of this week, Mr. Leo Abse is to introduce a Bill to remove some of the worst injustices associated with the laws relating to homosexual behaviour. Though this falls far short of the Wolfenden recommendations which I, for one, would like to see implemented, I urge you to give this Bill your support. It is not asking very much, but every little helps and I dont see how it could offend any but the most prejudiced extremists whose views are not worthy of considera-tion.

Yours sincerely,

[redacted] (Mrs).

CR1477/8/34X
EW

[redacted]

Mr Shuffrey 27/2/62

Williton
Taunton
Somerset

TREAT OFFICIALLY
-5 MAR 1962

3rd March 1962

H.O. ... GEN. REGISTRY
-5 MAR 1962

Dear Sir,

I write to urge you to at once ~~the~~ pass the Sexual Offences Bill which is planned to amend the existing monstrous laws governing male Homosexual offences.

The existing laws, never debated, never properly understood are a disgrace to a civilised nation and should be reformed completely on the lines of the Wolfenden Report. The amendments recommended by Mr Leo Abse will at least bring some sanity into the existing state of affairs and in particular stop the sadistic witch-hunting and refrain from prosecuting the

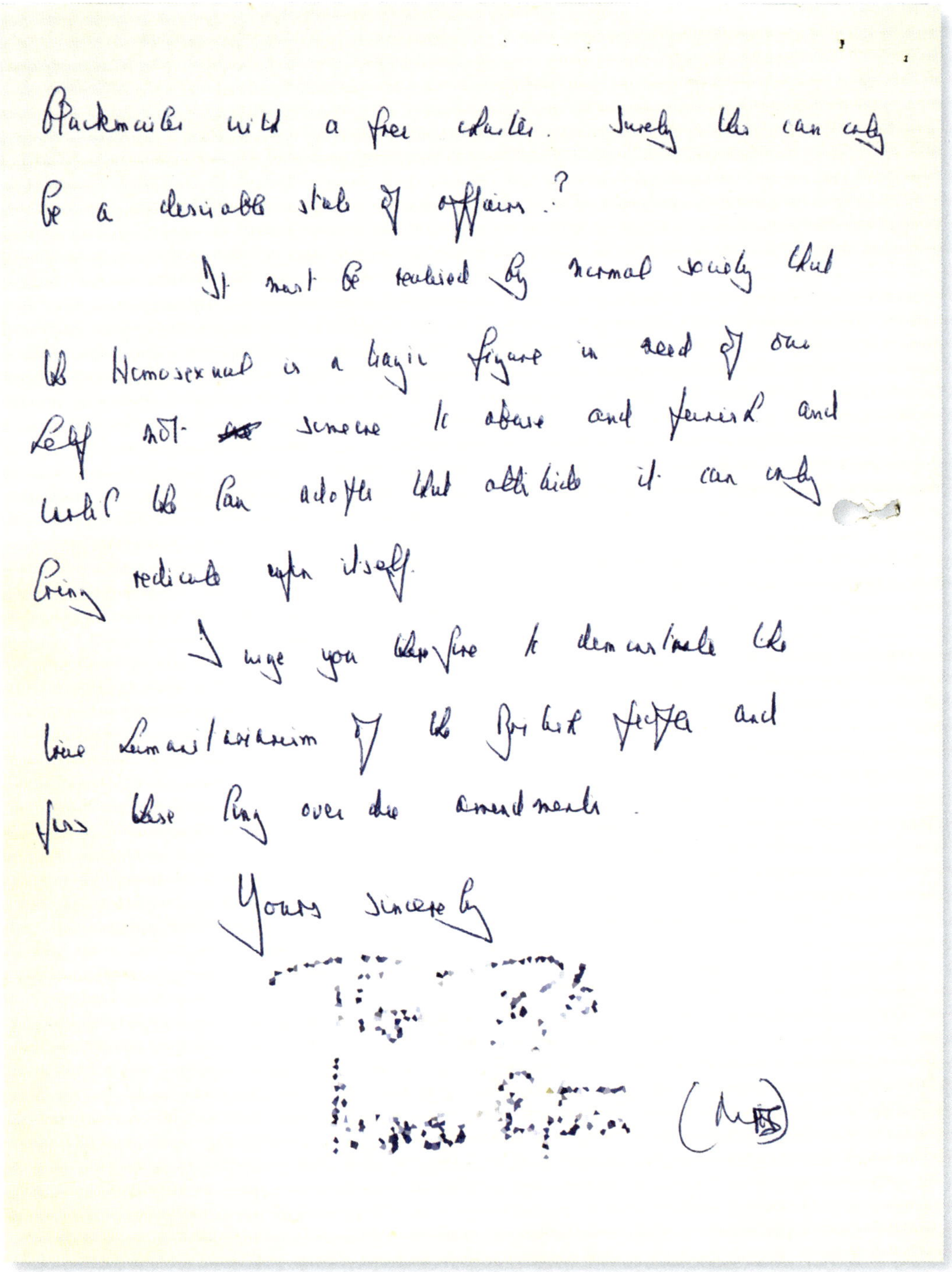
blackmailer with a free charter. Surely this can only be a desirable state of affairs?

It must be realised by normal society that the Homosexual is a tragic figure in need of our help not ~~sincere~~ to abuse and punish and until the law adopts that attitude it can only bring ridicule upon itself.

I urge you therefore to demonstrate the true humanitarianism of the British people and pass this Bill over the amendments.

Yours sincerely

(Mrs)

[redacted]

Williton

3rd March 1962

Taunton

Somerset

Dear Sir

I write to urge you to at once pass the Sexual Offences Bill which is planned to amend the existing monstrous laws governing male Homosexual Offences.

The existing laws, never debated, never properly understood are a disgrace to a civilised nation and should be reformed completely on the lines of the Wolfenden Report. The amendments recommended by Mr Leo Abse will at last bring some sanity into the existing state of affairs and in particular stop sadistic witch-hunting and refrain from presenting the blackmailer with a free charter. Surely this can only be a desirable state of affairs?

It must be realised by normal society that the Homosexual is a tragic figure in need of our help not someone to abase and punish and until the law adopts that attitude it can only bring ridicule upon itself.

I urge you therefore to demonstrate the true humanitarianism of the British people and pass the these long over due amendments.

Yours sincerely

[redacted]

[redacted] (Mrs)

Shooting at the Berlin Wall

The Cold War and the fight to stop the flow of people to the West

1967

When a telegram to the West German government in Bonn reported the fatal shooting of an East German man who was trying to escape life under Communism, the message conveyed shock at the brutality of the gunfire that had left the victim 'collapsed in a pool of blood'. Being at the height of the Cold War, the Western source also capitalised on this opportunity to present its Communist opponents in a bad light, condemning the 'senseless and inhuman orders' that East German soldiers were bound to follow, and contrasting this with the liberty of those who lived in 'the free part of Berlin'.

At the time of the shooting, the Berlin Wall had been in place for nearly six years. It had been constructed in August 1961 by the East German authorities in an attempt to stem the flow of people moving to West Germany because they perceived that the job opportunities and living standards were better there. Indeed, between 1949 and 1961, the equivalent of a town's worth of people per year had moved from Communist East Germany to capitalist West Germany. In the war of words between East and West, this was a propaganda nightmare for the East German leadership; people were voting with their feet, and if emigration continued at the same rate there would be no one left in the East. To some extent, building an impenetrable wall provided a solution. When Berliners went to bed on the night of Saturday 12 August they were able to move freely between both parts of the city, but when they woke up on Sunday 13 August this was no longer the case. Erected in haste and desperation, the Berlin Wall became the most powerful symbol of ongoing Cold War divisions.

The Wall stood for 28 years, acting as a physical barrier between East and West Germany, which were formally divided into two countries after the Second World War in 1949. During that time, those Germans living behind the Iron Curtain could only travel within East Germany and the wider Communist Eastern Bloc. East Germans could apply for visas to visit friends or relatives in West Germany, but whether such applications were granted was entirely at the whim of the authorities. Those who applied to leave East Germany for good were marked down as politically unreliable, subject to career blocks and were often put under surveillance by the Stasi, the East German secret police.

A small minority of the 16 million people living in East Germany, including the unfortunate victim described in this letter, tried to escape illegally, knowing that they faced the serious risk of being shot at and killed by their own country's border police. The boundary with West Germany was observed by approximately 50,000 border guards in watchtowers and on the ground, not to mention the landmines and self-firing devices placed on the border strip as deterrents. Five thousand East Germans nonetheless managed to escape successfully. They employed a variety of clever ruses to bypass the border, from digging underground tunnels to scuba-diving, to hot-air ballooning and stowing away in car boots. But 138 individuals paid the ultimate price of their lives in their bid for freedom.

RECEIVED IN ARCHIVES No. 6
-2 JUN 1967
RGS 4/3

(7)

TOP COPY

p 82/6

En Clair

PRIORITY BERLIN TO FOREIGN OFFICE

Telno. 220 1 June, 1967

UNCLASSIFIED

Addressed to Bonn telegram No. 241 of 1 June.
Repeated for information to: Foreign Office

Shooting Incident at Wall.

At 1016 hours today a man aged about 30 attempted to run through the Sandkrug Bridge crossing point from East to West Berlin. The Berlin Border Brigade Guards fired one shot at him as he was passing the East German barrier which was at that moment open. The bullet clearly hit him but he continued across the Bridge. When he was about 12 to 13 feet short of the demarcation line painted on the roadway a second shot hit him in the right leg and he collapsed in a pool of blood. A BBB Guard came out and dragged him back out of sight behind the barrier, which was then closed. The crossing point remained closed from 1018 until 1045 hours.

2. Commenting on this incident the British Press Officer issued the following statement this afternoon:

"The British Commandant deplores this brutal shooting which is yet another reminder of the senseless and inhuman orders under which armed East German soldiers have to prevent their fellow citizens from entering the free part of Berlin."

General Nelson

Sent 1500Z 1 June
Recd. 1520Z 1 June

DEPARTMENTAL DISTRIBUTION
Western Dept.
W.O.C.D.
Northern Dept.
J.R.D.
J.I.R.D.
J.I.P.G.D.
News Dept.
D.I.S.M.O.D.

=====

On 17 August, 1962 the 18-year-old Peter Fechter from East Berlin was shot down by Soviet zonal border guards while trying to escape over the Wall in Zimmerstrasse. The wounded boy was left lying on the Soviet sector side of the Wall for over an hour without any help being brought to him. He was then carried away by border guards without a stretcher. It is presumed that he was already dead.

For 'all women everywhere'

Ford Dagenham women strike for equal pay

1968

In 1968 how did a group of women cause fear in the British government, prompting statements such as 'disastrous' and 'a critical problem for British economy'?

The strike by women at Ford Motor Company's Dagenham plant in 1968 has been the subject of popular culture depictions, but records from The National Archives show these women workers really did panic the Wilson government.

The action started on 7 June 1968, when 187 women walked out of Ford's Dagenham plant, led by several key women: Rose Boland, Eileen Pullen, Vera Sime, Gwen Davis and Sheila Douglass. Prime Minister's Office files on this subject show the government tensions through fraught telegrams, alongside a handwritten letter signed the 'Women Workers at Fords of Dagenham'. The letter from these women workers boldly declares, 'We are fighting a great fight equal pay for women'.

In a regrading exercise, the women's work had been graded as less skilled, and therefore they were paid less. Contrary to popular belief, the women were not directly asking for equal pay, but for their technical skills used to make seat covers to be ranked at the same grade as that of their fellow male workers.

As the strike continued, production of the seat covers stopped. Three weeks into the strike Barbara Castle, First Secretary of State and Secretary of State for Employment, was sent to intervene on the 27 June.

With the threat of Henry Ford visiting England, the pressure was upped. Strained telegrams from the government stated the productions of 2,200 cars had been brought to a halt and had caused the cancellation of export orders exceeding eight million, with the threatened complete closure of all Ford plants in Britain, affecting 40,000 men. The women workers state in their letter they are sorry for the disruption to the men's work, 'but more sorry for ourselves'. Their impact on the economy could not be ignored.

Women had long been campaigning for equal pay; in the suffrage era, women saw the vote as a means to influence the government on equal pay. In the 1930s the Six Point Group, a women's rights organisation, lobbied the government around six principle issues, one of which was 'equal pay for men and women teachers.'

The Court of Inquiry appointed by Barbara Castle reassured the women it would look fully into their problem of regrading; it gave them the understanding that, subject to ratification, the women's rate was to be increased from 85 per cent to 90–92 per cent of the men's rate. The women workers settled for this agreement.

On 28 July, Mr Batty, the Managing Director of Ford Britain, telegrammed the Prime Minister thanking him for his intervention. By 8 July, production had restarted in the plants.

Contrary to popular perception, the women did not directly win their demands – the grading of their work did not change. However, this case was fundamental in the passing of the Equal Pay Act 1970 by Barbara Castle, for which women had been fighting for decades. As the women of Dagenham stated in their letter, this fight was for 'not only us at Fords all women everywhere'.

The Dagenham strikers with their placards, 1968.

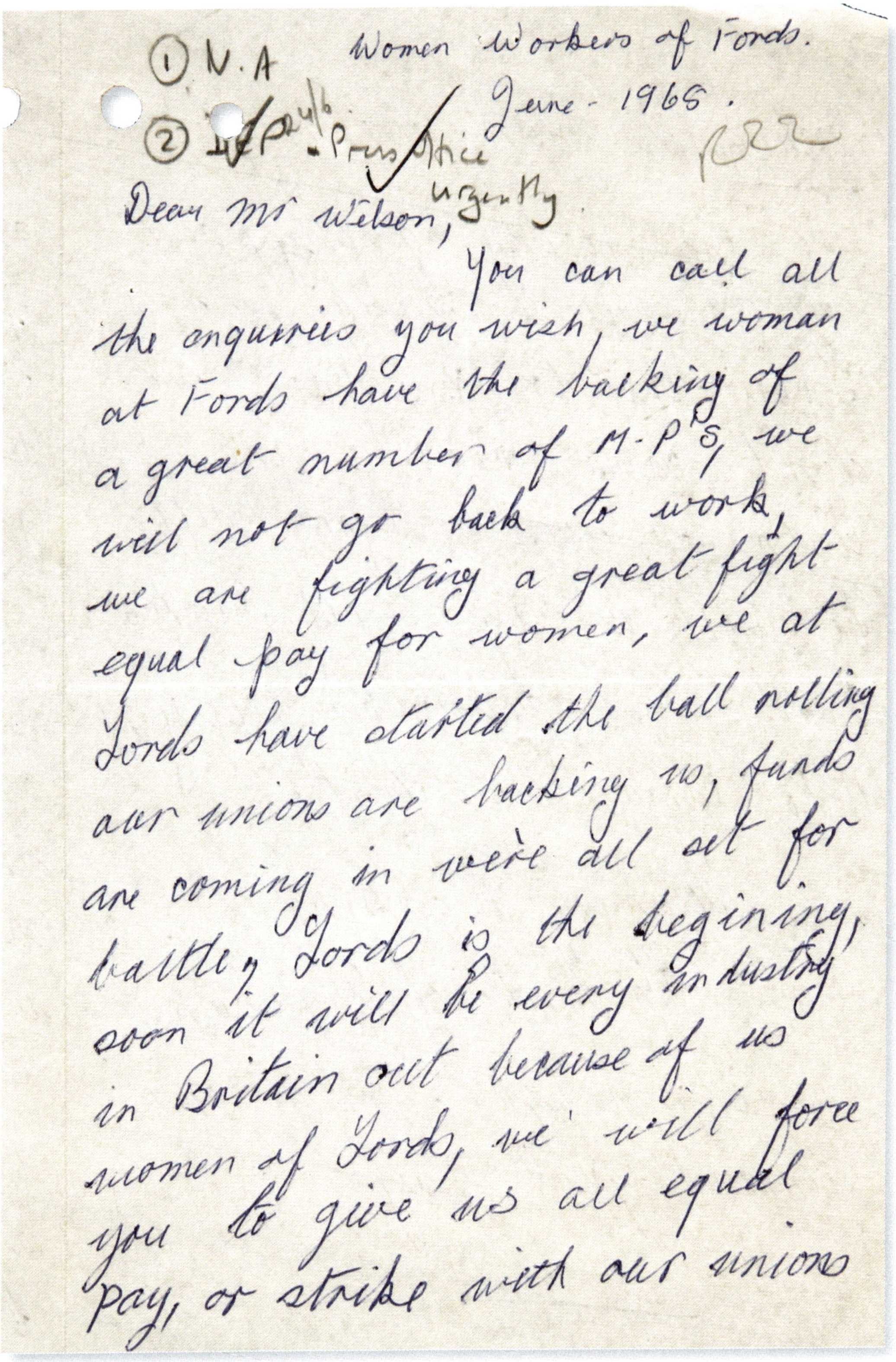

① N.A

② ~~?~~ P ?/6 - Press Office urgently

Women Workers of Fords.

June - 1968.

Dear Mr Wilson,

You can call all the enquiries you wish, we woman at Fords have the backing of a great number of M.P'S, we will not go back to work, we are fighting a great fight equal pay for women, we at Fords have started the ball rolling our unions are backing us, funds are coming in were all set for battle, Fords is the begining, soon it will be every industry in Britain out, because of us women of Fords, we will force you to give us all equal pay, or strike with our unions

2/ blessings, we're sorry for
Fords, sorry for the men
out of work, but more sorry
for ourselves its all for us
now. Some women may be hard up
we'll help them from our
growing funds, make no mistake
most of us have husbands
still working, thats why
we can fight you all, we
are only our own money
short, we will live. Give
us what we want, not only
us at Fords all Women
everywhere, we refuse to go
back, so what can you
and the government & Mrs
Castle & Jack Scamp do.

3/

<u>Nothing</u> I mean <u>nothing</u>,
we are sitting pretty, our
unions are backing us.
Show this to Barbara, we
dont care M.P's are
with us, soon everyone will
be with us we will make
Fords shut down completly,
who cares we dont.

Women Workers
at Fords of Dagenham.

Give us what our unions
demand equal pay.

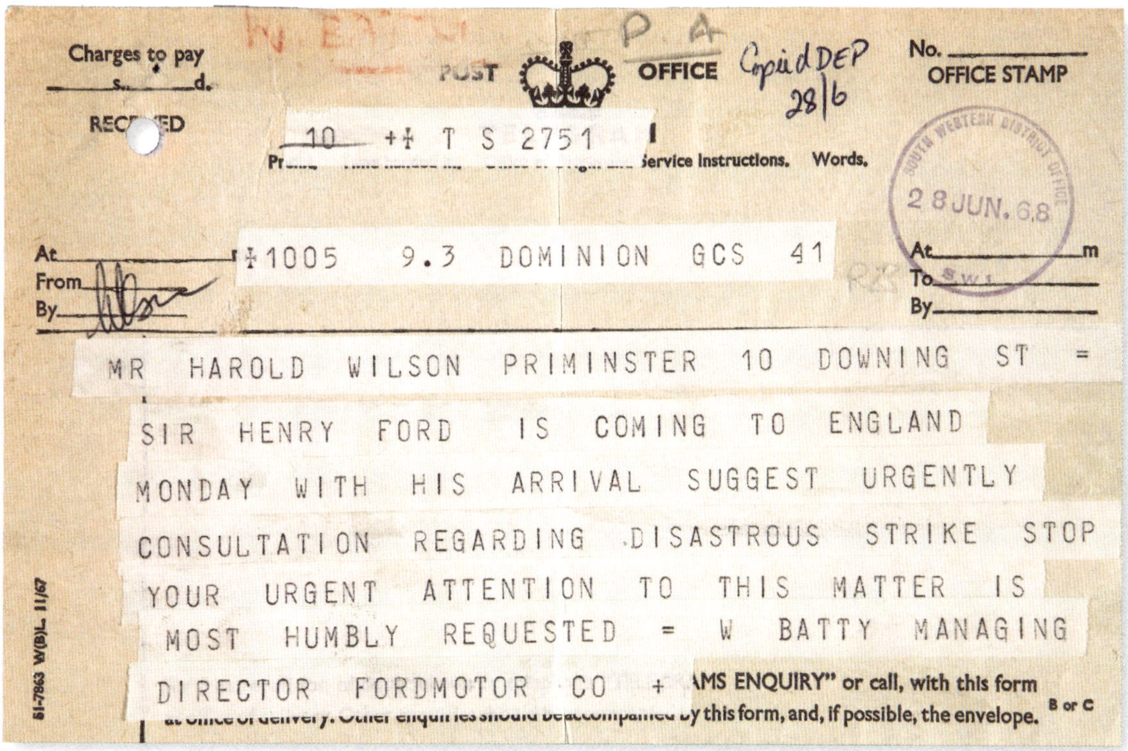

Charges to pay
s. d.
RECEIVED

POST OFFICE

P.A

Copied DEP 28/6

No.
OFFICE STAMP

10 +½ T S 2751

Service Instructions. Words.

SOUTH WESTERN DISTRICT OFFICE
28 JUN. 68
S.W.1

At ½1005 9.3 DOMINION GCS 41 m
From
By

At m
To
By

MR HAROLD WILSON PRIMINSTER 10 DOWNING ST =
SIR HENRY FORD IS COMING TO ENGLAND
MONDAY WITH HIS ARRIVAL SUGGEST URGENTLY
CONSULTATION REGARDING DISASTROUS STRIKE STOP
YOUR URGENT ATTENTION TO THIS MATTER IS
MOST HUMBLY REQUESTED = W BATTY MANAGING
DIRECTOR FORDMOTOR CO +

AMS ENQUIRY" or call, with this form
by this form, and, if possible, the envelope.

B or C

51-7863 W(B)L 11/67

Scandals, loopholes and murder

Can a child be deemed an animal?

The case of James Stannard – child welfare in the 19th century

1855

In September 1855, Charles Wright, the Clerk to the Board of Guardians in charge of the Mitford and Launditch Poor Law Union, wrote to the General Board of Health to ask for legal advice in a remarkable and unsettling case.

Poor Law Unions were set up around the country under the Poor Law Amendment Act of 1834. The Unions, controlled by elected Boards of Guardians, formed the centre of what we would now call the social security system, providing 'relief' to destitute paupers. Unions also took on many of the powers we today associate with local government, including overseeing local public health. Under the Nuisances Removal Act of 1855, Unions were empowered to deal with 'nuisances' that endangered public health – from polluted wells and open sewers to pigs kept in filthy sties next to houses.

However, one nuisance to public health that the Act did not make a provision for was one caused by a filthy 11-year-old boy – James Stannard of Litcham. James had been left disabled by an attack of small pox in 1854. However, because James's parents were in 'full employment', the family were not entitled to any assistance for his care, financial or otherwise. Subsequently, whether because of incompetence, inability or malice, James's condition deteriorated under his parents' care. According to letters sent regarding this case written by Wright at a later date, James had been visited six months into his confinement to bed, when concern was raised about how 'emaciated' he was. In August 1855, concern for James's condition was raised with the Union again, and the local medical official was dispatched to the house to investigate.

James was found in a deplorable condition. His mother, on questioning, revealed '*she had never washed him nor even seen his back for more than a year*'. Lying in a year's worth of his own filth, James, according to Wright, was in '*such a state of putrescence [literally rottenness] as to be not only in imminent danger himself but a nuisance to and injurious to the health of his parents and their neighbours*'. The Union's Relieving Officer (a kind of Victorian social worker) took decisive action to address the danger James's life was in, paying for nurses to attempt to save him, and prevent his filthy condition damaging anyone else's health. Whether he survived or not is unclear.

However, despite the Union's initial generosity in the face of James's ordeal, they were also keen to recover their costs (Wright, in another letter, puts these at 30 shillings a week, about £100 in today's money), and punish James's parents in some way. Neglect of a child was not made a formal criminal offence until the early 20th century, so although Wright's remarks that prosecuting James's mother (his father does not seem to be held culpable) would be 'advisable', it was however 'feared that no such punishment can be inflicted'.

Clearly desperate to find some way to punish the parents, and more importantly recover the Union's costs, Wright seizes on a bizarre and disheartening course of action: asking the General Board of Health whether James's father might be prosecuted under the Nuisances Removal Act, for keeping 'an animal in a nuisance state'. The 'animal' in this case, Wright explains, would not be a pig in an unclean sty, but a desperately ill child, left neglected and unwashed for a year. To make clear his point, Wright explicitly asks: *You will oblige me by your opinion whether the Child in question may be deemed "an animal" with the meaning of the 18 & 19 Vict. Cap. 121 [1855 Nuisances Removal and Diseases Prevention Act] and whether and what proceedings can be instituted under that statute or otherwise for the abatement of the nuisance, the recovery of the Expenses, or the Punishment of the Parents.*

The reply from Tom Taylor, the General Board of Health's Secretary, is curt, either reflecting distaste at what was asked or the same indifference: 'Sir, I am directed by the General Board of Health to acknowledge the receipt of your Letter of the 3rd instant, and to state in reply to your question with reference to 18 and 19 Vict. Cap. 121 [1855 Nuisances Removal and Diseases Prevention Act], that the word "animal" does not appear to this Board to include "a child".'

This letter, and poor James's treatment, is a startling glimpse into British society before universal healthcare or child-neglect legislation were introduced, when a man was more likely to be prosecuted for keeping a dirty pig than for neglecting his son.

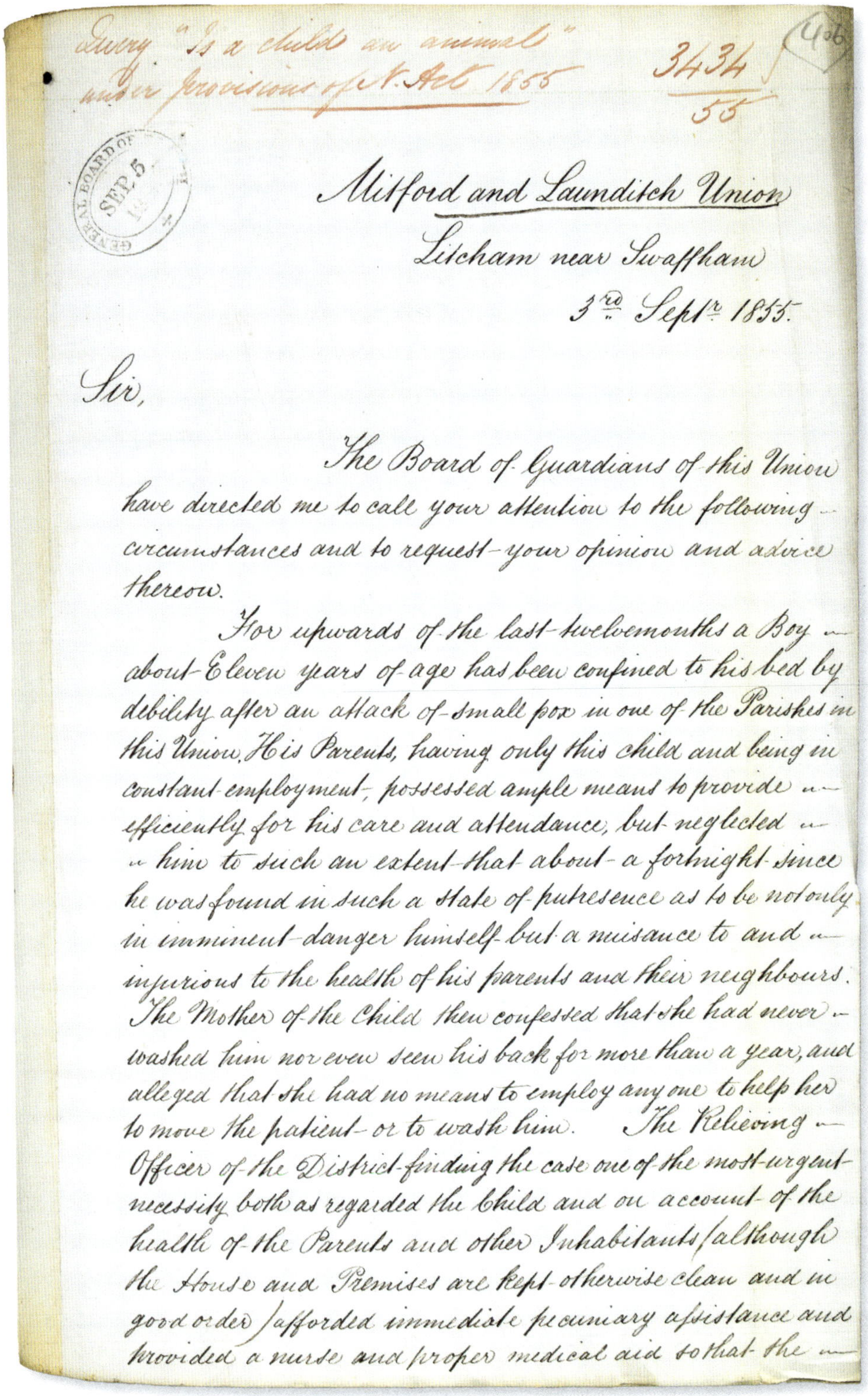
Query "Is a child an animal" under provisions of N. Act 1855

3434 / 55

(406)

Mitford and Launditch Union

Litcham near Swaffham

3rd Septr. 1855.

Sir,

The Board of Guardians of this Union have directed me to call your attention to the following circumstances and to request your opinion and advice thereon.

For upwards of the last twelvemonths a Boy about Eleven years of age has been confined to his bed by debility after an attack of small pox in one of the Parishes in this Union. His Parents, having only this child and being in constant employment, possessed ample means to provide efficiently for his care and attendance, but neglected him to such an extent that about a fortnight since he was found in such a state of putresence as to be not only in imminent danger himself but a nuisance to and injurious to the health of his parents and their neighbours. The Mother of the Child then confessed that she had never washed him nor even seen his back for more than a year, and alleged that she had no means to employ any one to help her to move the patient or to wash him. The Relieving Officer of the District finding the case one of the most urgent necessity both as regarded the Child and on account of the health of the Parents and other Inhabitants (although the House and Premises are kept otherwise clean and in good order) afforded immediate pecuniary assistance and provided a nurse and proper medical aid so that the

nuisance and the anticipated danger therefrom is ab
and it is hoped the life of the Child will be
ultimately saved; but as these Measures have bee
already, and will probaly continue to be, attended wi
considerable Expense it is desired that, if possible,
Proceedings should be taken against the Father of
the Child permanently to abate the Nuisance and
recover the expenses which have been and will be
incurred before the Boy is sufficiently restored to
It would moreover be advisable to punish the Mo
for her neglect but it is feared that no such
punishment can be inflicted.

You will oblige me by your opinion wheth
the Child in question may be deemed "An Anim
within the meaning of the 18 & 19. Vict Cap. 121. an
whether any and what proceedings can be instituted
under that Statute or otherwise for the abatemen
the Nuisance — the recovery of the Expenses, or th
Punishment of the Parents.

Your earliest reply will be esteemed a favor.

I have the honor to be,

Sir,

Your most obedient Servt

Charles W. [illegible]

Clk to the [illegible]

I. Taylor Esqr

Secretary

General Board of Health

London.

Mitford and Launditch Union
Litcham, near Swaffham
3rd Septr. 1855

Sir,

The Board of Guardians of this Union have directed me to call your attention to the following circumstances and to request your opinion and advice thereon.

For upwards of the last twelvemonths a Boy about Eleven years of age has been confined to his bed by debility after an attack of small pox in one of the Parishes in this Union. His Parents, having only this child and being in constant employment, possessed ample means to provide efficiently for his care and attendance, but neglected him to such an extent that about a fortnight since he was found in such a state of putrescence as to be not only in imminent danger himself but a nuisance to and injurious to the health of his parents and their neighbours. The Mother of the child then confessed that she had never washed him nor even seen his back for more than a year, and alleged that she had no means to employ any one to help her to move the patient or to wash him. The Relieving Officer of the District finding the case one of the most urgent necessity both as regarded the Child and on account of the health of the Parents and other Inhabitants (although the House and Premises are kept otherwise clean and in good order) afforded immediate pecuniary assistance and provided a nurse and proper medical aid so that the nuisance and the anticipated danger therefore is abated, and it is hoped the life of the child will be ultimately saved; but as these measures have been already, and will probably continue to be, attended with considerable Expense it is desire that, if possible, Proceedings should be taken against the Father of the Child permanently to abate the nuisance and recover expenses which have been and will be incurred before the Boy is sufficiently restored to [health].

It would moreover be advisable to punish the Mother for her neglect but it is feared that no such punishment can be inflicted.

You will oblige me by your opinion whether the Child in question may be deemed "an animal" within the meaning of the 18 & 19 Vict. Cap. 121 [1855 Nuisances Removal and Diseases Prevention Act] and whether any and what proceedings can be instituted under that statute or otherwise for the abatement of the nuisance, the recovery of the Expenses, or the Punishment of the Parents.
Your earliest reply will be esteemed a favor.

I have the honour to be,
Sir
Your most obedient servant,

Charles Wright
Clerk to the Union

T Taylor Esqr.
Secretary
General Board of Health
London

Copycat Rippers

Letters to the police from 'Jack the Ripper'

1888

On 31 August 1888, a woman named Mary Ann 'Polly' Nichols was found dead in London's East End; her throat was slashed and her body disembowelled. This was the first murder by so-called 'Jack the Ripper'. Eight days later Jack struck again, and Annie Chapman was discovered in a backyard in Spitalfields. Like Polly, she had had her throat cut and her guts had been removed.

Nearly a month after Polly's death, on 29 September, a letter arrived at the Central News Agency, claiming to be from the killer. The writer taunted the police with an early theory that the killer was another wanted man who went by the name of 'the Leather Apron'. The author went on, boasting how he had evaded capture and ending with a taunt that he was ready to it again and detailing one of the mutilations he would perform (see page 222).

Shortly after this letter came to the police, the murderer claimed two further victims. The body of Elizabeth Stride, a tall woman known as 'Long Liz', was found in Berner Street. Just 45 minutes later, a second body was found close by in Mitre Square. The body of Catherine Eddowes had been severely maimed and part of her innards had again been removed.

The very next day, the police received another 'Ripper note'. This time it was smeared with blood: *'I was not [kidding] dear old Boss when I gave you the tip, you'll hear about Saucy Jacky work tomorrow double event this time number 1 squealed a bit couldn't finish straight off had not time to get ears for police. Thanks for keeping last letter back till I got to work again. Jack the Ripper.'*

Believing that both the letters were written by the serial killer, the police decided to publish them, in the hope that someone might come forward and identify the handwriting. To this end, the letters were printed in the press.

However, instead of producing any helpful information, the publication of these letters led to a huge stream of letters from would-be Jack the Rippers, containing crude, threatening messages, stating their intention to murder again.

Most of the copycat letters were signed 'Jack the Ripper' and they borrowed the language of the original two – repeating the use of 'Boss', and 'ha ha', as well as the threats to mutilate the bodies of their future victims. The quality of the writing in the letters varies hugely: some pay heed to grammatical rules and the spelling is accurate, others are littered with spelling mistakes; some are legible, others are not.

One further murder, of Mary Jane Kelly, five weeks later on 9 November, inspired a new spate of letters from copycat Jack the Rippers, but this stream of correspondence eventually slowed to a trickle.

It is mystifying to consider why so many people wrote to the police pretending to be the notorious mass murderer. What motivated them to pen these appalling letters? Perhaps surprisingly, given Jack the Ripper's purported hatred of prostitutes, the only two copycats who were caught were both women: one from Bradford, the other from South Wales. Obviously it's possible that the first two letters were written by the murderer himself, but they also might have been written by a well-informed journalist in the hope of attracting attention to the story. This latter scenario seemed more plausible to the police, and they believed that a journalist called Tom Billing was the author.

The huge volume of Ripper letters, as well as their evidently varied styles and levels of literacy, suggests that a good number of people were assuming the Jack the Ripper persona on paper. But what made them want to be associated with such brutal and violent crimes remains a mystery.

An extract from *The Penny Illustrated News*, 13 October 1888, showing Kate Eddowes and a sketch of a man thought to be implicated in the case.

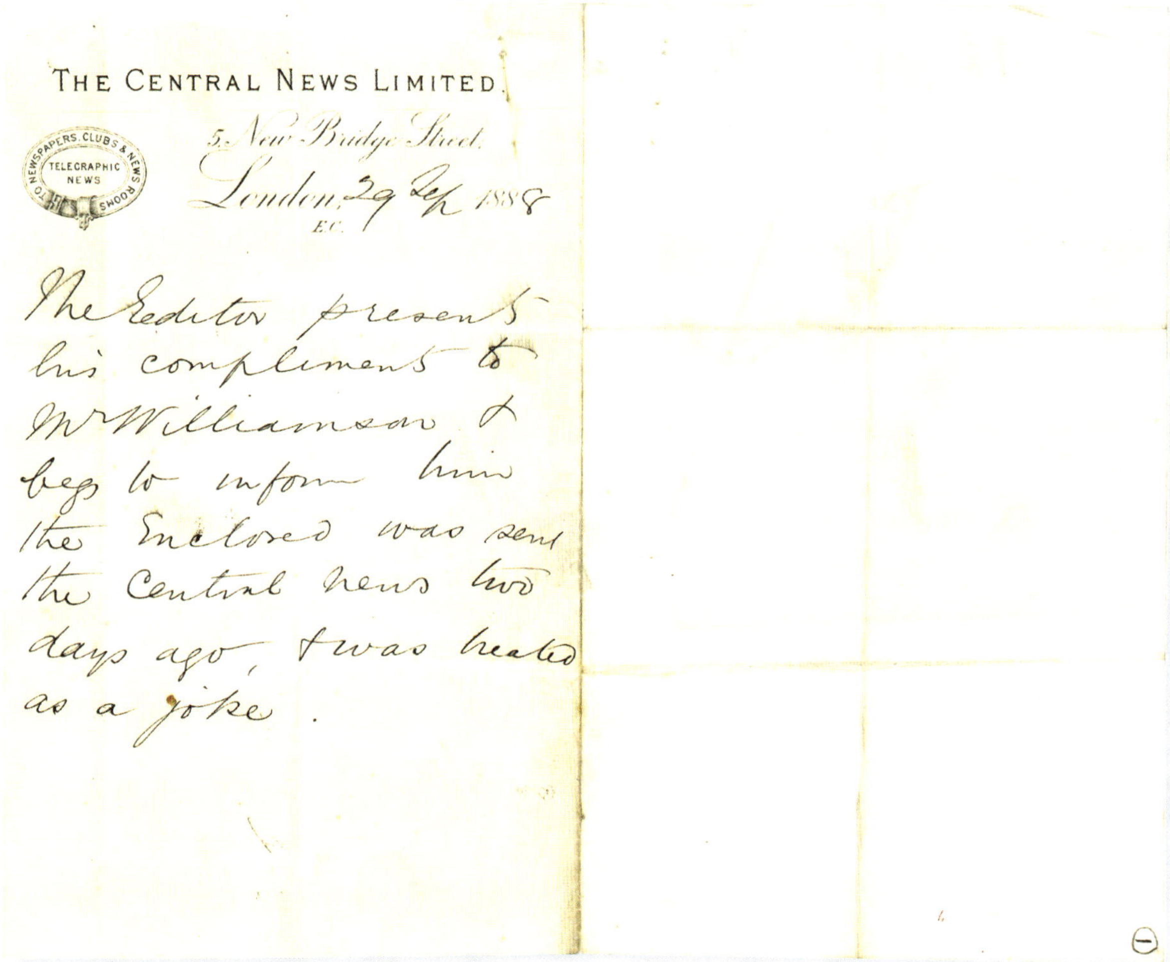

THE CENTRAL NEWS LIMITED.

TO NEWSPAPERS, CLUBS & NEWS ROOMS
TELEGRAPHIC NEWS

5, New Bridge Street,
London, 29 Sep 1888
E.C.

The Editor presents
his compliments to
Mr Williamson &
begs to inform him
the Enclosed was sent
the Central News two
days ago, & was treated
as a joke.

5 New Bridge Street
London E.C., 29 Sept 1888

The Editor presents
his compliments to
Mr. Williamson &
begs to inform him
the enclosed was sent
the Central News two
days ago, & was treated
as a joke.

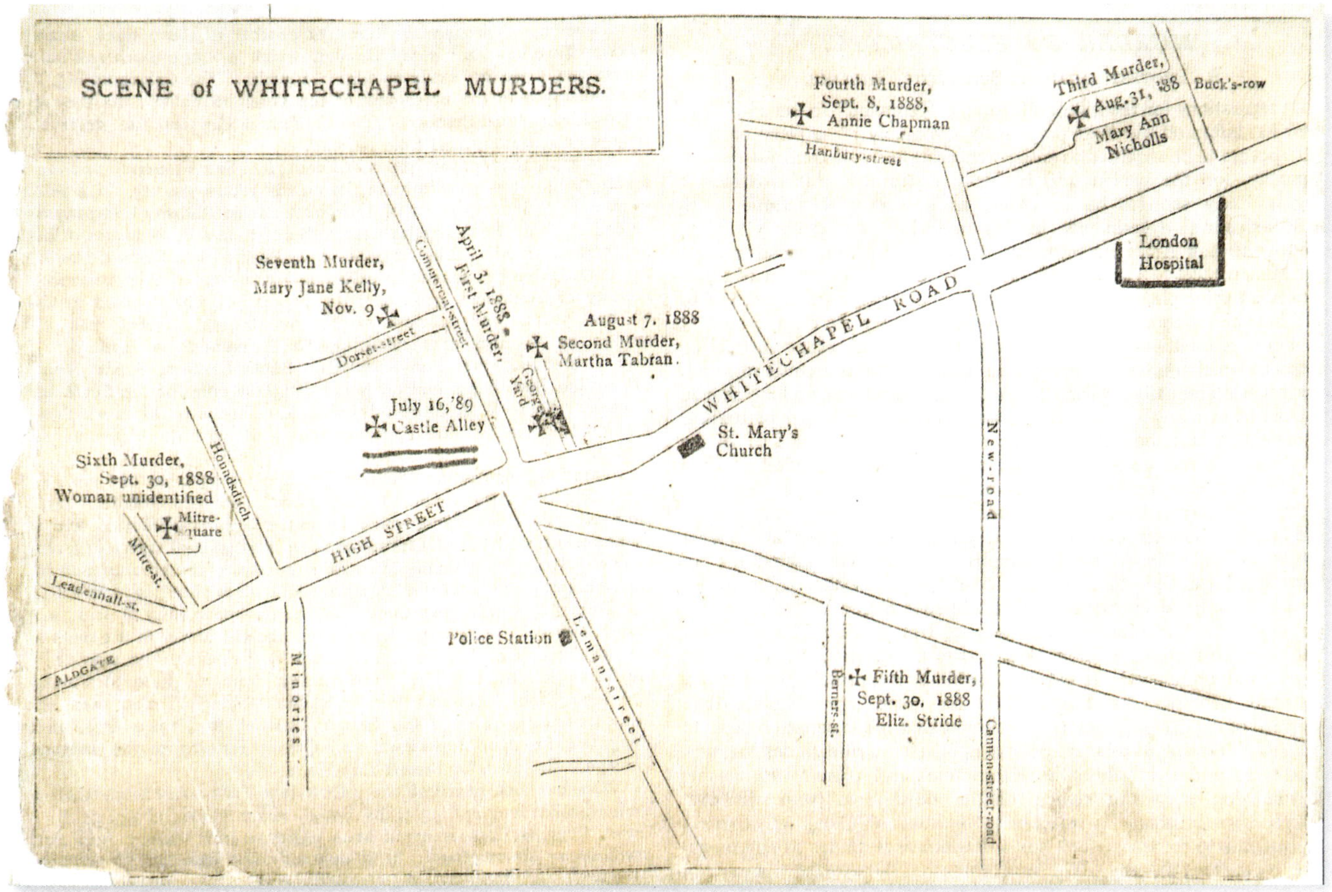
SCENE of WHITECHAPEL MURDERS.
Fourth Murder,
Sept. 8, 1888,
Annie Chapman
Hanbury-street
Third Murder,
Aug. 31, '88
Mary Ann
Nicholls
Buck's-row
London
Hospital
Seventh Murder,
Mary Jane Kelly,
Nov. 9
Dorset-street
Commercial-street
April 3, 1888,
First Murder,
August 7. 1888
Second Murder,
Martha Tabran.
George Yard
WHITECHAPEL ROAD
July 16, '89
Castle Alley
St. Mary's
Church
Sixth Murder,
Sept. 30, 1888
Woman unidentified
Mitre-
square
Houndsditch
Mitre-st.
Leadenhall-st.
HIGH STREET
ALDGATE
Minories
Police Station
Leman-street
New-road
Berners-st.
Fifth Murder,
Sept. 30, 1888
Eliz. Stride
Cannon-street-road

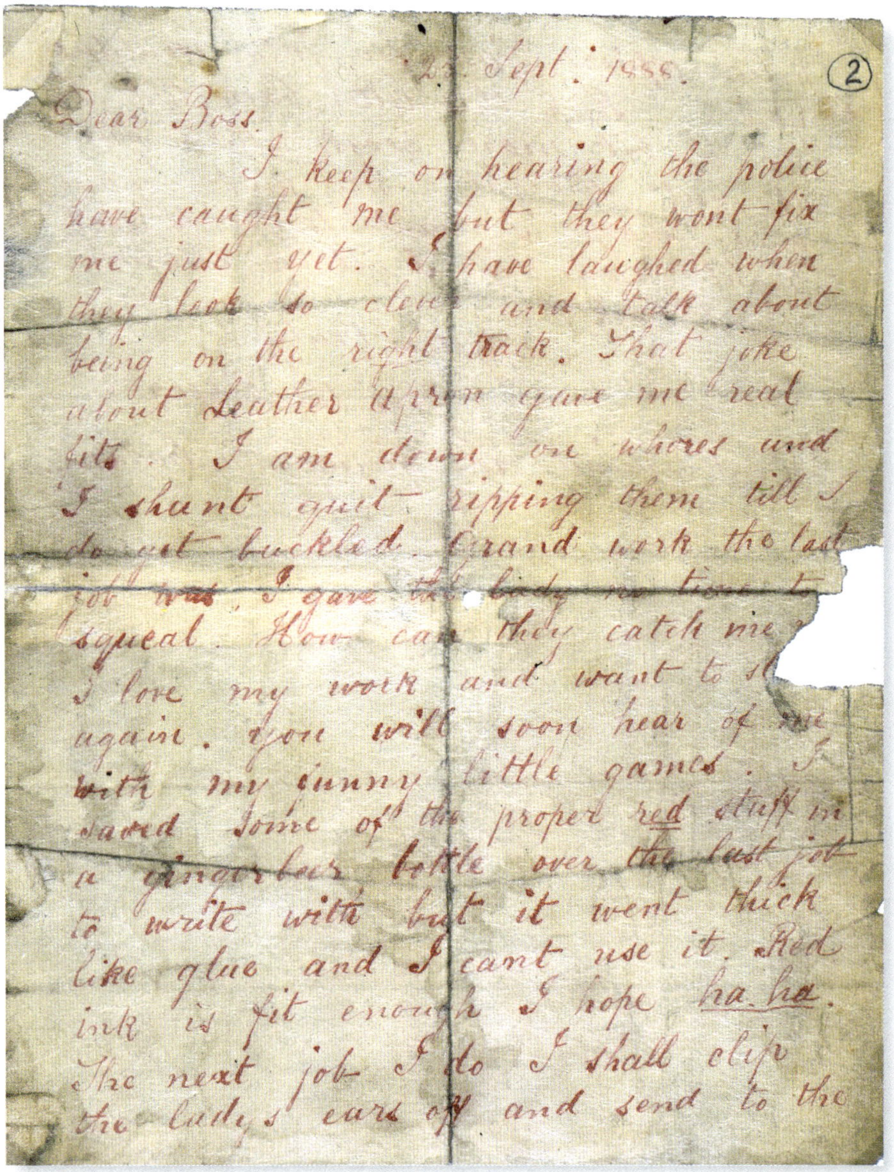

25 Sept. 1888.

(2)

Dear Boss.
I keep on hearing the police
have caught me but they wont fix
me just yet. I have laughed when
they look so clever and talk about
being on the right track. That joke
about Leather Apron gave me real
fits. I am down on whores and
I shant quit ripping them till I
do get buckled. Grand work the last
job was. I gave the lady no time to
squeal. How can they catch me
I love my work and want to s
again. You will soon hear of me
with my funny little games. I
saved some of the proper red stuff in
a ginger beer bottle over the last job
to write with but it went thick
like glue and I cant use it. Red
ink is fit enough I hope ha. ha.
The next job I do I shall clip
the ladys ears off and send to the

The Boss
Central News.
Office
London City.

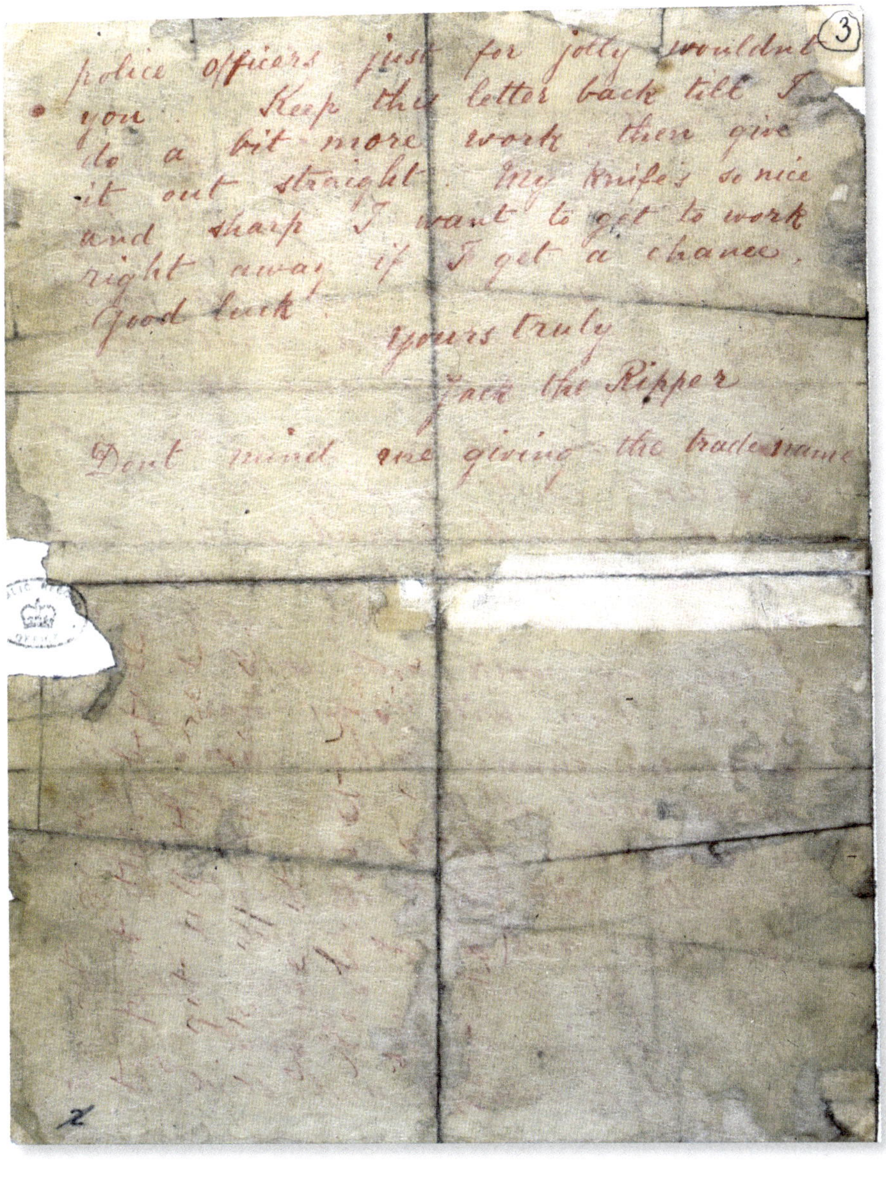

3

police officers just for jolly wouldnt
you. Keep this letter back till I
do a bit more work then give
it out straight. My knife's so nice
and sharp I want to get to work
right away if I get a chance.
Good luck.

Yours truly

Jack the Ripper

Dont mind me giving the trade name

2

Dear Boss,

I keep on hearing the police have caught me but they won't fix me just yet. I have laughed when they look so clever and talk about being on the right track. That joke about Leather Apron gave me real fits. I am down on whores and shant [sic] quit ripping them till I do get buckled. Grand work the last one was I gave the lady no time to squeal. How can they catch me now. I love my work and want to start again. You will soon hear of me with my funny little game. I saved some of the proper red stuff in a ginger beer bottle over the last job to write with but it went thick like glue and I can't use it. Red ink is fit enough I hope. Ha ha. The next job I do I shall clip the ladies ears off and send to the police officers just for jolly wouldn't you. Keep this letter back till I do a bit more work and give it out straight. My knife's so nice and sharp I want to get to work right away if I get a chance.

Good luck.

Yours truly,

Jack the Ripper.

Don't mind me giving the trade name.

18

A pattern emerges and a serial killer is uncovered

The case of the 'Brides in the Bath' murders

1915

On the evening of 10 December 1913, George Joseph Smith shuffled across the streets of Blackpool in search of lodgings, his cheerful, newlywed wife Alice Burnham in tow. Knocking on Margaret Crossley's door at 16 Regent Road, they found bed and board for 10 shillings per week and, in the words of Alice, had a 'splendid night's rest'. After an uneventful two days, Margaret's daughter Alice drew a bath for her guest and namesake, and returned to the kitchen to sit with her husband Joseph before he left for work. A short time later, Alice Crossley heard a panicked George calling for her from upstairs. She climbed the stairs to meet George and, on reaching the bathroom, found Alice Burnham drowned. Although an inquest would judge this to be an accidental death; time, curiosity and a great deal of investigation would identify it for what it really was: the second of the 'Brides in the Bath' murders.

Smith was born in Bethnal Green, London, in January 1872. After a childhood spent in a reformatory, he married his first wife in 1898 in what would be his only legal marriage. He encouraged her to steal on his behalf, for which crime both spent time in prison, before she fled to Canada to escape the marriage. Once released from prison, he went on to marry three more women over the next few years, stealing their savings and belongings with a depressing predictability, before marrying the first of the 'Brides in the Bath', Bessie Mundy, in August 1910.

Bessie's death in July 1912 would set the precedent for the following murders. In the days before her death, she wrote a will in favour of Smith, she extolled his virtues to her friends and relatives and she made a needless visit to her doctor, complaining of vague ailments. She was then found, by Smith and behind an unlocked door, drowned in a bath. A year later it was Alice following this pattern and then, in December 1914, it was Margaret Lofty. Margaret was married on the 17 December, made a will in favour of her husband the very same day, and was then found dead in the bath the next day.

As this letter makes clear, however, this pattern did not go unnoticed. A brief story in the *News of the World* newspaper covered Margaret's death, and was seen independently by both Joseph Crossley and by Alice's father, Charles Burnham. Each wrote a letter to the police (Joseph's is pictured) remarking on the similarity between

Margaret's death and that of Alice's a year earlier. The letters reached the desk of Divisional Detective Inspector Arthur Neil, who began pulling together a case immediately.

As the details emerged, Neil began to question the inquests that had given accidental death verdicts, doubting the possibility of three healthy women drowning in small baths in a few inches of water. Working with the pathologist Bernard Spilsbury, who had made his name in the Crippen case five years previously, the pair theorised that pulling the legs out from someone in a bath could cause a sudden rushing of water up the nose, rendering the victim unconscious and thus unable to pull themselves from the water. They tested this theory on a willing participant, who, unfortunately for her but fortunately for the case, was rendered unconscious and required artificial respiration.

With the case falling into place, Neil arrested Smith on 1 February 1915, catching him on the way to collect Margaret's life insurance, a policy taken out in the weeks before her death. At first, Smith was charged with making a false entry in a marriage register, but on 23 March he was charged with murder. The June trial focused on Bessie's murder but, in a legal first, Justice Scrutton allowed Smith's method of murder with respect to Alice and Margaret to be used as evidence. The prosecution's case made much of these similarities, and Smith was found guilty on 1 July, following a short deliberation by the jury. Smith's appeal was dismissed on 30 July, and he was hanged on 13 August 1915 at Maidstone Prison.

George Joseph Smith and the first of his victims, Beatrice Mundy.

DEATH IN A BATH

BRIDE OF A DAY FOUND DROWNED.

The death of Margaret Elizabeth Lloyd, aged 38 years, who was found dead in a bath at Bismarck-road, London, formed the subject of an inquest at Islington yesterday. Her husband is a land agent, and they were married at Bath on December 17. They came to London the same day, and took furnished rooms at the above-named address. She complained of pains, and saw a doctor, who found she was suffering from influenza. About half-past seven the next evening she went to the bathroom to take a bath, and owing to the length of time she was away her husband went to the bathroom. Getting no reply, he opened the door, and found her lying in the water dead. The room was in darkness, a candle which she had taken with her having become extinguished. Death was due to suffocation by drowning.

Mrs Batch, the landlady, stated that before going to her bath Mrs Lloyd appeared in a happy mood.

The jury returned a verdict of "Accidental death."

c/o Mrs Crossley
3 Clifton St
Blackpool.
Jany 3. 15

Dear Sir

I have been v. much struck with the enclosed account and its striking similarity to a case which happened here just 12 months previously
bath - pains in head - doctor & inquest.

I thought this might possibly be of some use. I shall be v pleased to answer any questions you like

Yrs truly
Joseph Crossley

c/o Mrs Crossley
3 Clifton St
Blackford
July 3, 15

Dear Sir,

I have been v. much struck with the enclosed account and its striking similarity to a case which happened here just 12 months previously. bath. pain in head. Doctor at inquest. I thought this might positively be of some use. I shall be v pleased to answer any questions you like.

Yours truly,
Joseph Crossley

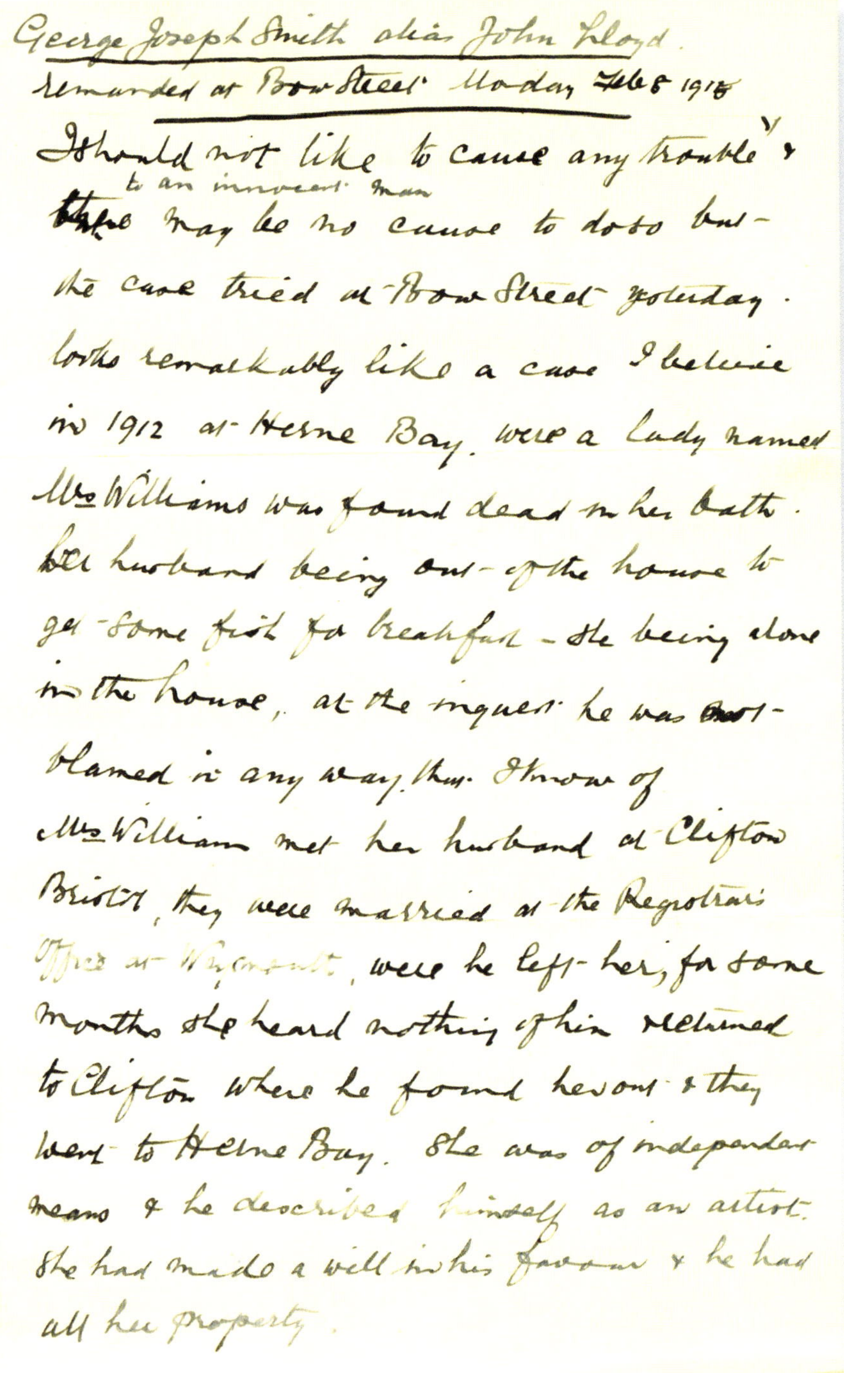
George Joseph Smith alias John Lloyd.
remanded at Bow Street Monday Feb 8 1915

I should not like to cause any trouble to an innocent man & ~~there~~ may be no cause to do so but the case tried at Bow Street yesterday looks remarkably like a case I believe in 1912 at Herne Bay. where a lady named Mrs Williams was found dead in her bath. her husband being out of the house to get some fish for breakfast – she being alone in the house, at the inquest he was ~~not~~ blamed in any way thus I know of Mrs William met her husband at Clifton Bristol, they were married at the Registrar's Office at Weymouth, where he left her, for some months she heard nothing of him returned to Clifton where he found her out & they went to Herne Bay. She was of independant means & he described himself as an artist. She had made a will in his favour & he had all her property.

George Joseph Smith alias John Lloyd

remanded at Bow Street Monday Feb 8 1915

I should not like to cause any trouble to an innocent man there may be no cause to do so but the case tried at Bow Street yesterday looks remarkably like a case I believe in 1912 at Herne Bay were a Lady named Mrs Williams was found dead in her bath. Her husband being out of the house to get some fish for breakfast – she being alone in the house, at the inquest he was not blamed in any way that I know of. Mrs Williams met her husband at Clifton Bristol, they were married at the Registrar's Office at Weymouth, were he left her for some months, she heard nothing of him returned to Clifton where he found her out and they went to Herne Bay. She was of independent means and he described himself as an artist. She had made a will in his favour and he had all her property.

A storm in a whiskey tumbler

Diplomatic drinking in prohibition America

1929

The Eighteenth Amendment to the United States Constitution, ratified in January 1919 and coming into effect in January 1920, prohibited the manufacture, sale, transportation, importation and exportation of alcohol within the country, and, it was hoped, marked the beginning of a 'dry' era for the American people. The reality on the ground, however, failed to match legislative ambitions. With bootlegging becoming a popular pastime and speakeasies flourishing, the irony was that alcohol came to define the period that tried to ban it.

This letter, written by James T Carter of Lynchburg, Virginia on 18 April 1929, is a product of this gulf between the ideal and the reality, and takes aim at an unexpected target, the British Embassy. Carter addresses the awkward point that, while border crossings were patrolled and warehouses raided across the country, the British ambassador and addressee Sir Esme Howard was free to sip whisky in the nation's capital behind a veil of diplomatic immunity. His is perhaps not the most reasoned of arguments, relying upon emotional blackmail with its references to the US's 'enormous sacrifice' and 'immense service' during the First World War, but it seemed to strike a chord with Howard who felt moved enough to offer a reply.

Unfortunately for Howard, his reply, issued through his private secretary a week later, was a little too honest. Although stressing the nature of his immunity and the law as it stood, he said that he'd be happy to abide by the law if it was changed in this matter, an offer that implicitly placed responsibility for the situation with the White House. Carter, sensing an opportunity, forwarded this letter to President Hoover on 14 May, quoting Howard's offer before saying: 'I judge from this that you can help make Washington a model city so far as whiskey drinking is concerned'. With no reply forthcoming, Carter went to the press with the ambassador's comments.

Howard soon faced ire from all sides. Hoover was angered by the ammunition it gave an already powerful 'dry' lobby, potentially forcing his hand in delicate matters of diplomacy. Other embassies worried about the implications for diplomatic immunity or, at the very least, their drinks cabinets. The British Foreign Office, meanwhile, stood to pick up the flak for an unauthorised announcement by one of their own. Howard had, through his fairly innocuous words, created what *The Times* called a 'flurry in the capital, which can be created by nothing so promptly and so acutely as by the public discussion of some aspect of the prohibition question'.

Attempts to control the story began immediately, with Howard issuing a statement to the press that made it clear he spoke only for himself, not for the British government as a whole, nor for the diplomatic community in Washington DC. Howard then met with the Secretary of State, Henry Stimson, and further reiterated that he spoke on a personal basis. However, rather than stopping there, Howard promised Stimson that he would no longer be importing alcohol for his own use, citing his own unease at the situation. He told Stimson of the 'sword of Damocles' he felt hanging above his head, and his fear that 'some day some American guest may be seen issuing forth from the embassy … in a state of intoxication'. His employers were unimpressed, with the Foreign Office questioning the idea of having a 'dry' ambassador 'representing a country which is not so and in the company of 54 colleagues all of whom import liquor', and noting Howard's over-sensitivity to attacks from the 'dry' lobby.

With this confused, half-hearted response, it's little surprise that attacks continued against the immunity enjoyed by diplomats. In June 1929, Senator Carraway of Arkansas submitted a successful resolution to the Senate, which called for the publication of a list of diplomats caught driving while intoxicated during the previous 13 years. The resulting list of 35 people was quickly picked up by the press before it was realised that the list covered all driving offences, not just those involving alcohol. As such, the only ambassador on the list, the German von Prittwitz, faced the wrath of the press for little more than a minor parking offence.

The hysteria generated by diplomatic drinking, and fuelled by comments such as Howard's, would only end with prohibition itself. The Twenty-first Amendment was ratified in December 1933, which in turn repealed the Eighteenth. What Hoover had termed the 'noble experiment' was over.

70 312

c o p y

EPPERSON LUMBER COMPANY

LYNCHBURG, Va.

April 18th, 1929.

British Ambassador,

Washington, D.C.

Dear Sir:

Referring to the enclosed clipping and the newspaper comment and criticism which has touched upon this instance, as a citizen of this country I am writing to suggest that you as the Dean of the Diplomatic Corps now at Washington, abolish the possession of whiskey, whiskey drinking and drunkenness from your premises in Washington and try to persuade the other Public servants of foreign countries in Washington on duty, to follow you. This is the wish of millions of tax-payers and voters of this country who are making a fight for humanity and to eliminate whiskey drinking in the lives of our people.

Such a step on your part, would in my estimation increase immensely your popularity personally and the popularity of your government and tend to cement the bonds of friendship between the two countries.

Of course you realize without having your memory refreshed on the subject, that our country at an enormous sacrifice rendered you an immense service some 10 years back with our Army and Navy and it does seem to me that we rendered to the French an even greater service. This being the case, both the English and the French should be most anxious and happy to comply with the wishes of the better classes of people in this country.

I hope you can see your way clear to carry out this wish immediately and will be glad to have an expression from you. Respectively,

(SD.) J.T.CARTER

Destroying barrels of alcohol during the Prohibition.

'Impassioned Obscenity'
The Cerne Abbas Giant

1932

Ancient monuments litter the British Isles, with most posing more questions than they answer. The Cerne Abbas Giant, a chalk monument carved into a hill in Dorset, is no exception – with little known of its origins, its purpose or its meaning. As well as raising questions, however, the monument has also raised eyebrows, and none more so than Walter L Long's, the writer of this letter.

The Giant itself is a crude depiction of a nude man holding a club aloft, complete with an erect penis, and is thought to be of ancient origin, despite 1694 being the earliest record of it. Long himself produced a fairly accurate sketch, which you'll see at the top of the letter, hidden beneath a self-censoring flap of paper. One theory sees the Giant as a product of Romano-British culture, with its resemblance to Hercules emphasised, a theory that received a boost with the recent archaeological discovery of a since-disappeared cloak or pelt on the Giant's left arm, a hallmark of depictions of Hercules. Others either doubt its ancient status, pointing to the lack of records before the 17th century, or else go back even further to Celtic Britain.

It is, of course, not a historical controversy that bothers Long, but rather the Giant's 36-foot-long genitalia. His letter asks that something be done about the Giant's 'impassioned obscenity' for the sake of the 'rising generation', citing the support he has garnered from local religious figures and the previous appeals he has made to the National Trust. His request is not for the removal of the penis altogether, but rather for its conversion into a 'simple nude', although how this would be achieved, and what the end result might be, is left open.

The official reply he received from the Home Office was restrained, if a little blunt, informing Long that the Secretary of State 'cannot see his way to take any action in the matter'. The archival file, however, betrays the true thoughts of the recipients and, perhaps more so, the frustrations of life as a civil servant. SW Harris was tasked with dealing with the matter and considered with colleagues what would make Long content, asking if he wished the Home Office to report such indecency to the police or if he'd be happy with a small grove of fig trees planted in a strategic position. Harris noted how the monument had stood for 2,000 or 3,000 years without complaint, 'or from 1/3 to one half the Biblical age of the Earth', before decrying that 'it is hard to be patient; it is harder still to be serious'.

Harris's frustration would, however, eventually turn to amusement. In 1939, he shared the letter with a colleague, describing it facetiously as a 'valuable record for the archives of the Home Office'. The reply from his colleague is perhaps the kind of response Harris had dreamed of sending to Long seven years previously: *'He is an old scandal, but he has stood there and scandalised for thousands of years and I hope [he] will do so for thousands more.'*

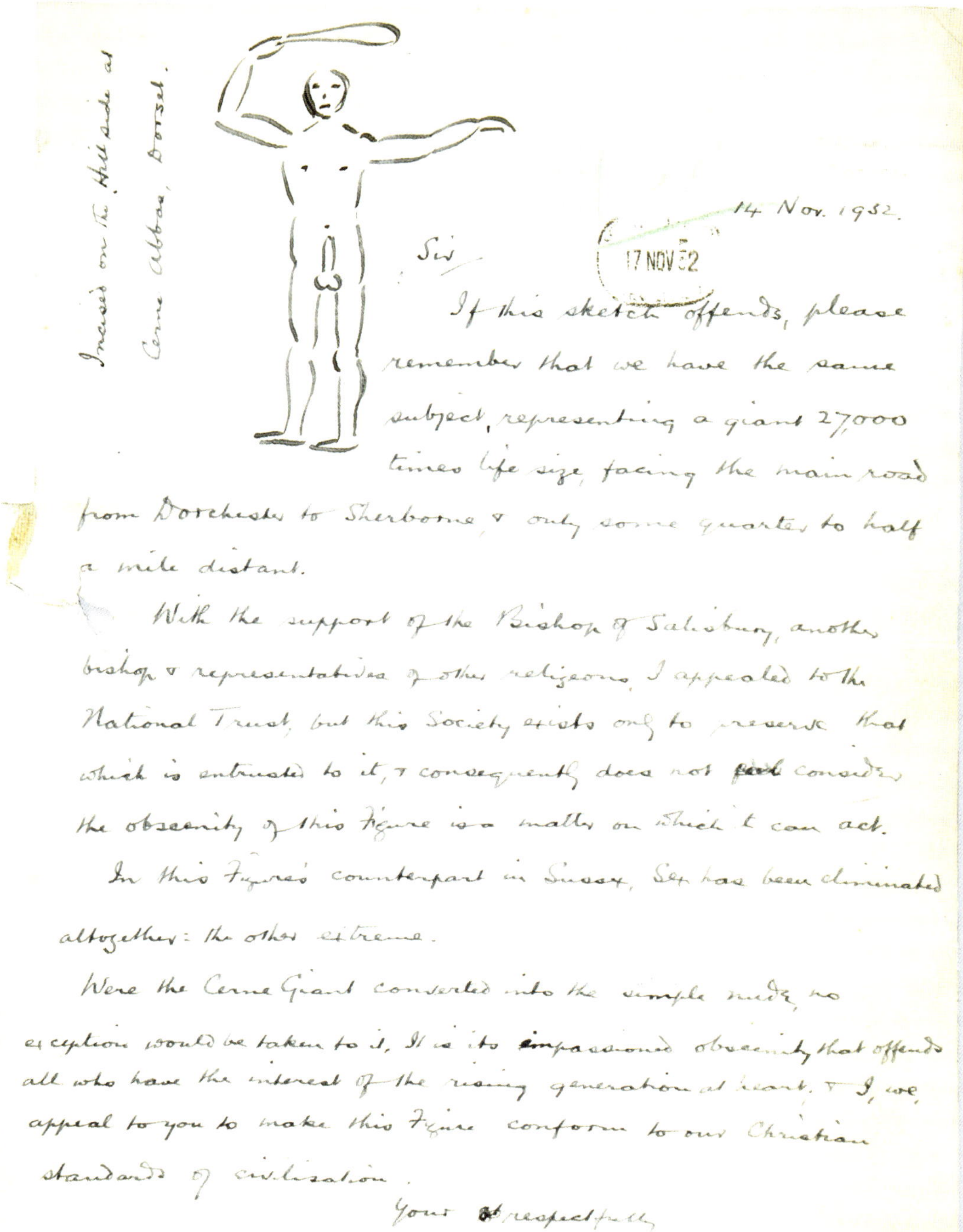

Incised on the Hill side at Cerne Abbas, Dorset.

14 Nov. 1952.

17 NOV 52

Sir,

If this sketch offends, please remember that we have the same subject, representing a giant 27,000 times life size, facing the main road from Dorchester to Sherborne, & only some quarter to half a mile distant.

With the support of the Bishop of Salisbury, another bishop & representatives of other religions, I appealed to the National Trust, but this Society exists only to preserve that which is entrusted to it, & consequently does not ~~feel~~ consider the obscenity of this Figure is a matter on which it can act.

In this Figure's counterpart in Sussex, Sex has been eliminated altogether: the other extreme.

Were the Cerne Giant converted into the simple nude, no exception would be taken to it. It is its ~~impassioned~~ obscenity that offends all who have the interest of the rising generation at heart, & I, we, appeal to you to make this Figure conform to our Christian standards of civilisation.

Yours respectfully

Walter Long.

30th No

655265/1.

Sir,

With reference to your letter of the 14th November, I am directed by the Secretary of State to say that he has caused inquiry to be made and finds that the prehistoric figure of which you complain - the Giant of Cerne - is a national monument, scheduled as such, and vested in the National Trust.

In the circumstances the Secretary of State regrets that he cannot see his way to take any action in the matter.

I am, Sir,

Your obedient Servant,

(sgd) H Houston.

Walter L. Long, Esq.,
Oakleigh,
Wyke,
Gillingham,
Dorset.

Commander of the death camps

Josef Kramer, commandant of Bergen-Belsen, writes to his wife

1945

On 8 July 1945, Josi wrote to his wife Rosi from the Celle Prison, in Lower Saxony, Northern Germany. 'Please send me a pullover (grey with sleeves) (...) as I always have to do with the cold,' he asked her, 'and 2 pairs of the new socks because I have none left'. These were very ordinary words from a man who was no ordinary prisoner. Josef Kramer was the Commandant of the Bergen-Belsen concentration camp.

Born in Munich in 1906, Kramer joined the Nazi party in 1931 and the SS in 1932. He started his career as a concentration camp guard in Dachau in 1934, and was rapidly promoted, climbing up the SS ladder in Sachsenhausen and Mauthausen. In 1944, then bearing the silver pips and stripes of a SS-Hauptsturmführer (the equivalent of a captain in the army), he was appointed as Lagerführer (camp leader) of Auschwitz II-Birkenau, at the very heart of the 'final solution'. The first gas chamber had been operational there since March 1942, and Kramer supervised the gassing of newly arrived prisoners. In December 1944, he was sent to Bergen-Belsen.

'That so many people died in Belsen – I could not alter that any more – it is all fate,' he wrote, 'and maybe I shall even be punished for that'. There was no gas chamber in Bergen-Belsen, but Kramer behaved so inhumanly that he acquired the infamous nickname of 'the Beast of Belsen'. The camp was liberated on 15 April 1945 by the British, who found about 13,000 unburied dead and 60,000 prisoners who, in stark contrast with Kramer who acknowledged being 'in good health' and being given enough food in detention – were half-starved and severely ill.

For us, who have the sad benefit of hindsight, this letter to his wife is a disturbing mix of utter denial and uncanny normality.

Kramer alternated fatherly concern: ('*what are the children doing, Kurt, Karlheinz and especially Christel*?'), practical advice ('*liquidate my accounts – savings and banking accounts – at the Savings-bank in Bergen*'), loving words ('*the years which I could spend together with you were too beautiful for me*') and self-pity ('*at home I should have so much to do and here I do not know how to spend the day being so idle*'). This can certainly be expected from any prisoner writing to his loved ones, but it makes Kramer so human it is almost unbearable.

Above all, he displayed a lack of understanding of his own situation which is difficult to comprehend: '*all the time*,' he complained to his wife, '*I am asking myself why this misfortune came over me. How have I deserved this? What have I done that one has to treat me like a criminal*?' In the statement he gave before his trial, he blamed Himmler, Pohl and Glücks, who were at the head of the concentration-camp system, and added '*if Hitler knew what was going on, the responsibility of all this falls on him, but I do not think that he knew*'. He also claimed he hadn't '*personally committed any crime*'.

Kramer was tried by a British military court at Lüneburg during the Belsen Trials, which started on 17 September 1945, only two months after he wrote to his wife asking for a 'toothbrush. Nothing else'. Sentenced to death by hanging, he was executed on 13 December 1945. As he told her, 'it is fate and one cannot alter it'.

Josef Kramer (second right) pictured with Dr Josef Mengele (left) and Rudolf Hess (second left), commandant of Auschwitz.

Celle, July 8th 1945.

Dear Rosi!

Since 8 days I am again here, have heard from the Major that you were here twice to look for me. Rosilein (my little Rosi), I was terribly ashamed that you had to look for me in jail. That's where I got to now, that my wife and children have to look for me in a jail. The SS and the whole party is not worth it that I a, now taken for a criminal. But it is fate and one cannot alter it. It is 12 weeks since I was arrested – I wonder how you and the children go on in this time. I was always worried about you – do you draw assistance, have you got help, can you stay where you are or have you to move out? I have written from Belgium on the 1st of May but do not know whether the letter arrived under the present conditions. I wonder how your mother and my parents are. What are the children doing, Kurt, Karlheinz and especially Christel? All questions over which I am pondering all the time and no answers to them. Liquidate my accounts – savings and banking accounts – at the Savings-bank in Bergen. It is not much but it is a little help for you and I do not need the accounts anyway. I cannot tell you what is going to happen with me, I do not know it myself. How long they are going to keep me does not depend on me, I can only hope and wish that this time will soon be over. Apart from my nerves I am in good health, you need not worry about me personally. Please tell my parents the same, I myself cannot write to them. All the time I am asking myself why this misfortune came over me. How have I deserved this? What have I done that one has to treat me like a criminal? That so many people died in Belsen – I could not alter that any more – it is all fate and maybe I shall even be punished for that. My father used to say sometimes, I was not lucky. To-day I believe it only too well. The years which I could spend together with you were too beautiful for me. At home I should have so much to do and here I do not know how to spend the day being so idle. Dear Rosi, if it is possible for you, please send me a pullover (grey with sleeves) with a car, as I always have to do with the cold. Further 2 handkerchiefs and 2 pairs of the new socks because I have none left. Toothbrush. Nothing else. No food, I have enough here. Address – Prison Celle, I shall get it alright. I would rather prefer it if you could come yourself but do not know if i can ask you, once more to make this for you so very sad way. Besides you can not leave the children without supervision if you have not a help any more. I can only hope that this time of suffering will soon find an end and I shall again be with you.

Rosilein, all the best to you and the children, for the future. I shall always be with you.

Your Josi.

Love to Kurti, he should be good and help Mummy.

Letter addressed to:

Frau Rosine Kramer
Belse, Kreis Celle
Wiesener Strasse
Hut near Camp.

Translated July 10th 1945.

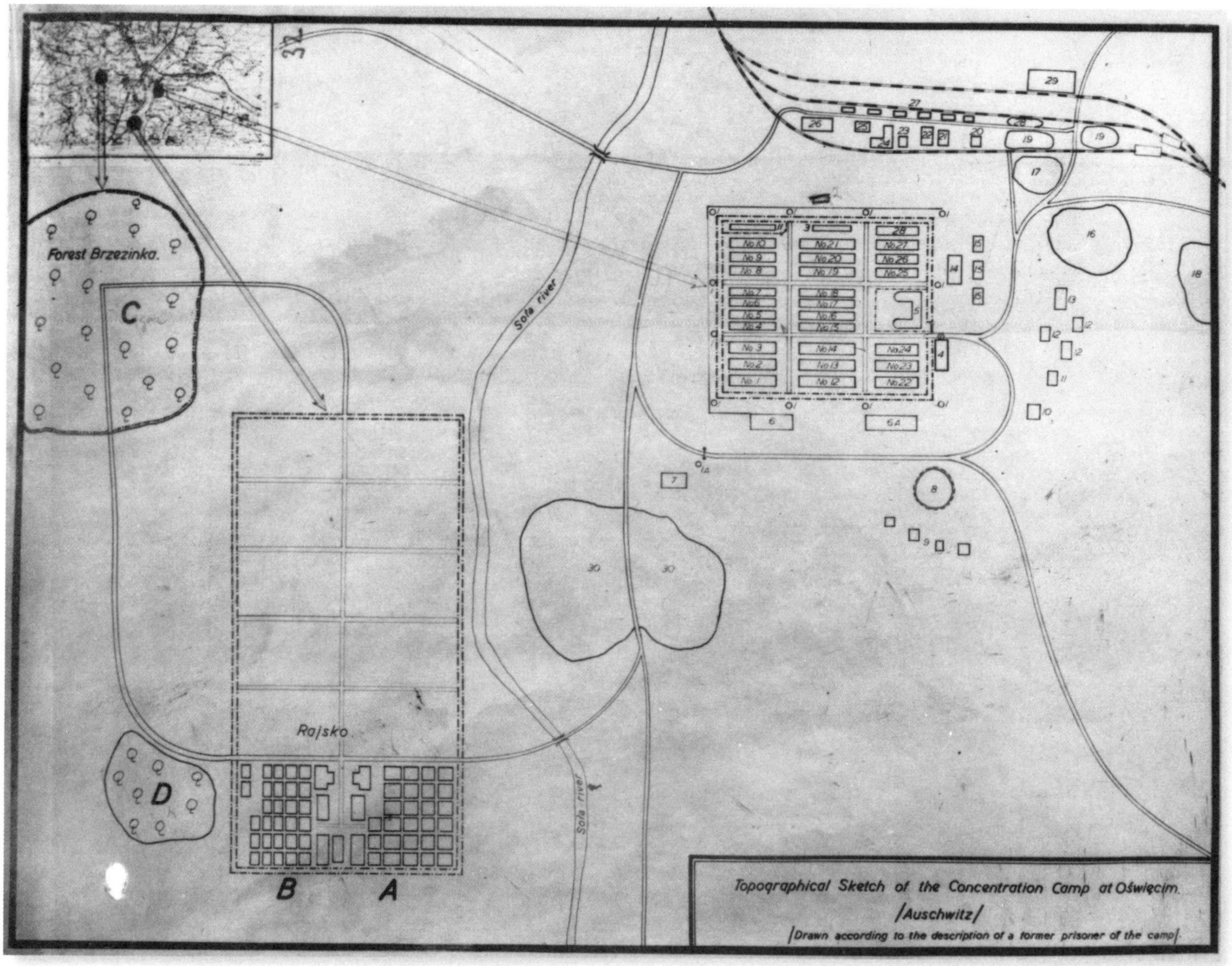

Topographical map of the concentration camp at Oświęcim (Auschwitz).

Christine Keeler and Stephen Ward

The scandal that rocked the early 1960s

1963

Christine Keeler was a young model whose affair with a married Cabinet minister shook the British establishment. The story began on 8 July 1961 with a party held at Cliveden, the Buckinghamshire estate owned by the 3rd Viscount Astor. Keeler, then 19 years old, was introduced to John Profumo, Secretary of State for War in the Conservative government of Harold Macmillan, and the two began an affair. However, she simultaneously became involved with Captain Yevgeny (Eugene) Ivanov, a Russian military attaché. Details of the events did not finally emerge for some time. In the context of the Cold War, there was great concern about the potential security implications of Keeler's liaisons. As rumours circulated, Profumo misled Parliament in March 1963 by denying impropriety, before ultimately resigning in disgrace.

The scandal also exposed behaviour that was out of tune with the prevailing moral sensibilities. Integral to this was Dr Stephen Ward, the man who introduced Keeler to both Profumo and to Ivanov. Ward was a well-connected 48-year-old osteopath, and his home in Wimpole Mews, Marylebone, provided the venue for many of Keeler and Profumo's encounters. Revelations of Ward's hedonistic lifestyle caused outrage. Lord Denning's report on the affair, published in September 1963, referred to him as an 'utterly immoral' man who 'did not confine his attention to promiscuity'. 'There is evidence that he was ready to arrange for whipping and other sadistic performances', it continued.

This letter from Conservative backbench MP Captain Henry Kerby to Anthony Barber, the Financial Secretary to the Treasury, illustrates the moral disapproval towards 'this disgraceful case'. With rumours and allegations swirling as to the true nature of Keeler's work, Kerby disparagingly refers to her as a 'so-called "model"'. He uses similar language in relation to Ward – a 'so-called "Dr"' – though it should also be noted that osteopathy was not at that time recognised as a branch of medicine. Kerby's main concern here, however, was Christine Keeler's tax affairs. Barber's reply, dated 3 May, did not comment specifically on Keeler or Ward. Referring to 'the activities of prostitutes and others living on immoral earnings', the minister noted that 'You will not be surprised to learn that such people are not in the habit of mentioning these activities by name in their Income Tax returns'.

Matters regarding income facilitated the criminal charges brought against Stephen Ward. The resulting trial shone further light on the lifestyle of Ward and his associates. Keeler testified against him, as did her former flatmate Mandy Rice-Davies. When Ward's defence counsel pointed out that Lord Astor denied having even met her, Rice-Davies famously replied 'Well he would, wouldn't he'. Ward was eventually convicted on 31 July 1963 of two counts of living off immoral earnings. The trial and verdict remain controversial, recently becoming the subject of a book by the distinguished barrister Geoffrey Robinson QC, entitled *Stephen Ward Was Innocent, OK: The Case for Overturning his Conviction*.

Ward was not in court to learn of his fate. He lay in a coma having attempted to take his own life the night before, and died on 3 August. In December 1963, Keeler was convicted of perjury for her testimony in the trial of Aloysius 'Lucky' Gordon, a former lover whom she accused of violence towards her. Sentenced to nine months in prison, Keeler withdrew from the media spotlight upon her release. John Profumo's marriage to the actress Valerie Hobson survived the scandal, and he dedicated the remainder of his life to charity work. He was awarded a CBE in 1975 and died in 2006.

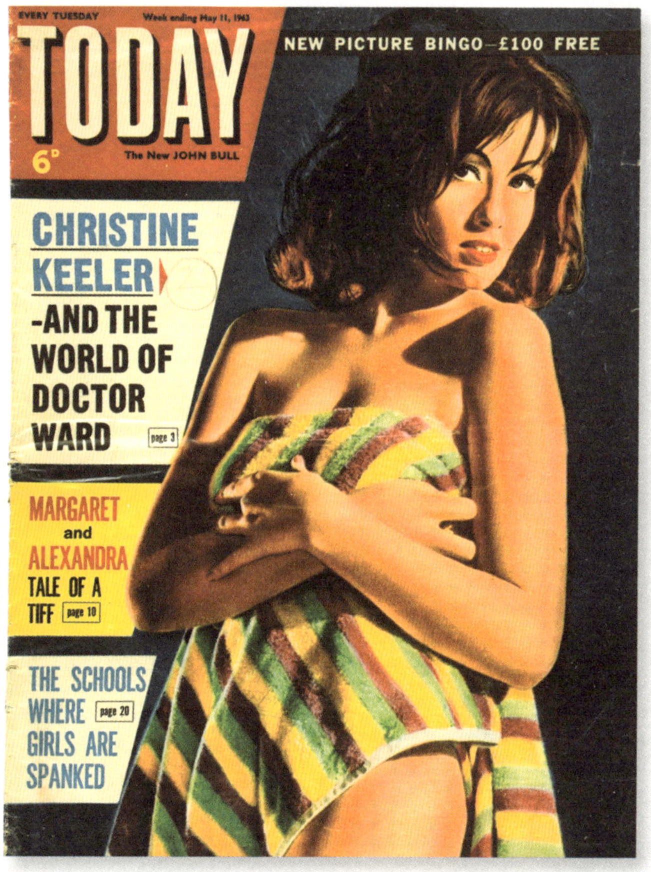

B3 545/63

10/5

6th April 1963.

CONFIDENTIAL

Anthony Barber Esq. M.P.
The Treasury
London. S.W.1.

Dear Tony,

'Model' Christine Keeler.

I know you will come back to me with the ~~checkered~~ dogeared old excuses about personal cases being 'out' etc. Nevertheless, in view of the tremendous, and still growing, and most unsavoury publicity which this disgraceful case, with its vast ramifications, has received, I would like an assurance from you about it. Is this so-called 'model' being chased for Income Tax? I hope she is.

As I understand it, a girl presumed to be earning fees as a model would have to return fees rendered on a self-employed basis unless she worked through an agency on a salary basis. If, however, her employment was used as a cover for immoral earnings what is the position then please? Would the Revenue report their suspicions to the Police for investigation? Have they done so?

Then again, what about any man behind such a set-up? Presumably it is next to impossible to trace him through Income Tax returns. He would deal in cash only handing it over to 'model' employees, and there need be no trace of it anywhere. If enforced to make a Return he would, undoubtedly, have a ready-made and plausible tale of some sort of legitimate self-employment - an artist, 'osteopath', or what-not. Would Inland Revenue at this point request a Police investigation?

In view of the tremendous public interest, not to say disgust, in this case, I would like your assurance that your Income Tax people are on the ball with regard both to Miss Keeler, and to so-called 'Dr.' Stephen Ward.

With all regards,

Yours ever,

Bob

P.S. A final point regarding cases of immoral earnings.

P.T.O.

Am I right in assuming that a rent-free residence, flat or what-have-you, is not taxable where the occupier has no right to rent? This would cover, presumably, a furnished flat which was provided for the purpose unless Revenue could contend that the purpose was illegal, and therefore outside the protection of the Finance Act. Is this so please? Revenue, in the absence of a Return on Income, issue assessments - do they not? - on an estimated basis. If the Tax is paid without question the usual practice - again is it not? - is to increase the assessment for the next and following years. Then the Inspector pounces and demands full disclosure from commencement, and unless I am much mistaken you can go back up to 20 years, although the Taxpayer can only go back 6 years. I wonder if the Tax Inspector has yet pounced on Christine Keeler. If not, it is high time that he did so. Do you not agree?

'The Kray twins done it'
Murder at the Blind Beggar

1966

The London of the 1960s is often remembered for its miniskirts and its Mini-Coopers, but while Carnaby Street was 'swinging', the East End of London was in thrall to the notorious Kray brothers, Ronnie and Reggie. This anonymous letter formed part of the murder investigation that, in the words of Scotland Yard's Detective Superintendent Harry Mooney, 'brought to an end the[ir] reign of terror'.

The Krays sat at the top of London's criminal hierarchy for much of the early 1960s, inspiring fear in the underworld for their ruthlessness while at the same time cultivating their celebrity through their legitimate businesses, namely as owners of Esmeralda's Barn, a nightclub in Knightsbridge which saw them mix with the likes of Frank Sinatra and Diana Dors. The victim mentioned in the letter, George Cornell, was part of the very same underworld that the Krays were coming to see as theirs by right. He worked with Charlie Richardson, one of the Kray's key rivals, was responsible for running numerous frauds and was known to be violent; the police report on Cornell states that he would have been charged with two counts of GBH had he not been killed. The statement of his wife, Olive, taken as part of the investigation, goes yet further. She stated that Cornell had been asked to murder Ronnie as revenge for the shooting of William Andrews on 4 March 1966, and that it was only Cornell's hesitancy that gave Ronnie the chance to get there first the following week, on 9 March.

On that evening, Cornell visited Andrews in hospital before heading to the Blind Beggar pub in Whitechapel. He arrived at 8.10pm and met with acquaintances John Dale and Albert Wood, finding a table by the bar. At the same time, less than a mile away, Ronnie Kray was leaving The Lion pub in Tapp Street ('The Widows') with John Barrie ('Scots Ian') in tow, and was about to climb into John Dickson's ('Scots Jack') borrowed Ford Capri. These three first headed to the Grave Maurice pub, where Ronnie went in and out within a minute searching for Cornell, but by 8:35pm were parked outside the Blind Beggar. Ronnie and Scots Ian entered the pub, leaving Scots Jack in the car. Once inside, Ronnie pulled out a Luger and shot Cornell in the forehead.

It's not clear if this letter comes from a witness to these events, someone who heard the story after the fact, or just from someone in whose best interests it was to see the

Krays behind bars, but for a long time this kind of anonymous finger-pointing was all the police had to rely upon. The Krays' notoriety made speaking out against them a huge risk, with an ID parade in August 1966 described as farcical by Mooney for the clear influence the Krays had over the proceedings. As such, it wasn't until the summer of 1968 that Ronnie and Scots Ian were charged with the crime, and only once members of their gang, 'the Firm', including the driver Scots Jack and the Teale brothers, had provided statements that contradicted their assertion that they had been in The Widows all along.

The trial began in January 1969 and was heard alongside that for the later murder of Jack 'The Hat' McVitie, for which Reggie was the main defendant. Ronnie and Scots Ian relied upon members of the Firm to support their alibi, but were let down by those who either refused to lie on their behalf or actively placed them at the scene of the crime. With their defence case in tatters, Ronnie and Scots Ian were convicted of the murder of Cornell on 4 March 1969 and sentenced to life imprisonment. Reggie was convicted as an accessory to the Cornell murder, for his role in covering up the crime, and also for the murder of McVitie. He was also sentenced to life imprisonment, bringing the Krays' rule over the East End to a close.

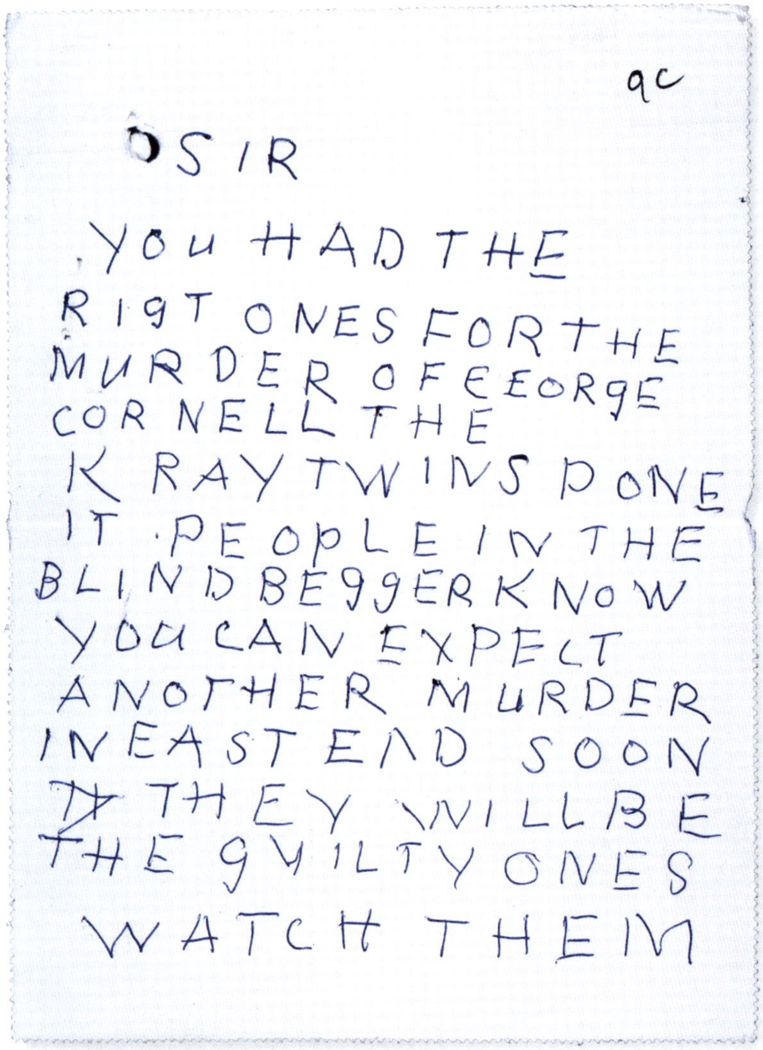

9c

SIR

YOU HAD THE
RIGT ONES FOR THE
MURDER OF GEORGE
CORNELL THE
KRAY TWINS DONE
IT PEOPLE IN THE
BLIND BEGGER KNOW
YOU CAN EXPECT
ANOTHER MURDER
IN EAST END SOON
~~T~~ THEY WILL BE
THE GUILTY ONES
WATCH THEM

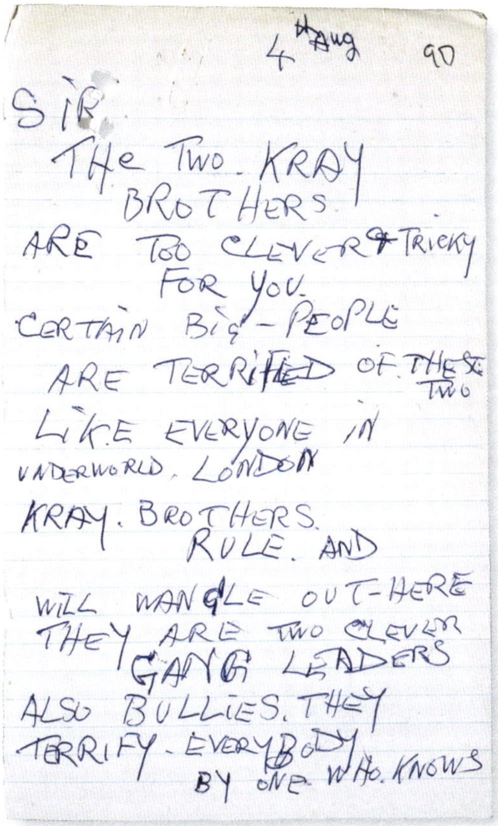

4th Aug 9D

SIR

THE TWO KRAY BROTHERS

ARE TOO CLEVER & TRICKY FOR YOU.

CERTAIN BIG-PEOPLE ARE TERRIFIED OF THESE TWO

LIKE EVERYONE IN UNDERWORLD. LONDON

KRAY. BROTHERS. RULE. AND WILL WANGLE OUT-HERE

THEY ARE TWO CLEVER GANG LEADERS

ALSO BULLIES. THEY TERRIFY. EVERYBODY

BY ONE WHO. KNOWS

C8

To

CHIEF. INS. DT. THOMAS BUTLER.

CRIME-SQUAD. SCOTLAND YARD.

LONDON S.W.1

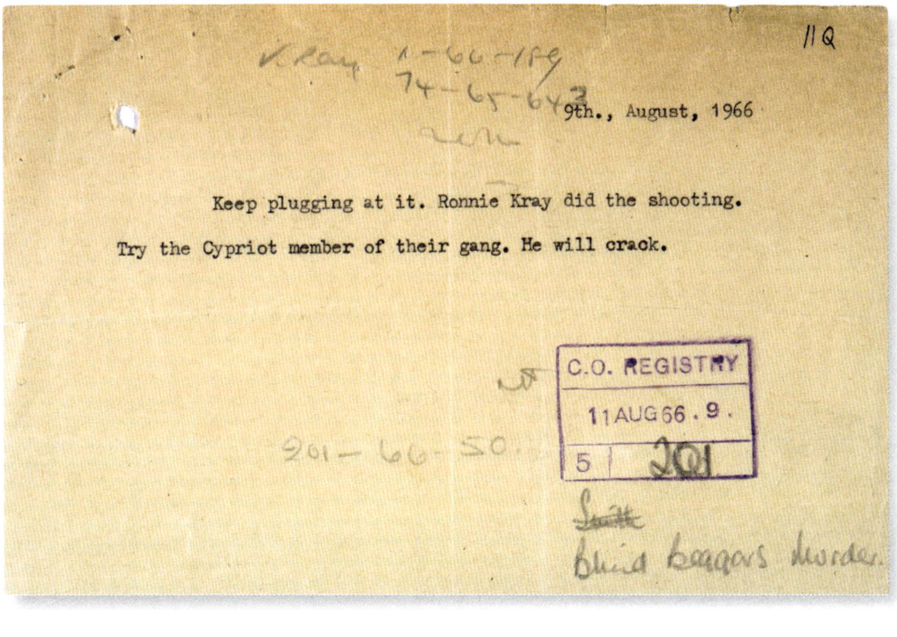

11Q

Kray 1-66-169

74-65-643

9th., August, 1966

Keep plugging at it. Ronnie Kray did the shooting.

Try the Cypriot member of their gang. He will crack.

C.O. REGISTRY

11 AUG 66 . 9 .

5 | 201

201-66-50.

~~Smith~~

Blind Beggars murder.

'One for the pot'
The World Cup is stolen

1966

On 30 July 1966, Bobby Moore held the Jules Rimet trophy aloft in a crowded Wembley Stadium, confirming England's as yet only victory in football's World Cup. Just a few months earlier, such a scene had been considered unlikely, if not impossible. This wasn't because England lacked talent, nor was it because of boycotts by the aggrieved African nations, but rather it was due to the fact that the Jules Rimet trophy had been stolen and, for a tense few days, faced the threat of the melting pot.

The trophy had arrived in the UK at the start of the year, entrusted to the British Football Association (the FA) on 6 January 1966, and was in turn loaned to Stanley Gibbons Limited on Friday 18 March, for use in a stamp exhibition at Westminster Central Hall. The following Sunday, with the exhibition closed to the public, the display case was broken into and the trophy removed. One of the four security officers on duty at the time, George Franklin, recalls going for coffee at 11am before returning at noon to an empty case, the back door to the exhibition having been forced open. Another, Frank Hudson, remembers seeing a man loitering around the toilets in the entrance hall at the time. Margaret Coombes, attending the Methodist Sunday School Service in the Hall, also remembers seeing a loitering man. Ultimately, however, the trophy was gone, its whereabouts unknown, with little to go on but these vague recollections.

Luckily, the thief was more a mercenary than a collector. Joseph Mears, Chairman of both Chelsea Football Club and the FA, received a call the next day telling him to expect a package, which duly arrived on the Wednesday. It contained the trophy's small gold lid and the letter shown, which promised 'if you are willing to pay me £15,000 in £5 and £1 pound notes you shall have your cup back', with the threat that the trophy would be 'one for the pot' if the demands were not met. Another call to Mears soon followed with the man, now calling himself Jackson, asking for £5 and £10 notes instead, and reiterating the Friday deadline.

That evening, Mears gave everything he had to Detective Inspector Leonard Buggy of the Metropolitan Police Flying Squad. As Friday approached, Mears's angina, exacerbated by stress, forced him to bed under doctor's orders and so Buggy had to put himself forward as the go-between. In a call on Friday morning, Buggy convinced

Jackson that he was 'Mr McPhee', Mears's assistant, and a meeting was arranged at Battersea Park, London, with Buggy borrowing Mears's Ford Zodiac and bringing a suitcase packed with £500 in bank envelopes, dressed up to look like the full £15,000.

Buggy pulled up on Park Gate Road and, as he had been instructed in the phone call, climbed out of the Zodiac and got back in. A man approached and introduced himself as Jackson, asking to see the suitcase. Buggy showed him and, seemingly satisfied, Jackson climbed into the Zodiac's passenger seat and began to direct Buggy, furtively looking out of the rear window on a journey of double-backs and false stops. A 'funny old van' that had been following the Zodiac was spotted by Jackson enough times to make him suspicious and, following a brief stop by Kennington Park, paranoia got the better of him and he jumped from the moving car. Buggy gave pursuit through a builder's yard, vaulting a couple of garden fences before catching Jackson in the garden of 111 Lorrimore Road, and detaining him on suspicion of theft.

It soon became apparent that 'Jackson' was in fact Edward Betchley, a second-hand car dealer and ex-serviceman with one previous conviction for theft in 1954. Betchley, insisting at all times that he was merely a middle-man, was later convicted of demanding the £15,000 with menaces with intent to steal, and was sentenced to two years' imprisonment. At the time of the arrest, however, the main concern was the location of the trophy. The tournament was fast approaching and the police pressed Betchley for a location. Betchley remained silent, perhaps realising the power of his position.

Before any kind of deal could be made, the trophy was found by David Corbett and his dog Pickles on an evening walk around his home in Upper Norwood, London. Pickles sniffed out the Jules Rimet trophy, which was hidden under a bush and wrapped in newspaper, on Sunday 27 March, and took his place in history as the dog that saved the World Cup. Whether Betchley had worked alone or not now seemed unimportant – the World Cup was back on and England, for once, stood a fighting chance of winning it.

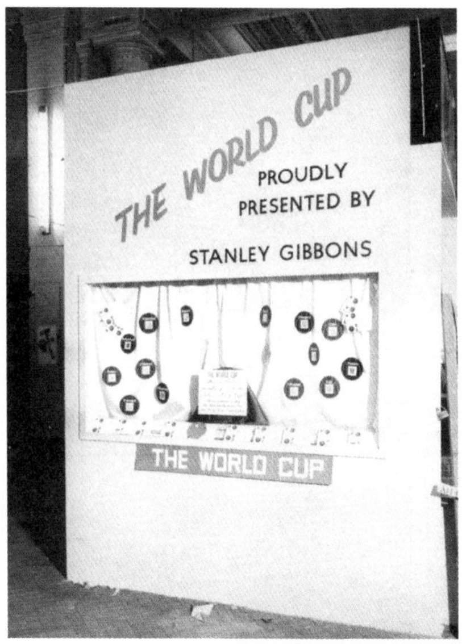

The Stanley Gibbons stand – minus the World Cup.

EXHIBIT NO. 6.

COPY

21 st March

Dear Joe
N
kno doubt you view with very great
concern the loss of the world cup to me
it is only so much weight in scrap gold
so if you want to see it again i suggest
you do as i say and follow my instruction

first if the press or police are inform
ed of this, this cup will go into the
melting pot ~~admitted i only get a~~
fraction of the money i want but i shall
be safe and you lose the cup forever
but if you are willing to pay me ££15,000
in £5 and £1 pound notes you shall have
your cup back and you will be satisfied
and so will the rest of the WORLD.

If you agree with this followT these
instructions .
insert in thursdays Evening News
Personal Column. Willing to do business
signed. Joe.
Second contact will be by phone to
Chelsea F.C.
Find enclosed top of World Cup. to prove
Genuine.

IS TRESS ONCE AGAIN THAT THIS CUP IS
ONLY SO MUCH SCRAP TO ME AND REPEAT
AND DO NOT INFORM PRESS OR POLICE.

It would be a great pity to
destroy this cup in view of
its great history and beauty
it portrays.

if i do not hear from you by
Thursdays or Friday at the
latest issume its one for the
POT.

The World Cup as it was retrieved,
wrapped in old newspaper.

COUPE DU MONDE
CAMPEON
1930
ITALIA
CAMPIONE
1934

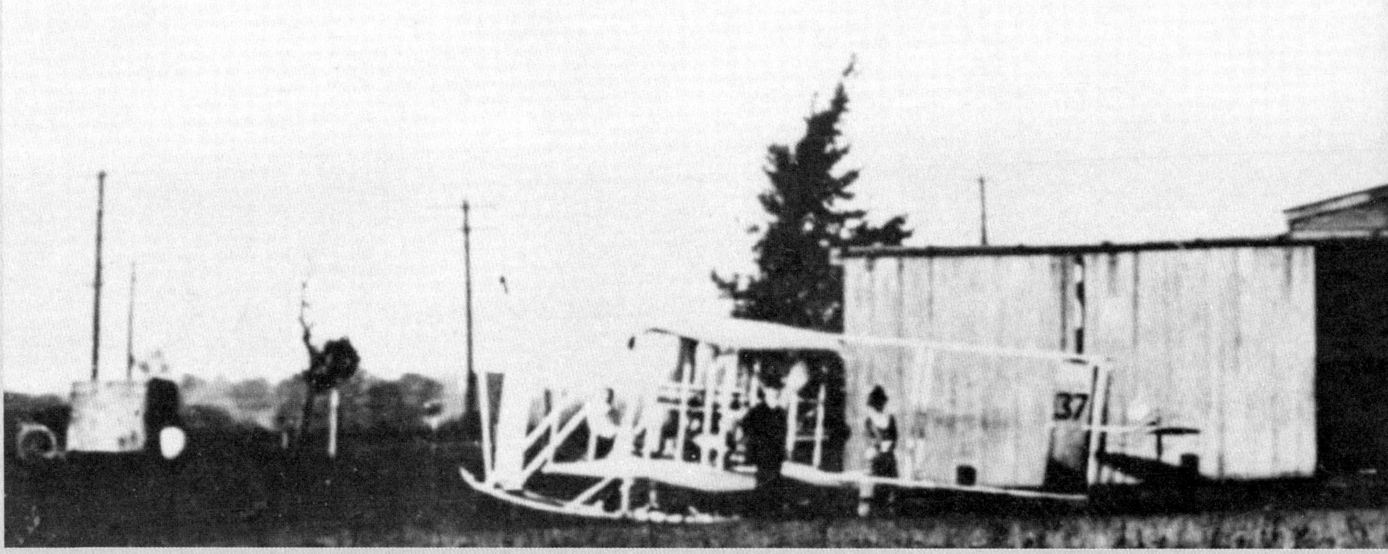
37

Cultural and technological change

The cantankerous father of computing
Charles Babbage and street-music noise

1861

Born in London in 1791, Charles Babbage is best remembered as the father of computing. After studying mathematics at Cambridge University, Babbage was elected a fellow of the Royal Society in 1816. He was a founding member of the Astronomical Society, and in 1828 was appointed Professor of Mathematics at Cambridge University. In the same year he moved to Dorset Street in Marylebone, which remained his home until his death in 1871. In his later years he gained a reputation as a cantankerous and argumentative old man. This aspect of the life is reflected in a lecture by Doron Swade and Alan Weissberger entitled 'Charles Babbage, "Irascible Genius", and the first computer', published in 2008.

In this letter written to the Home Secretary in 1861, Babbage complains about street musicians who were making his life 'intolerable'. To support his case, he attached a list of the most annoying examples of street music, contending that the public highways were solely for the transit of persons and goods, and not for the performance of music and entertainment. Babbage protested that the constant din prevented him from making calculations and drawings, and he sought sanctuary 'from the tyranny of the idle and ignorant over the industrious workman and the thoughtful mental labourer.'

A particular bugbear for Babbage was that the word of a householder was not sufficient to remove a street musician who continued to perform after being requested to stop. Equally disturbing was that if the offender was foreign, 'he is usually acquainted with a few words of English and those of the most vulgar and offensive kind'. Babbage was in despair that it took over 30 minutes to find a police constable to remove an organ-grinder, only to find him replaced by a bag-pipe player or brass band, and so he demanded that the law was changed to forbid all musical instruments at all times from being played in the street, and that the word of the householder should be sufficient to secure an arrest. The Home Secretary found the letter 'amusing', and suggested that the remedy proposed was too extreme. Until his death in 1871, Babbage continued to be disturbed by 'interruptions at almost all hours', and took to working on Sundays because it was the quietest day of the week.

Charles Babbage

Lucasian Professor of Mathematics in the University of Cambridge.

Engraved by Roffe, by permission from an original Family Painting.

Sir,

The increase of the nuisance arising from noises in the street of various kinds as well as from Street Music has become during the last few years so intolerable that I am induced to ask your attention to the very imperfect state of the law in regard to its suppression.

I do this with the less reluctance because I have been urged to it by many more silent victims than myself.

We ask relief from this tyranny of the idle and the ignorant over the industrious workman and the thoughtful mental labourer.

The principle – 'that no person has a right to use his own property so as to injure or disturb his neighbour in the use of his' – applies to all such cases even if the streets and Highways were the absolute property of the public or of the performers.

But the public highways are not the property of any individual. They were given up by the owners of the land to the use of the public for the transit of persons and of property.

During the last eight or ten years the nuisance has been constantly increasing. By putting in force clauses of the Police Act (2, 3 Victoria (illegible)) sections LVII & LXVI I have succeeded partially in mitigating the nuisance: but within the last two years the interpretation of the law has been altered, and the magistrate now refuses to convict except on evidence which it is next to im –

X see a list of these on the annexed sheet

possible to obtain.

Before this change whenever I was annoyed by Street Music, I sent my servant or went myself and desired the performer to go away. If he continued playing I sent or went for a constable to whom I gave the offender in charge. He was then taken to the Police Station and ultimately before the Magistrate and was almost invariably fined.

The cause [required to be stated by the Act] which I assigned to the Magistrate, and which was always deemed sufficient, was that these disturbances interrupted me in the normal pursuits of my life. —— that they prevented me from making the calculations and drawings without which I must dismiss those skilled workmen who during a long series of years have been earning their wages by the execution of the machinery which I have been contriving.

Within the last two years the interpretation of the Police Act has been changed and it is now held that

"a constable cannot legally arrest a street-musician who has continued his noise after being requested to desist by a householder, unless the constable is himself a witness of the fact of the warning and persisting."

The following is a case of continued recurrence.

In the midst of work requiring the greatest attention I am disturbed by an organ or other noisy instrument. I either send my servant or go out myself and desire him to desist. If the offender is a foreigner he is usually acquainted with but few words of our language and those of the most vulgar and offensive kind: these he applies freely and continues his noise. I now go in search of a constable (from the result of a large number of instances I believe I understate the time when I say that in an average it costs half an hour before I can find a constable and bring him to the spot where the offense was committed). If I can prevail upon the constable to return with me it is found, either:

That the organ grinder has collected his pence (?) and gone – or

That on the constable desiring him to go he desists and marches away.

Now as soon as the street is relieved from the presense [sic] of the constable another organ-grinder or perhaps a brass band or possibly bagpipes may take the place of its predecessor and after giving me another half hour's search for another constable may again make room for a similar successor.

In consequence of this view of the law I have been put to great expense and of further loss of time. Sir, actions for false imprisonment have been threatened or commenced against me. I put myself entirely in the hands of my legal advisors who settled these matters as they thought best.

Afterwards I obtained an elaborate opinion on those clauses of the Police Act which relate to the nuisances and street musicians from M. Denman Q.b. The result is that the present state of the law practically gives me no remedy. I may notice incidentally that during the day on which I was settling the case to be submitted to counsel I had seven interruptions from street musicians. These interruptions occur at almost all hours. At eleven and twelve o'clock at night I have been frequently disturbed. In order to carry on my work I am obliged to sit up at night and to reserve the most intricate part for Sundays.

The nuisances have greatly increased in the last few years and penetrate every part of London. I purchased my present residence about thirty years ago having selected it because it was in a very quiet street was detatched [sic] from the adjoining houses and stood in a garden of above ¼ of an acre. Large workshops and a fire proof building have been built upon it at considerable expense. It is not now within my power, even if I could find any other locality adapted to my object, to incur the loss of time and expense which removal would occasion.

With respect to the remedies to these which I would suggest whenever and amended police act is required that some amongst the following courses should be adopted.

1 To declare illegal - all noises not fairly necessary for the transit of passengers and good.

This is the fittest and most just course; if not adopted some of the following may be proposed:

2 To forbid all musical instruments at all times from being played in the streets.

3 To forbid them after a certain hour say 8 P.M.

4 Ditto in front of all hotels public houses beer-shops coffee shops

5 To declare that it is sufficient – that the householder or his servant forbid the music and that it is not necessary that the constable should have been present at the commission of the offense [sic]. Without this the present act is useless.

I should have been glad to explain to you more fully these and some other views of the subject: but aware of the very many demands on your time, I can scarcely expect you could find an opportunity of allowing me even a short interview.

I am sir

Your very obedient servant

C. Babbage

Annexed for a letter addressed to the Rt. Hon.
The Secretary of State

List of various Street Nuisances

1. Organs. Hurdy-gurdies. Fiddlers. Harps etc etc [these are innumerable]

2. Brass bands of various kinds with from 3 to 12 performers [these are numerous and frequent]

3. Fantocini [sic]. Various exhibitions usually accompanied by shrill pipes and noisy drums. [these are frequent]

4. Monkey and fiddle dancing. Or with guns or sword performing exercise.

5. Scotch bagpipes disturbing at a great distance.

6. Imposters with bagpipes more disagreeable even than the genuine performers.

7. The same accompanied by dancers who are either part of the troop or are collected from the children and idlers of the neighbourhood.

8. Black or coloured men beating a monotonous drum called a Tom-Tom to no time, but audible at a g reat distance.

10. Tumblers of various kinds generally with music or the audience collected by music.

11. Tall men on stilts looking inquisitively into drawing room windows.

12. Young girls on shorter stilts.

13. Children playing in the streets at all sorts of games – always making a great noise, occasionally breaking a window and sometimes putting out the eye of a passenger.

14. Amateur performers parading the streets with accordions, flutes, whistles and other instruments for their own instruction or pleasure ...

15. Groups of children occasionally get up a kind of concert of whistles accompanied by a few pieces of board beaten by sticks as a representation of drums. These children parade in a prolonged chorus in a snug corner of the street close to my residence.

16. Certain societies occasionally parade the streets with large bands. Volunteers pass with their bands. But it is certainly desirable that volunteers should not exercise these bands in the streets or at least that they should not be permitted to do so up to a very late hour in the night. Nor ought each isolated member of the band after the companies are dismissed to be permitted to play his own instrument on his way homeward.

17. Persons (generally young men of very powerfull [sic] voice) crying out the sale of some article in their very loudest tone. Two or more frequently shout out for the sale of their wares usually at the same moment. [This is one of the most tolerable nuisances and often occurs on Sundays]

18. Troops of men women and children singing religious songs and psalms. [There are almost always impostors.]

19. Indians and Mahometans pretending to be mad and followed by crowds of young children laughing and screaming.

The greater part of these nuisances ought to be deemed legal offenses [sic]. It ought not to be necessary as it is at present – that most of them can only become offenses by a house holder desiring the offender to desist and his subsequent continuance of the noise.

Electric trains

Seashore sabotage

1898

In the summer of 1893, Magnus Volk – an inventor said to have brought the first electric illuminations to Brighton – launched the Volks Railway: the first-ever electric railway in the UK, which ran along Brighton's seafront. The line was an enormous hit with visitors; on the August bank holiday after it opened, the single car carried roughly 1000 customers in just 11 hours.

Several years later, Magnus Volk put forward another idea to the Board of Trade: an extension to the rail line that would take it through to the town of Rottingdean. The difference between this extended part of the line, and the pre-existing Volks Railway, was that the extension – officially titled the 'Brighton and Rottingdean Electric Seashore Tramroad' – would actually run through the sea on stilts.

A plan for the tramroad sent to the Board of Trade in 1893 shows a two-tiered carriage connected to four 23ft steel stilts. The legs were designed to roll along a track situated on the sea bed and were tall enough to ensure that even at high tide the passengers (and the overhead electrical current supplying power to the vehicle) would be a safe distance from the water – though this didn't stop Volk from attaching a life boat to the carriage, just in case.

The tramroad earned the affectionate nickname of 'The Daddy Long Legs' and even enticed King Edward VII, then Prince of Wales, to journey on to it (a report from Ministry of Transport records states that he was 'much pleased with the novelty of the undertaking, and also with the pleasant sensation of travelling through the sea'). Despite being a success with the public, numerous seamen were slightly narked that their seashore had been hijacked by another tourist attraction: a series of letters between Magnus Volk and the Board of Trade reveal a series of complaints from displeased seafarers written in 1898. In this letter here, Volk – evidently very familiar with this particular complainant – writes: *...Your informant who poses as the long shoreman's friend, for some unknown reason is continually endeavouring to harass the undertaking and I hear that he has promised to secure the abolition of both the tramroad and the Electric Railway and that any communication that he may receive from the Board of Trade is slewn along the beach as evidence of his progress in the matter.*

Earlier in the year, enough complaints had been logged to prompt the President of the Board of Trade to announce he would 'take steps to protect the public and boatmen of Brighton from accidents in the enjoyment of their right to the seashore'. Several attempts to sabotage the running of the railway were also attempted: perpetrators had been stealing the firm's advertising boards from outside the boarding points.

How these disputes were resolved we do not know, but irritated locals did not have to wait long for the railway to be removed. Remarkably, despite the surprising combination of sea water and electricity, it was not an electrical mishap that prematurely ended the life of the Brighton and Rottingdean Seashore Electric Tramroad. A number of events – including corporation changes to the seafront, and a diminished set of funds for development following reconstruction work necessary after the tramroad was hit by storm damage – sadly led to its abandonment in 1902. The Volk's Railway, however, continues to occupy parts of the seafront today and is still operating in 2016.

The controversial 'Daddy Long Legs'.

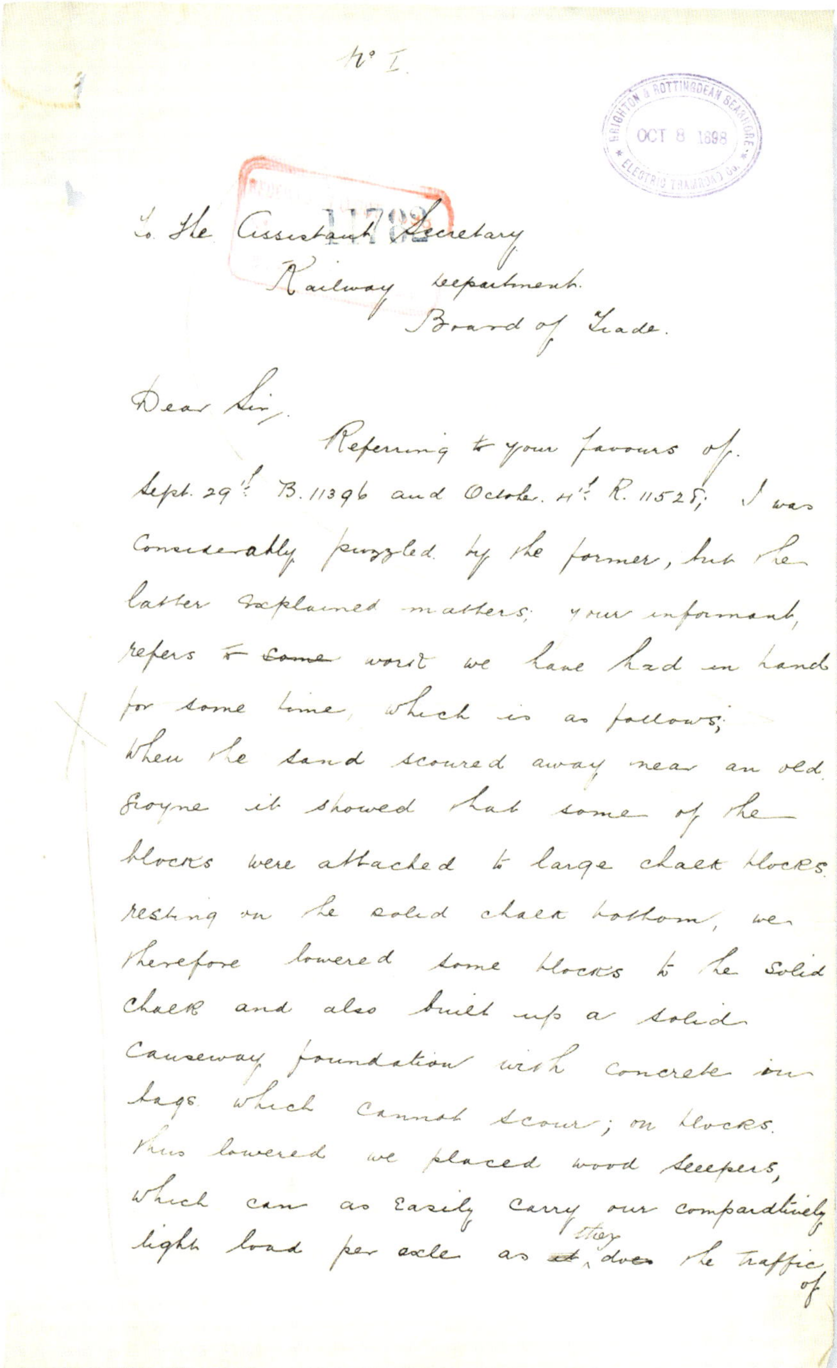

No I.

BRIGHTON & ROTTINGDEAN SEASHORE ELECTRIC TRAMROAD Co.
OCT 8 1898

11782

To the Assistant Secretary
Railway Department.
Board of Trade.

Dear Sir,

Referring to your favours of Sept. 29th B.11396 and Octobr. 4th R.11528, I was considerably puzzled by the former, but the latter explained matters; your informant refers to ~~some~~ work we have had in hand for some time, which is as follows;
When the sand scoured away near an old groyne it showed that some of the blocks were attached to large chalk blocks resting on the solid chalk bottom, we therefore lowered some blocks to the solid chalk and also built up a solid causeway foundation with concrete in bags which cannot scour; on blocks thus lowered we placed wood sleepers, which can as easily carry our comparatively light load per axle as ~~it~~ they does the traffic of

No II

of ordinary railways.

Some few other thin blocks are slightly damaged, but the line is under constant inspection and as opportunity offers we are making a continuous causeway. Taken altogether, considering the novel nature of the line, there has been very little trouble with it, and every care is taken for the safety of the traffic.

I may add that your informant, who poses as the longshoreman's friend, for some unknown reason is continually endeavouring to harass the undertaking & I hear that he has promised to secure the abolition of both the Tramroad & the Electric Railway, and that any communication that he may receive from the Board of Trade is shewn along the beach as evidence of his progress in the matter.

I remain

Yours faithfully

Magnus Volk

Acting Secretary for
THE BRIGHTON & ROTTINGDEAN
SEASHORE ELECTRIC TRAMROAD Co.

To the Assistant Secretary

Railway repairmen

Board of Trade

Dear Sir,

Referring to your favours of Sept 29th B11396 and October 4th R11525, I was considerably puzzled by the former, but the latter explained matters; your informant refers to some work we have had in hand for some time which is as follows:

When the sand scoured away near an old groyne it showed that some of the blocks were attached to large chalk blocks resting on the solid chalk bottom. We therefore lowered some blocks to the solid chalk and also built up a solid causeway foundation with concrete in bags which cannot scour; on blocks, thus lowered we placed wood sleepers which can as easily carry our comparatively high load per axle as they do the traffic of ordinary railways.

Some few other thin blocks are slightly damaged, but the line is under constant inspection and as opportunity offers we are making a continuous causeway. Taken altogether, considering the novel nature of the liner, there has been very little trouble with it, and every care is taken for the safety of the traffic.

I may add that your informant who poses as the long shoreman's friend, for some unknown reason is continually endeavouring to harass the undertaking and I hear that he has promised to secure the abolition of both the tramroad and the Electric Railway and that any communication that he may receive from the Board of Trade is slewn along the beach as evidence of his progress in the matter.

I remain

Yours faithfully

Magnus Volk

Acting Secretary for The Brighton & Rottingdean Seashore Electric Tramroad Co.

‘A flyer capable of carrying a man’

The Wright brothers’ negotiations with the British government

1906

With a firm place in history’s hall of fame, the Wright brothers have come to dominate our view of early aviation. For 12 seconds on 17 December 1903, Orville Wright took to the air above Kitty Hawk beach, North Carolina, in the world’s first powered and controlled heavier-than-air flight, while his brother Wilbur looked on. The significance of the Wrights’ achievement, however, was not very keenly felt at the time. In the years that followed this flight the brothers spent as much of their time trying, and often failing, to convey the importance of their findings to potential investors as they did tinkering with wing angles. This letter, written by Wilbur, forms part of protracted negotiations with the British War Office, and details one such attempt to get the money they needed to turn their findings into a business.

Initial discussions between the Wrights and the British were opened in late 1904 and continued into 1905, but failed to make any progress. A letter from the Wrights to the War Office in November 1905 sums up the stalemate, with the Wrights unwilling to divulge anything more than photos and witness statements without a contract in place, but the British equally reticent about signing a contract without more information. With the prospect of any kind of deal looking bleak, the Wrights came back to the British with a refined offer in May 1906. The Wrights offered a flyer, instructions for its use, the data required to progress the design and, most importantly, ‘the confidential disclosure of the original discoveries in aeronautical science’.

This, according to Colonel Superintendent Capper, showed ‘a much more practical intention of coming to terms’. As head of the Army Balloon Factory in Farnborough, the closest thing the British had to an aviation research outpost, Capper took the lead in the negotiations and so was an important man for the Wrights to please. Unfortunately, Capper’s praise ended there. He remained unconvinced, and requested further details from the brothers.

The result was this letter of 10 July 1906, personally signed by Wilbur. In a way that was characteristic of the Wrights’ correspondence up to this point, it continued the sales pitch without adding much that the British didn’t already know. Discussions with the French government are noted, perhaps appealing to a sense of cross-Channel rivalry, and regards are sent to Capper and his wife who had been received with 'special pleasure' when they visited two years previously, but specifics are avoided.

It was at this point that Lieutenant Colonel Gleichen, the British Military Attaché in the USA, was asked to contact the Wrights in a more direct attempt to flesh out the details of their offer. A letter was duly sent and, at last, in a letter of 31 July 1906 the details emerged: it would cost the British $100,000 for a flyer and the rights to reproduce the plane and an extra $100,000 for details of the science behind it. For Capper, this marked the end of negotiations, with, in his mind, the prices being 'out of all proportion to the benefits to be gained'. Gleichen was less dismissive, visiting the Wrights personally and producing a report that noted that they had 'little or none of the usual braggadocio of the Yankee inventor' and reiterated their achievements to date. This fell on unsympathetic ears. Capper asked Gleichen to formally decline the Wrights' offer in November 1906.

Undeterred, the Wrights would try to persuade the British Government once more in April 1908. Capper, still at the helm of the Balloon Factory, asked again for their terms before expressing some of his own, which included five separate trials testing speed, altitude, duration, capacity and observation potential. There were, however, more horses in the race by this point, a couple of which were from Capper's own stable. One of these, Samuel F Cody, made the first powered, heavier-than-air flight on British soil in October of that year at the Balloon Factory's site in Farnborough, making the Wrights' offer redundant in the eyes of the British government.

With their fame growing and contracts with the US government signed, it's unlikely that the Wrights were too disheartened by this rebuff. A change of tack saw them carry out demonstrations across the world, turning them into international celebrities and wealthy businessmen by the end of the decade. Meanwhile, in Britain, with the government ceasing funding in early 1909, official attempts at heavier-than-air aviation stalled. It wouldn't be until the First World War that the significance of this new form of flight was widely recognised by the establishment.

Wilbur Wright.

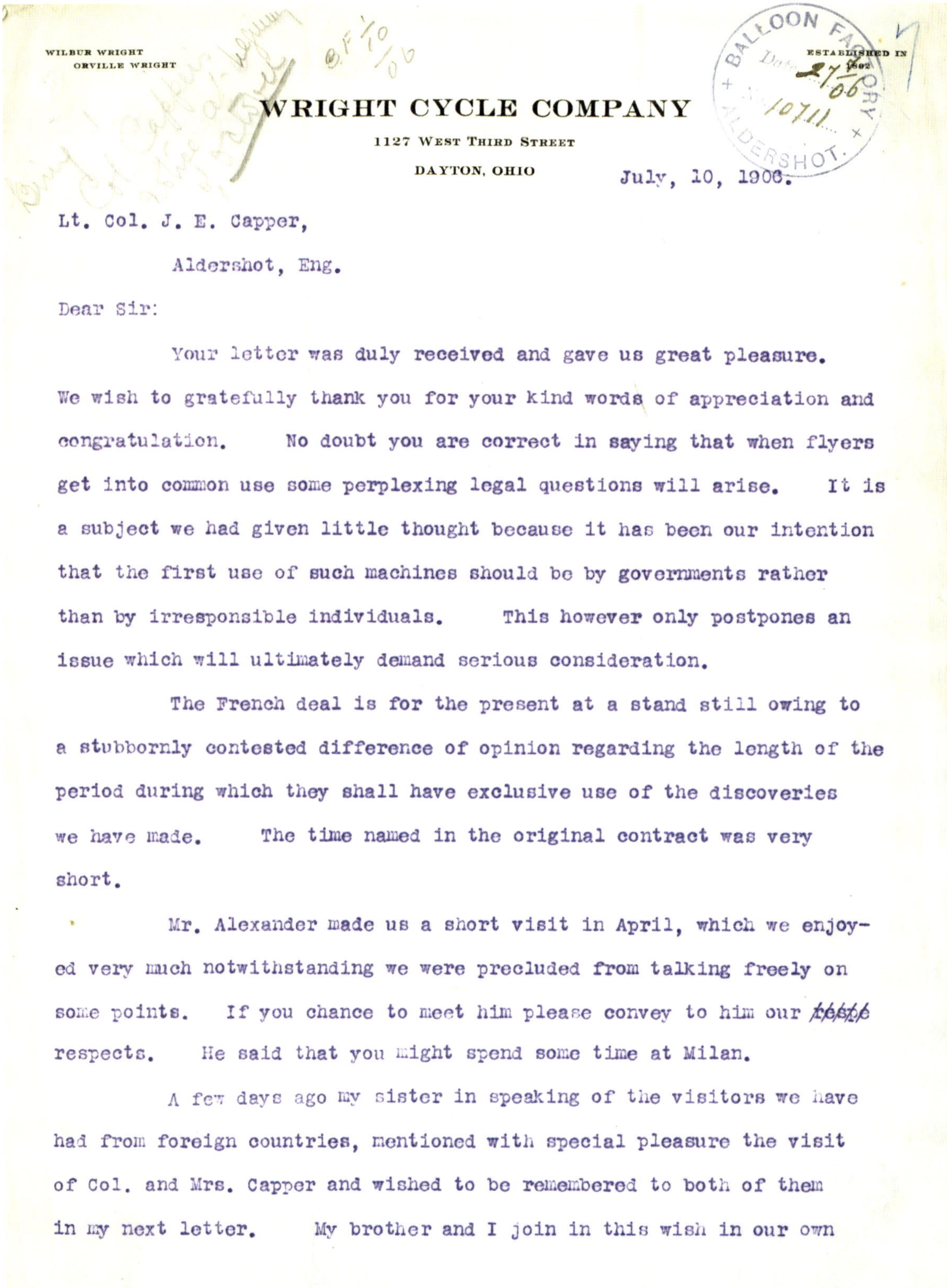

WILBUR WRIGHT
ORVILLE WRIGHT

ESTABLISHED IN 1892

BALLOON FACTORY
Date 27/7/06
No 10711
ALDERSHOT.

WRIGHT CYCLE COMPANY

1127 WEST THIRD STREET

DAYTON, OHIO

July, 10, 1906.

Lt. Col. J. E. Capper,

Aldershot, Eng.

Dear Sir:

Your letter was duly received and gave us great pleasure. We wish to gratefully thank you for your kind words of appreciation and congratulation. No doubt you are correct in saying that when flyers get into common use some perplexing legal questions will arise. It is a subject we had given little thought because it has been our intention that the first use of such machines should be by governments rather than by irresponsible individuals. This however only postpones an issue which will ultimately demand serious consideration.

The French deal is for the present at a stand still owing to a stubbornly contested difference of opinion regarding the length of the period during which they shall have exclusive use of the discoveries we have made. The time named in the original contract was very short.

Mr. Alexander made us a short visit in April, which we enjoyed very much notwithstanding we were precluded from talking freely on some points. If you chance to meet him please convey to him our respects. He said that you might spend some time at Milan.

A few days ago my sister in speaking of the visitors we have had from foreign countries, mentioned with special pleasure the visit of Col. and Mrs. Capper and wished to be remembered to both of them in my next letter. My brother and I join in this wish in our own

WILBUR WRIGHT
ORVILLE WRIGHT

ESTABLISHED IN 1892

WRIGHT CYCLE COMPANY

1127 WEST THIRD STREET

DAYTON, OHIO

behalf. Please believe me with great respect,

Yours truly,

Wilbur Wright.

10

(84/W/5424)

28

Wright Brothers,
1127 W.Third Street,
Dayton, Ohio.

(Copy)

April 10. 1908.

The Secretary,
War Office,
London,S.W.

Dear Sir,

The increased interest now taken in the different countries in aeronautics, prompts to again call your attention to our aeroplane. The machines as now designed, are suitable for military scouting, being capable of carrying two men (an operator and an observer), and sufficient fuel for long flights.

We are prepared to undertake the manufacture of one or more of these machines under a contract; or, if the Government would prefer to build machines for itself under our British patent, we will grant license to operate on payment of suitable royalties on the machines so manufactured.

The United States Government has lately entered into contract with us for one of our two-men machines.

Very respectfully,

(sd) Wright Brothers,
O.W.

31

Orville Wright flying in *Kitty Hawk* in 1911.

No women drivers allowed

Men from the London Trades Council threaten to strike

1917

Why in 1917 did 100,000 men threaten to strike against women drivers?

The First World War necessitated women moving into many roles previously unknown to them, from dentistry to clay digging. However, one of the most controversial appears to have been driving. The role of vehicle drivers was important to both the front line and the home front, from ambulance units in France to the day-to-day public transport used to move around the essential wartime workforce. As the war continued, men increasingly moved to the front line, making women's work in these roles necessary. The War Office stated female omnibus drivers were a 'matter of urgent military importance'.

In the climate of the First World War, with its growing female union membership and vibrant, militant pre-war suffrage movement, it seems surprising that the male union movement would be so adverse to women's progress in the workforce.

However, the image of women cycling or driving was generally controversial, with only a few women being afforded this freedom prior to the war. Suffragette Vera Holme was a rare example of this: in 1909 she became Emmeline Pankhurst's driver; she wore masculine clothes, smoked and lived by independent means – for many at the time these were not positive associations.

The freedom that motor cars provided was simple but vital, often meaning that women could not be chaperoned and they therefore began to gain a freedom of movement they had often not previously had. In practice, it often meant women had to change their clothing to more practical trousers, and more 'masculine' wear – this led to a fear of subversion: women acting like men were seen as a threat because they questioned the accepted social hierarchy.

When, in 1917, the absence of men on the home front necessitated the increase of female omnibus drivers, the subject of licensing women drivers was met with controversy at the Home Office. The letter this article is concerned with is from the London Trades Council, giving an ultimatum demanding the repeal of women's driving licences and threatening a strike of their 100,000-strong workforce – just to prevent women driving. The union noted there were 'strong moral grounds why women should not be so employed'. The male trade unionists felt women entering the workforce would drive down men's wages upon their return. Why would anyone prefer to employ men who were more expensive, if women had proved they could do the work just as well during the war?

In a deputation from the Home Office, the unions were reassured that as a compromise women would have omnibus licences only for the duration of the war. A letter to the Home Office from the Women's Freedom League, who continued to fight for women's equality during the war in numerous ways, dated 16 March 1917, made their position clear: *We feel that at a time like the present when women are being called upon more and more to take part in the work of the nation (pleasant and unpleasant) it would be a very dangerous thing for those in authority to concede to any section of men the right of refusing to allow women to enter their industry.*

It is often represented that war hastened change. However the issue of women drivers shows that even in the unique environment created by the war it was hard to break down these gender barriers.

Despite the controversy, many women did successfully contribute to the war effort through driving. The following image from the War Office publication *Women's War Work* (September 1916) shows a pride in the work women were undertaking for the war effort.

A female van driver during the First World War.

HOME OFFICE
17 MAR 1917
RECEIVED

275410

Telephone: Museum 1429.
Telegrams: Despard, Museum, 1429 London.

Colours: Green, Gold and White.
Weekly Paper: "The Vote" 1d.

VOTES FOR WOMEN.

WOMEN'S FREEDOM LEAGUE.

OBJECTS: To secure for Women the Parliamentary Vote as it is or may be granted to men; to use the power thus obtained to establish equality of rights and opportunities between the sexes, and to promote the Social and Industrial well-being of the community.

President: Mrs. C. Despard.
Hon. Treasurer: Dr. E. Knight.
Hon. Organising Secretary: Miss Eunice Murray.
Head of Political and Militant Department: Miss C. Nina Boyle.
Secretary: Miss F. A. Underwood.
Auditor: Mrs. Ayres Purdie.
Bank: London & South Western.

OFFICES:
144 HIGH HOLBORN,
LONDON, W.C. 1.

16th March, 1917.

The Rt. Hon. Sir George Cave, K.C., M.P.,
Home Office,
Whitehall, S.W.

Dear Sir,

The Women's Freedom League notes with regret the threat of the taxi, tram and bus drivers to strike against the licensing of women drivers.

We feel that at a time like the present when women are being called upon more and more to take part in the work of the nation (pleasant and unpleasant) it would be a very dangerous thing for those in authority to concede to any section of men the right of refusing to allow women to enter their industry.

We therefore urge you not to yield to the demand of the men on this matter, since the success of a threat as is being made would not only have a bad effect on the spirit of the women of the country, but might also serve to hinder the efficient working of the National Service Organisation.

We have the honour to be, Sir,

Your obedient Servants,

C. Despard

(President)

E. Knight

(Hon. Treasurer.)

Anne. E. Corner

(Acting Political Organiser.)

Florence A. Underwood.

(Secretary.)

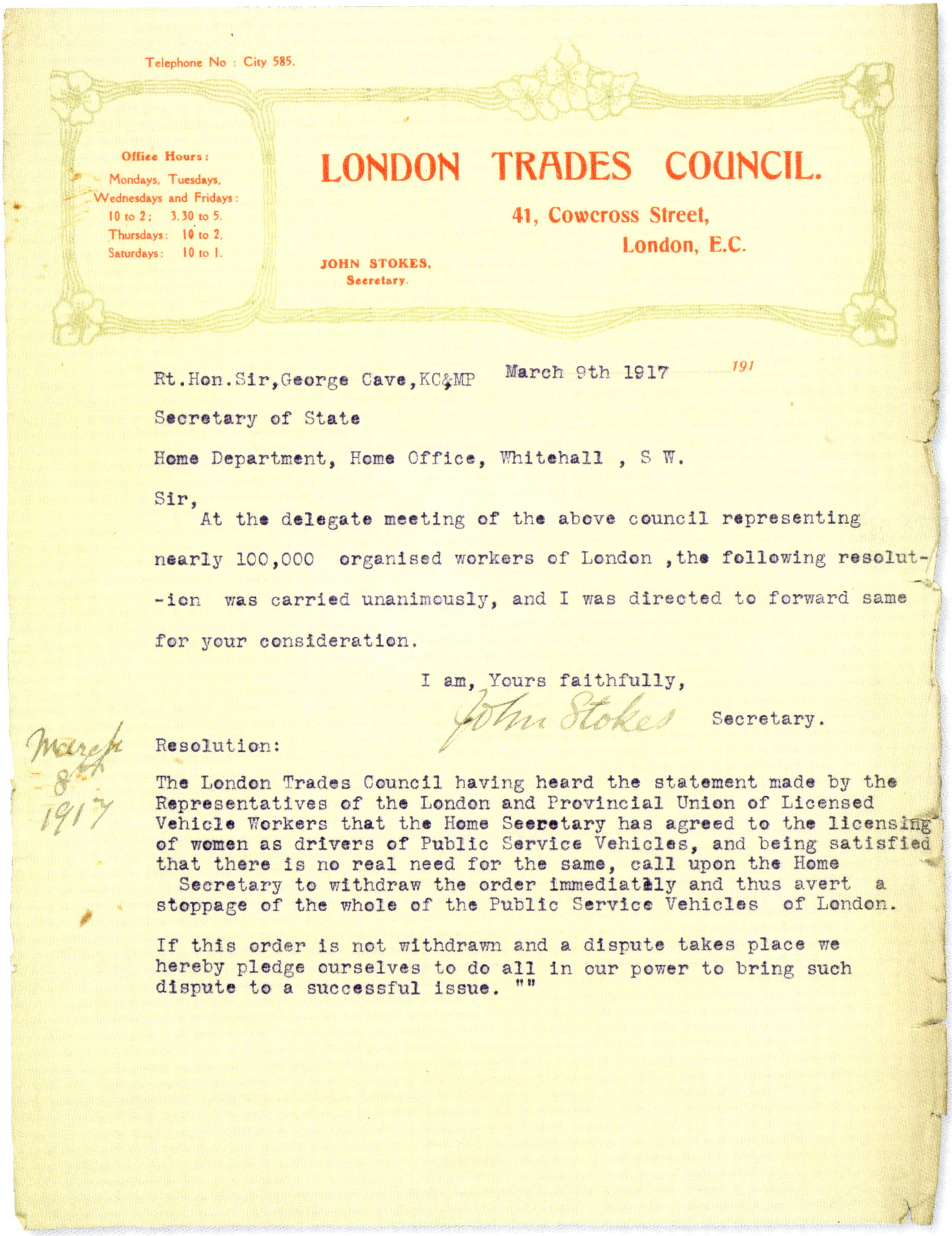

Telephone No : City 585.

Office Hours:
Mondays, Tuesdays,
Wednesdays and Fridays:
10 to 2; 3.30 to 5.
Thursdays: 10 to 2.
Saturdays: 10 to 1.

LONDON TRADES COUNCIL.

41, Cowcross Street,
London, E.C.

JOHN STOKES,
Secretary.

Rt.Hon.Sir,George Cave,KC&MP March 9th 1917 191

Secretary of State

Home Department, Home Office, Whitehall , S W.

Sir,
At the delegate meeting of the above council representing nearly 100,000 organised workers of London ,the following resolut--ion was carried unanimously, and I was directed to forward same for your consideration.

I am, Yours faithfully,
John Stokes Secretary.

March 8th 1917

Resolution:

The London Trades Council having heard the statement made by the Representatives of the London and Provincial Union of Licensed Vehicle Workers that the Home Secretary has agreed to the licensing of women as drivers of Public Service Vehicles, and being satisfied that there is no real need for the same, call upon the Home Secretary to withdraw the order immediatly and thus avert a stoppage of the whole of the Public Service Vehicles of London.

If this order is not withdrawn and a dispute takes place we hereby pledge ourselves to do all in our power to bring such dispute to a successful issue. ""

Women from the WRA (Women's Reserve Ambulance) Corps learning to drive an ambulance, c.1914.

Disappointed fiancées

The right of married women to work in the civil service

1946–1947

What happened in 1947 if you found yourself a 'disappointed fiancée'?

Before October 1946, if you worked in the Civil Service and wanted to marry, you had to leave your job – that is, if you were a woman. In many areas of public life the marriage bar prevented women from working after marriage. Women were expected to focus on their husband and their family.

In the Civil Service, a marriage bar prevented all but six married women from taking civil service jobs before 1925. A Treasury document after the repeal of the marriage bar shows the continuation of negative attitudes and gendered assumptions towards married workers. This is summed up in a document dated shortly after the Act from 1947–51, stating 'Naturally, their home comes first with them, and if their husbands or children are ill, they regard it as their duty to remain at home and look after them'. The same record notes married women were considered 'a perfect nuisance' by the Treasury.

What is interesting is how some women readily accepted these gendered expectations after the marriage bar had been removed: many women still left work for marriage.

The letter in this piece is found in a Treasury file from after the removal of the marriage bar entitled 'Disappointed fiancées'. The file details many women's individual experiences of leaving the service for marriage, only to be 'disappointed' in their relationships, and therefore asking for their jobs back. This illustrates wider attitudes concerning women and social roles that, despite the removal of the marriage bar in the civil service by this time, women themselves largely expected to leave work upon marriage. The Civil Service was progressive in this area, and many other professions had still not removed the marriage bar – indeed the Foreign Service did not waive the marriage bar until 1973.

Interestingly, these were not women forced to leave the service by the marriage bar; this had ended the year before. These were women who left due to the expectations placed on women to look after the home and raise children, only to be disappointed in their love lives. Sometimes this was due to philandering, other times due to death and illness, or family disapproval.

CV Millett wrote to the Home Office in 1947 to ask whether she could be reinstated in her previous position. Millett had been betrothed to a man in Canada, arrangements were made at the Guildford Registrar's office, only for him to be repatriated to Canada and to marry a Canadian woman, citing differences of religion. In response, W Kees of the Treasury wrote, 'As her resignation was owing to a mistaken belief that she was to be married and the general war circumstances, possibly sympathetic consideration could be given to her reinstatement. She is a very useful all round officer'.

A survey at the end of the war concluded that 24 per cent of married women didn't believe in work after marriage, agreeing with the statement, 'A woman's place is in the home', with 35 per cent of single women saying the same. And yet of those women who worked during the war and were asked to give the advantages of war work, the two top answers are 'money helps out' and 'company, never lonely', followed by 'more independence' – clearly many married women did feel the benefit of working.

This collection of letters from 'disappointed fiancées' seems to fundamentally illustrate that social change was often slow to follow legal change, and women themselves had many preconceptions about their own role in society.

Women at work, c.1920.

24

Copy

c/o Mr. J.E. Maren,
175, Highland Road,
Kensington, Johannesburg.

10.12.46.

Dear Sir,

I resigned my appointment with the Board of Trade, C.M.L. Buildings, Birmingham on the 20th July, 1946, as Established Superintendent of Typists, to proceed to South Africa to be married. Owing to unforeseen circumstances the marriage will not now take place and I am returning to England by air in January all being well. Under the said circumstances, I wish to make formal application for re-instatement as an established officer, and ask you to give my case your very sympathetic consideration please.

If there is not a vacancy in my grade in the Board of Trade, Birmingham, I would be grateful if you could pass my letter on to the Civil Service Commissioners informing them of my circumstances, to see if they could find me a vacancy in any other Department. I realise, of course, that I would have to be prepared to go where the vacancy occurs in or out of Birmingham.

My parent Department was the National Savings Department, where I was for 7 years before transfer to the Board of Trade Midland Regional Office.

If you are unable to reply to my letter before the 10th January, please address communications to :-

248, Church Road, Yardley,
B'ham, 25, England.

Thanking you in anticipation,
I am, Yours faithfully,

(sgd) Marjorie M.A.King.

E. 3193

E. 2392/019

40

27th August, 1947.

Dear Mr. Cox,

You wrote to Mr. Kees on 24th July about an application for reinstatement from Miss O.V. Millett a former Clerical Assistant who resigned in May 1946 with the intention of getting married.

Normally in such cases, provided the officer applies reasonably soon after resignation, we allow her resignation to be cancelled and the break in service is regarded as leave without pay.

Miss Millett resigned over a year ago but has since been in temporary employment and her actual break in service is only a matter of months.

If, as I imagine is the case, Miss Millett has since 7th November, 1946 been carrying out the duties of a C.A. post, we are prepared to agree that her resignation may be regarded as cancelled and the break in service recorded as leave without pay. Her period of service from 7th November may reckon for increment and also in full for superannuation.

Yours sincerely,

O.M. Tregurtha

H.A. Cox, Esq.,
Tithe Redemption Commission.

Finsbury Square House,
33-37 Finsbury Square,
London,
E.C.2.

The introduction of the contraceptive pill

Allowing 'improper demands' by women?

1961

With the introduction of the contraceptive pill, it became possible to separate sex from reproduction. This newfound ability to have sex without the risk of conception called into question the nature and purpose of sex. Were human beings driven by an instinct to reproduce, or were they above all moved to seek physical sexual pleasure? Did men seek sex, but women seek babies and providers for them? Were men even capable of love? These are some of the thorny questions raised by medical developments over the course of the 20th century.

This letter relates to the invention of the contraceptive pill, which was the first oral method of birth control. Sent from the pharmaceutical company GD Seale & Co. on 20 January 1961, it warns the Ministry of Health of its plans to introduce the product on the UK market. Behind the scenes in Westminster, this news caused grave concern about the widened availability of contraceptives for social purposes, with fears that there might be 'improper demands' by single women, and a general moral decline. Setting the tone for the 'Swinging Sixties', perhaps?

Attitudes towards birth control fluctuated over the course of the century. Indeed, in spite of the growing availability of contraception in the 20th century, at its start abortion was popularly considered far less immoral than mechanical or chemical contraception. Contraception required planning ahead and mentally deciding not to risk pregnancy. Abortions, by contrast, could be interpreted as the simple restoration of a woman's health by 'bringing back the monthlies' as they were called. In Britain, for example, slippery elm was sold by many ordinary chemists and marketed as 'remedies for menstrual irregularity'. All of these methods to get rid of an unwanted child were culturally acceptable; abortion was illegal in the UK until 1967, but most people did not consider it criminal.

And though it was common at the beginning of the century to doubt the morality of birth control, with the invention of the diaphragm at the end of the 19th century by a German gynaecologist, and its mass manufacture during the First World War as a result of developments in rubber production, use of contraception increased markedly. The same benefits aided condom production. However, wartime casualties and the resulting shortage of men led to serious concern about falling birth rates and dwindling military strength. Accordingly, some countries brought in laws intended to prevent access to contraception. In France, a law punished all those who distributed contraceptives or advocated their use. And though Weimar Germany had been a European front-runner in terms of providing access to birth control, all of this was reversed with the Nazi seizure of power as they disbanded all such activities in favour of pro-natalism in 1933.

After 1945, changes in military technology meant that there was no longer a direct correlation between a high birth rate and military might. Suddenly boosting the birth rate was no longer a priority, which naturally had a knock-on effect on governments' attitudes to the use of contraceptives. Indeed, by the 1960s, opposition to birth control decreased significantly in most European countries. Nonetheless, the very fact that GD Searle & Co felt they 'should write to give advance notice of our plans for the introduction of an oral birth control tablet' speaks volumes about the ongoing sensitivities surrounding the use of contraception.

Ultimately, both wider access to birth control across Europe, and the capacity of women to be in charge of it, meant that women were able to look beyond their biological function and plan when they had children. This is reflected in the fall in the average number of births per couple in Western Europe. In the mid-19th century, the average woman in Western Europe had five or six children; by the mid-20th century, she had two.

G. D. SEARLE & CO., LTD.

ETHICAL PHARMACEUTICALS
LANE END ROAD
HIGH WYCOMBE, BUCKS

Telephone: High Wycombe 1770
Telegrams/Cables: SEARIN High Wycombe

CONFIDENTIAL

20th January, 1961.

The Chief Medical Officer,
Ministry of Health,
Savile Row,
London, W.1.

Dear Sir,

We felt we should write and give advance notice of our plans for the introduction of an oral birth control tablet. The product has already been on the market in the U.K. for over three years under the trade name Enavid for gynaecological use. We have not previously recommended it for birth control.

Our birth control product will be sold under the name Conovid. It is a prescription only product, and the method of introduction will be by letter to the medical profession only. There will be no advertising even in medical journals. We propose to inform wholesalers by letter on 23rd January, the retail trade on 26th January and the medical profession on 30th January.

A copy of the Reference Manual which will be sent to the medical profession is enclosed. This gives details of the extensive trials which have been carried out in the field for which we now recommend it. It is already on sale in the U.S.A. and Canada and is at present undergoing trials by the Family Planning Association in this country.

We ask that this information be treated as confidential until we make our announcement to the medical profession.

Yours faithfully,
G.D. SEARLE & CO., LTD.

H.A.R. Gough

H.A.R. Gough,
General Sales Manager.

Enc.
HARG/FMA

DIRECTORS: JOHN G. SEARLE, (U.S.A.) (CHAIRMAN) LT.-GEN. SIR ERNEST BRADFIELD, M.S., F.R.C.S. WESLEY M. DIXON, JNR. (U.S.A.) FRANKLIN P. O'BRIEN, (U.S.A.) D. I. WILSON G. G. ROBERTSON

Workers at a pharmaceutical factory packing cartons of the contraceptive pill in 1965.

OVULEN

'A good thing to be laughed at'

Harold Macmillan approves of his TV satirisation

1962

This is a handwritten note from Conservative Prime Minister Harold Macmillan to the Post Master General, John Reginald Bevins, regarding the BBC television satire show *That Was The Week That Was*. It gives an interesting insight into Macmillan's character, and makes clear that he chose not to take action against the BBC. According to Asa Briggs, in *The History of Broadcasting in the United Kingdom*, Macmillan 'liked the way Rushton [William] impersonated him'. His note was written on the day that Hugh Carleton Green, Director-General of the BBC (1960–69) had apologised to the Prime Minister's Office about a sketch in the previous week's show.

The live TV comedy programme aimed to take a swipe at politicians and public figures, and was part of the general boom in satire from the newly launched *Private Eye* to the revue *Beyond the Fringe* in the 1960s. Macmillan and John Profumo were early subjects for the new show, which went on air in November 1962. It was devised, produced and directed by Ned Sherrin, and presented by David Frost.

After two seasons, the programme was taken off the air by the BBC at the end of 1963, possibly out of fear for any political influence it might bring to bear as Britain faced another General Election.

Broadcasting (Gen)

Urgent

Admiralty House
Whitehall. S.W.1

Post Master General

I hope you will not repeat not take any action about "That was the week that was" without consulting me.

It is a good thing to be laughed at.

It is better than to be ignored.

HM

10.12.62

Broadcasting (Gen)

Urgent

5

PRIME MINISTER

Admiralty House
Whitehall, S.W.1

Post Master General

I hope you will not repeat not take any action about "That was the week that was" without consulting me.

It is a good thing to be laughed at.
It is better than to be ignored.

HM

10.12.62.

Aliens in the Mendip Hills

Correspondence to and from the Ministry of Defence

2004–2005

For 60 years, the Ministry of Defence (MoD) collected reports on and sightings of Unidentified Flying Objects (UFOs). The reason for the collection was not to prove or disprove the existence of aliens, but to ensure the safety of British airspace. In November 2009 the UFO Desk at the Ministry of Defence closed. An increase in sightings, social media and press reports then called for the disclosure of 'the truth'. The MoD released digital copies of the files, redacted, to The National Archives. The closure was partly to save money, and partly due to no evidence being found of a UFO threat to Britain or British airspace. The files contain a varied amount of reports, from those easily explained, such as the rise in the use of Chinese lanterns or the fall of Russian satellite booster rockets to earth; to those indicating assumed withholding of information on alien activity, such as the Lightning aircraft crash in the North Sea in 1970.

One file contains correspondence from an avid Ufologist, dated from around 2000. This is an excellent example of an individual's interest in the existence of aliens. The writer informs the MoD of the existence of aliens living in Somerset, especially under the Mendip Hills. He explains the aliens are working with the Moonies and using Black Magic to overthrow the government and monarchy. He also mentions writing to the President of the USA about the existence of aliens in Somerset.

The initial response of the MoD is along the lines that the MoD does not have an interest or expertise in UFOs, and there is no evidence to substantiate the existence of these alleged phenomena.

The correspondent continues to write and send in various articles, including a piece by the West Country Unidentified Flying Object Research Association. He even suggests he will visit Whitehall, the MoD are quick to point out they have a limited interest in UFOs. A subsequent suggested visit sends the MoD into turmoil, with an internal memo stating, 'If he does arrive he is not to be admitted, but if he is admitted then a guard must be present at all times.' The MoD continues to state they have limited interest in UFO sightings, and they have no evidence to substantiate the existence of these alleged phenomena.

All the letters are signed with varying words and phrases, with the writer even declaring he has worked for MI5 for 25 years, with no pay (signed KEN MI5). There is no response to the request for a gun to shoot the aliens. He even requests a government grant and a Geiger counter. The letters report the aliens are the size of 10-year-old children, and that they can be found outside the local supermarket. The police submit a report on the author of the letters, and thus we have an explanation of the author. The final letter in this file states he is Lord Mountbatten's grandson.

This is a unique set of letters; others within this correspondence file are slightly more straightforward. Not all the letters and reports are from members of the public. The United States Air Force reported a UFO sighting in Thetford Forest in 1980; and various police officers around the country have reported everything from hovering lights, to cylindrical shapes, to strange beings while on patrol.

The Freedom of Information requests for information regarding the crash of the Lightning aircraft in 1970 and the set of lights across the night sky, show how our imagination sometimes gets the better of us.

There is no proof of alien life, but the individual's imagination will always trigger that desire to know if 'the truth is out there'.

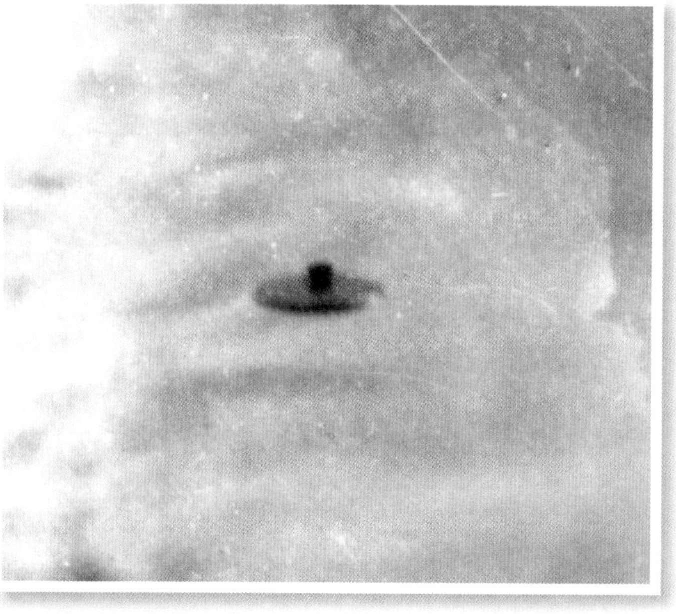

An image of a supposed UFO or 'flying saucer.'

24/4/2004

From [redacted]

I am writing to you again because I have enclosed some paper work at what I hope you will find of most interest

It is the beginning at a book I am writing also I have enclosed a photo of me at one of my (Sky watches) at Pole Mill Chingford in the early 1970s. I am standing on a ???? at Pole Mill in my open Jacket [PTO]

and wool hat.

Sorry about my handwriting I am having problems with my (right hand)

I will come and see you in the middle of May with my Deputes [redacted information] PS I keep an (Exorcise)

Yours sincerely

Code name (Ken MI5) Alaska FBI

Green Blue Red

Swordfish

Grandad

Combe Move if the Undertaker

President & Founder

WCUFORA Founder March 1976

Lord Mountbaton or Lord [redacted] or Lord [redacted]

what am I [redacted] I again sorry about my handwriting

From: [redacted]

Directorate of Air Staff (Secretariat) 3a

Ministry of Defence etc

Dear [redacted]

Thank you for your letter dated 24 April 2004

Also thank you for your draft letter and photograph.

You will be aware from our previous correspondence, of our policy on 'UFOs'

Your letter, draft book and copy of your photograph have all been placed on our files

Yours sincerely

[redacted]

28/5/2005

From [Redacted]

Dear [Redacted]

I am writing to you because you should be told about the situation in the West Country today. Please tell Geof Hoon ok

We are sighting aliens, they look like children, they are the (three foot six people)

I have written to the American president [PTO] to tell him the situation in the West Country

The Aliens are under ground at Burrington Combe (Somerset). They also have a base at Edith Mead

Please tell me what you want me to do in my position for it is also I am also President and founder of the WCUFORA

Also my understanding is I am a Lord, is this correct, if so I wish….

From: [redacted]

Directorate of Air Staff (Secretariat) 3a

Ministry of Defence etc

Dear [redacted]

Thank you for your letter dated 28 May 2005

As stated in previous correspondence, the MOD does not have any expertise or role in respect of 'UFO/Flying Saucer' matters to the question of the existence or otherwise of extra-terrestrial lifeforms, about which it remains totally open-minded. I think I should add to that to date, the MOD knows of no evidence which substantiates the existence of these alleged phenomena.

Also, your comments have been noted and your letter will be placed in our files

Yours sincerely

[redacted]

7/11/2005

I am writing to you because I feel that you should be told about the situation in the West Country today concerning the Aliens at Burrington Combe and Edith Mead both in Somerset

Also we ??? Black Magic ?? Black Witches at [PTO] Hutton Park Caravan site, Weston Super Mare.

If I were you I would move the army across the airfield at Hutton park, also move a troop train out ??? the caravan site with Hercules onto the airfield in a rapid deployment first against the Black Witches

Also Weston-Super-Mare police on this side of the witches

I have written to President Bush about the situation concerning Aliens at Edith Mead and Burrington Combe in Somerset. I told hime, if I were him I would move the US Marines up the Bristol Channel and move the 8th Airbourne Devision on to the Mendips. I aim to come to London sometime in the New Year for a debriefing. OK Sir Hoon mush be smashed [PTO]

Yours sincerely

Code Name

Green Blue Red

Swordfish

Grandad Combe

Alaska FBI SAS

Move in the Undertakers

Lord [redacted] or am I Lord Mountbatton

Or Lord [redacted]

President & Founder [redacted]

Index

Project coordinators

Timothy Cross • Edward Field • Hester Vaizey • Carianne Whitworth

Contributors

Paul Carter • Randolph Cock • Christopher Day • Juliette Desplat • Richard Dunley • Edward Field • James Fleming • Katie Fox • Rachel Hillman • Andrew Holt • Clare Horrie • Victoria Iglikowski • Jeff James • Andrew Janes • Ela Kaczmarska • Roger Kershaw • Katy Mair • Keith Mitchell • Jess Nelson • Stephen Twigge • Hester Vaizey • Carianne Whitworth • Lauren Willmott

With thanks to

Adrian Ailes • Paul Johnson • Linda Stewart

SOURCES FOR LETTERS AND IMAGES

The National Archives

Companions, comrades, lovers: 16–19: SC 1/3/182, the transcript (p.18) is from Anne Crawford's Letters of the Queens of England, Sutton Publishing, 1997; **20–23:** SP 1/167 f.14; **24–29:** SP 53/10/84; **30–33:** HCA 30/258/2 no. 106; **34–37:** WO 138/35; **38–41:** RAIL 253/516; **42–45:** T 172/696; NSC 5/11; **46–49:** MH 47/60; **50–53:** MEPO 3/75; DPP 2/224 (3); **54–57:** DO 131/88; DO 131/15; **58–61:** CO 981/15, no 44

Espionage and deception: 64–67: FO 371/2201; MPK 1/426; **68–71:** WO 141/82; COPY 1/44; **72–75:** KV 2/3874; **76–79:** WO 106/5921/20; WO106/5921/19; **80–83:** WO 204/3930; **84–87:** KV 2/3004/1; **88–93:** HS 9/612 (1-3); HS 9/612 (039-041); **94–99:** FCO 158/25; FCO 158/26; FCO 158/6

Allies, diplomacy and foreign relations: 102–107: FO 27/599; J 76/4/1 (part 1); **108–109:** HO 45/9366/36228; **110–113:** FO 371/7733 f. 2; PRO 30/69/944; CO 1047/57 (1 of 20); **114–117:** PREM 1/331A; INF3-47; **118–121:** MH 56/221; INF13-171 (3); **122–129:** CAB 66/13/46; **130–135:** CAB 130/3; ES1/495 (3); **136–139:** FCO 57/401

Protest, revolution and rebellion: 142–145: SC 1/30/81; **146–149:** SP 14/216/2; **150–155:** HO 52/7 (231); HO 52/7 (229); **156–159:** MH 12/9232/46; MH 32/60; **160–163:** MT9/920A/1 (19); COPY 1/566 (56506); MT 9/920C (526); **164–167:** WO 32/5460 (1, 2, 4); **168–171:** WO 371/345; CN11-8 (2); **172–177:** WORK 11/227; WORK 11/176; **178–181:** FO 371/34550; **182–185:** MH 55/1656; **186–191:** DO 119/1478; **192–197:** HO291/125; **198–201:** FCO 33/263; FO 371/163600 (4) (12); **202–207:** PREM 13/2412 (6); ZLIB 17/129A

Scandals, loopholes and murder: 210–215: MH 13/231; **216–223:** MEPO 3/3153; HO 144/221-A49301I f3; **224–229:** MEPO 3/225B; **230–233:** FO 371/13540; **234–237:** HO 45/18033; **238–241:** WO 235/12 (67); FO 371/42806; **242–245:** IR 40/16656; CRIM/4140; **246–249:** MEPO 2/10922; CRIM 1/5006; **250–253:** DPP 2/4167

Cultural, technological change: 256–263: HO45/7195; **264–269:** MT 6/1109/2; ZSPC 11/669/44; ZSPC 11/669/47; **270–275:** AIR 1/728/176/3/33; **276–281:** HO 45/11164; MH 47/142/1; **282–285:** T 275/137; STAT 20/416; **286–289:** MH 135/108; **290–291:** PREM 11/3668; **292–299:** DEFE 24/2062/1

Getty Images

14, 19, 21, 29, 31, 34, 35, 39, 47, 59, 62, 64, 69, 83, 99, 100, 103, 108, 117, 123, 137, 139, 140, 142, 147, 155, 169, 183, 187, 199, 203, 208, 215, 217, 223, 225, 233, 235, 239, 254, 257, 271, 275, 281, 289, 290, 293

Juliette Desplat

110